THE
HIGH SIGN

THE
HIGH SIGN

DAVID S. HEEREN

The High Sign
Copyright © 2015 by David S. Heeren. All rights reserved.

Author's Preface

THE PURPOSE OF this book is to assist Christian believers to prepare for the final great event in world history—the Second Coming of Jesus Christ. An unusual trait of this book resides in the fact that even those readers who disagree with its theme may receive assistance to become ready for the Day of the Lord.

The motion picture *It's a Mad, Mad, Mad, Mad World* began with Jimmy Durante telling a group of comical characters that they could find treasure by looking "under the Big W" in a park in a California coastal city. The treasure seekers scurried aimlessly about the park to the disgust of one of their wives. She watched their clueless search, shaking her head. But then a look of recognition appeared on her face and she said in a hesitant voice to a bystander, "I know what it is." She was looking at the Big W: It was a cluster of palm trees, growing in the shape of a W, silhouetted clearly in her line of sight against a backdrop of sky.

An analogy can be stretched beyond reason but, like the woman in the movie, I discovered something important at a time when I wasn't looking for it. The Lord has called it a sign, and signs are for recognition and identification. This sign isn't supposed to be another Bible mystery. It will stretch across the sky in brilliant illumination to herald the Second Coming of Jesus, according to the account of the Lord Himself (Mat. 24:27-30).

I think I know what it is.

Here's how this came about: Ten years ago I began reading the biblical book of Isaiah. When I came to the eighth verse of the sixth chapter, I stopped. Isaiah had heard the voice of God saying, "Whom shall I send, and who will go for Us?"

Responding enthusiastically, Isaiah said: "Here am I! Send me." And the rest of the book of Isaiah consists of great visions given supernaturally to the prophet, including many about the Day of the Lord when Jesus will return.

After reading this verse I prayed the same prayer Isaiah had prayed, and I meant it. During the next few days, as I read through the book of Isaiah, I started seeing prophetic imagery associated with that day which I hadn't noticed during many previous readings of the same Scriptures. I began compiling a list of the images and recognized what I thought were noteworthy similarities between them. I compared the Isaiah verses with each other and with Jesus' words as recorded in Matthew chapter 24. By the time I had finished reading the book of Isaiah this thought was in my mind:

I know what the sign of Jesus' return will be.

After another decade during which I have made frequent studies of the book of Isaiah and all the other biblical prophecies related to the Second Coming, I am more positive now than I was in the beginning. I feel like the woman in the park in the movie, knowing something, yet wondering when and how this information should be disclosed. Will anyone believe me if I tell them the unconventional idea that I am convinced is true?

The sign of Jesus' Second Coming will be a comet.

How, for the past ten years, have I been developing this thought? First of all, the evidence of about twenty cometic images in the book of Isaiah that originally put the idea in my head has grown over the years. By the time there were forty of them, in 2007, I wrote a book entitled *The Sign of His Coming,* which didn't have much impact on the Christian book industry. But now, eight years later, there are 54 of these images plus much more independent evidence.

Besides the 14 additional cometary images in Day of the Lord Scriptures, I have found evidence that 25 major events described in the Bible can be associated with the appearance of comets. These include the great Flood of Noah, destruction of the Tower of Babel, annihilation of Sodom and Gomorrah, the plagues of Exodus, the Red Sea crossing, the Long Day of Joshua and four events associated with Jesus. A total of 131 pieces of factual information add to the evidence that the 25 are cometic. Nothing significant—not a single scientific fact or verse of the Bible that I have found—contradicts any of this, and I have located relevant texts in 53 of the Bible's 66 books.

The first 24 of the 25 events already have happened, with descriptive details from many sources indicating that they were indeed associated with the appearance of comets. The only one of the 25 yet to occur is the return of Jesus. Identifying the celestial object that will herald the Day of the Lord, and encouraging believers on that day to proclaim the gospel of salvation with joy to "multitudes, multitudes in the valley of decision," is what this book is about (Joel 3:14).

PART ONE

THE SHORT PERIOD

Chapter One

The Great Flood

ONE OF MY favorite pastimes is doing puzzles. I enjoy puzzles of all kinds, but especially crosswords, jigsaws and Sudoku. Usually there is a picture of a jigsaw puzzle solution on the cover of its box. A good way to start a jigsaw puzzle is to find and set apart the straight-edge pieces. After completing the frame, the next step is to collect pieces of similar coloring and put them together to complete segments of the puzzle before fitting them all together to finish the project. It is helpful to take frequent looks at the picture on the box cover.

The theme picture of this book is a comet that has visited Earth three times and will make a fourth appearance to herald the Second Coming of Jesus on the Day of the Lord. The straight-edged pieces forming the frame of the puzzle are 54 objects mentioned in the Bible to signify comets such as this one. The inner portion of the puzzle includes a centerpiece of 25 biblical events involving comets and 131 important facts about these events.

The first biblical event we are to consider is the great Flood of Noah. Beginning with the Flood, using the jigsaw puzzle analogy, we shall show how God has employed comets for His purposes during critical times in world history. We shall conclude with three chapters giving evidence that He also will use a comet as the celestial sign heralding the Second Coming of His Son (Mat. 24:30).

And, finally, after completing the puzzle we shall have a clear view of the most important thing: God's people, recognizing the sign of Jesus' Second Coming, will have a chance to share the gospel of salvation with unbelievers, who will be terrified in the "valley of decision" during the days leading up to the wonderful events that will happen on the Day of the Lord (Joel 3:14).

It is the Lord's will that all should be saved and come to the knowledge of the truth (1 Tim. 2:4). The Day of the Lord comet will be the last and perhaps the greatest evangelism tool in world history. If God's people are faithful to do their part, millions upon millions of unbelievers will be urged to repent and turn to the Lord for eternal salvation during the final days of opportunity. All of Billy Graham's crusade audiences combined didn't have so much eternal potential.

The First Earthquakes

The early part of the biblical book of Genesis makes clear that the direct cause of the Flood was the hand of God.

He made the decision to inundate the Earth because of decadent behavior, especially an extreme of sexual immorality: "The sons of God saw the daughters of men, that they were beautiful; and they took wives for themselves of all whom they chose." (Gen. 6:2)

Various interpretations of this verse have been offered. If the sons of God were men, marrying and having intercourse with women, this would have pleased the Lord, who established and hallowed man-woman marriage. So, these sons of God must not have been men. The only other creatures likely to be described as sons of God were the angelic beings of God's creation. Angels faithful to God would not have done such a vile thing as to copulate with human beings. But all kinds of depravity have been engaged in by corrupted angels known as demons.

In a footnote to his translation of Josephus' account of the Flood, translator William Whiston wrote: "This notion, that the fallen angels were, in some sense, the fathers of the old giants, was the constant opinion of antiquity."[1]

Walt Brown's remarkable hydroplate theory provides one of the most meticulous and comprehensive scientific models of what occurred beneath the surface of the Earth during the Great Flood. Brown summarized: "Before the global flood, considerable water was under the earth's crust. Pressure increases in this subterranean water ruptured the crust, breaking it into plates. The escaping water flooded the earth."[2]

But what incited the pressure increases?

The key Bible verse identifying the two producers of the floodwaters was Genesis 7:11: "In the six hundredth year of Noah's life, in the second month, the seventeenth day of the month, on that day all the fountains of the great deep were broken up, and the windows of heaven were opened."

There must have been tectonic forces at work causing multiple breakages in the crust of the Earth that suddenly released the stored waters. Before the Flood, there were bodies of water contained within subterranean pockets beneath the oceans. But what generated these earth-rending quakes so suddenly after the Earth had existed for 1,656 years in comparative placidity?

The proposition here is that it was a large comet. In order for a comet to make a close approach to Earth, the model of the Solar System shows it would probably happen either in the spring or fall. In the case of the Flood, it happened in spring (second month in the Hebrew calendar), so our model is reasonable thus far.

As the comet came closer and closer, seismic activity would have been generated by the clashing gravitational fields of Earth and the intruder. The immediate result of this would have been enormous tidal disturbances in Earth's massive magma interior. These, in turn would have exerted tremendous pressures on the planet's mantle resulting in the breakups releasing vast quantities of previously buried waters.

To get an idea how much pressure can be exerted by Earth's liquid magma interior on Earth's solid mantle, you need to know only these facts. Earth has a solid iron/nickel core surrounded by magma that extends all the way to the mantle. The mantle (surface) occupies 22 miles. The magma covers a distance of more than 3,200 miles.

The earthquakes in which subterranean depths were fractured during the great Flood were described: "Enormous reservoirs of water were stored under the earth. This mighty collection of waters was called *t'hom*, 'the great deep' (cf. Gen. 1:2). These subterranean waters, confined by creative power on the second day of creation, were unleashed to pour forth in volume and in violence defying description. It was not an ordinary flood, but a giant tidal wave that broke suddenly upon a startled populace. *Baqa* indicates a terrestrial convulsion that split asunder every restraining barrier that had existed. It was a tumultuous breaking loose of indescribable destruction. Man cannot imagine the fury and the destructive might of the eruption, nor the awfulness of the display of God's power to destroy sinful beings. The complete corruption of men was far worse than any of us can imagine. The destruction was necessary."[3]

The First Rain Storm

There wasn't any rainfall during the first 1,656 years of human history. Earth was watered at that time by droplets, perhaps dews, condensing from a misty atmosphere (Gen. 2:6). There were no violent storms until the Flood of Noah, which produced the first rainfall and the first rainbow (Gen. 9:12-13). God designated that rainbow as the sign of His covenant with Noah that He would not destroy the Earth and its air-breathing creatures a second time by means of floodwaters (Gen. 9:14-16).

Those vast waters came from both above and beneath the Earth's surface, and they were released, according to the Bible, at precisely the same time (Gen. 7:11). This was either a monumental coincidence, or both outpourings resulted from a common cause. The hydroplate theory accounts for the subterranean waters, but what about torrents of rain falling for forty straight days and nights out of a sky that previously had not produced a single raindrop?

Waters emerging from beneath the Earth would not immediately evaporate, producing clouds generating forty straight days of torrential worldwide rains. Surface waters of the world today fill a volume comparable to the Flood era, but since the Flood at no time has it rained upon all of the world's oceans simultaneously for forty successive days.

The traditional ways of interpreting the forty days of rain described in Genesis chapter seven are to brush it aside as if it were a tall tale or a local event, or to try to explain it by saying there was a vapor canopy surrounding Earth that suddenly condensed, producing torrential rainfall.

The first two options are out, for we dare not corrupt the inspired Word of God (2 Tim. 3:16-17). Moreover, for the water level to rise more than twenty feet above the 17,000-foot Mount Ararat, where the ark landed a year later, would require a worldwide flood, not a local one: The world-encircling ocean waters seek universal levels. This means that if the water reached a height of 17,000 feet in the Middle East, it would reach the same height everywhere else in the world. The Flood was indeed a worldwide event, for there are historical traditions describing it in the artifact remains of ancient cultures all over the Earth.[4]

This leaves option number three. But if the suggested canopy contained enough water vapor to produce hundreds or even thousands of inches of worldwide rainfall, why didn't it rain before that time? And where did all that water come from? During the author's lifetime, the most intense rainfall was 21 inches during a 24-hour period in Fort Lauderdale. Sustain this rate of precipitation for forty days and you would have more than 800 inches of rain. The impression is given from the wording of Scriptures that there may have been a lot more than 800 inches of rainfall during the first forty days of the duration of the Flood.

So much rain certainly did not come from a vapor canopy. If Earth's atmosphere was that heavy with water vapor—and it is doubtful if it's possible that this could have been so—there would have been other torrential rains during the first millennium and a half of world history.

The only reasonable answer to this question is that, in order to produce the dual calamities that changed the face of a previously placid planet, there must have been an outside force. We reiterate the postulation that this force was a comet.

A comet alone of all celestial objects known to approach the Earth contains a sufficient quantity of water to dump torrential rains onto the surface of the Earth for forty days and forty nights. The coma (head) of a comet is huge. In the area of its orbit near the sun, it can be larger in dimensions than a planet, even as large as the sun. It consists of a comparatively small rocky core, surrounded by vast layers of ice and gases.

If a comet approached close enough to Earth so that it could be drawn at least temporarily into an orbit around the planet, the interacting gravitational fields of the two bodies would cause breakage on or near the solid surfaces of both. The comet's gases would dissipate and its ice layer would be broken up.

With a weight much heavier than the comet, Earth would draw to itself much of the gas and all of the ice that was breaking off the comet's coma. The ice would plummet through Earth's atmosphere and the frictional heat generated by the descent would melt the ice, causing it to fall as rain onto the planet's surface. There is so much ice in the comas of many comets that this process could continue for forty days, if the comet remained in proximity to Earth for that long. And this is something a comet is capable of doing.

Equally important is an explanation for the fact that, as suddenly as the downpour began, it ended. This too may be characteristic of a comet event. It could have happened that either the last of the comet's ice fell and melted on the fortieth day or that the comet moved away from its proximity to Earth at that time.

In the book *The Biblical Flood and the Ice Epoch*, author Donald W. Patten theorizes that a wayward planet, perhaps Mercury, caused the Flood. Patten's model of the event was well-constructed. It suggested that during the year of the Flood the celestial visitor made two complete orbits around the Earth before escaping once again into space.

Patten speculated that the intruder's two revolutions around Earth consumed about eight months of the year of the Flood. Early in that period of time ice breaking away from the visitor fell to Earth, melting along the way and generating the deluge.

It is possible that our comet premise and Patten's planet both may be correct. Recent observations have disclosed that attached to Mercury is a rudimentary tail similar to that of a comet, though less prominent. Perhaps at one time the planet Mercury was a comet, which had its orbit changed and its tail shortened during a lengthy encounter with Earth that resulted in the Flood.

But the two great new water producers were not enough to engulf a world boasting mountains topping off with Everest's 29,029 feet. Even Mount Ararat's 17,000-foot elevation would have stood far above the new waters generated by aspects of the Flood we have discussed so far. So how do we account for the Bible's statement that the floodwaters stood 22.5 feet (15 cubits) above the tops of the mountains for five months (Genesis 7:20-24)?

The depth of the deepest ocean today is about 36,000 feet. If all the water in the world could be distributed over a flat surface, it would rise to a height of about 12,000 feet above that surface.[5] But of course the Earth's surface is not now, nor has it ever been flat. From the beginning there was a land mass with varying elevations and a vast sea.

The new water generated by rain from ice that melted as it broke away from the comet and by the breaking up of water-filled subterranean caverns could have brought about a worldwide rise in sea level of two or three thousand feet. But how was it possible for waters of such depth to cover Earth's highest mountains?

The First Tall Mountains

The most logical answer to this question is that Earth's tallest mountains today did not exist before the Flood. At that time, the highest elevation of Earth was nowhere near the peak of Everest, or any other mountain taller than a few thousand feet. But, if that is true, there must have been mountainous uplift at some time during the Flood year to account for the new heights of Ararat, where the ark landed, and other peaks. Ararat is known to be volcanic.[6] It may have been uplifted during the massive seismic activity that broke open "the fountains of the great deep." But is there any other evidence of such uplift during the Flood?

Psalm 104:5-9 discusses the Flood: "Thou didst cover [Earth] with the deep as with a garment; the waters stood above the mountains. At thy rebuke they fled; at the sound of thy thunder they took to flight. The mountains rose, the valleys sank down to the place which thou didst appoint for them. Thou didst set a bound which they should not pass, so that they might not again cover the earth." (rsv)

This summarizes key points during the Flood year. It concludes with God setting boundaries above which He promised floodwaters would not rise to cover the Earth a second time. Although there is a reference to creation in the same context, this part of the text is not speaking of the creation event but of the unique promise of God to Noah after the Flood that He would not destroy life on Earth again with floodwaters (Gen. 9:11). It could not refer to the creation for that would make God a liar. He did cause floodwaters to cover the Earth after creating it.

During the Flood God covered the Earth with the *deep*, a word commonly used for deep waters or oceans. "The waters stood above the mountains" describes most of the first 150 days of the Flood, when the entire land mass was covered and all air-breathing creatures other than those in the ark were drowned (Gen. 7:23).

Elsewhere in the Bible, when the creation is described, there is similar terminology. But nowhere in these contexts does it say that the originally created waters covered mountaintops. The Bible verse describing the peak height of the waters during the great Flood was this: "And the waters prevailed exceedingly on the earth, and all the high hills under the whole heaven were covered." (Gen. 7:19)

This verse supports the idea that much new water was introduced by the breaking up of the ocean depths and also by the ice melting into rainfall as it plummeted through Earth's atmosphere after breaking away from the coma of the comet. It supports the idea that the Flood did indeed cover the entire pristine land mass of Earth, which would be impossible if the same topography existed then as does today.

The Hebrew word *har* usually translated *mountains* in the Bible, here in the NKJV appropriately is rendered *high hills*. The translators of the New King James and the original King James versions may have had scientific insight, or perhaps Holy Spirit guidance, because they used *high hills* instead of *mountains* in Genesis 7:19, during the initial phase of the Flood. This word can mean *mountains, high hills* or *a range of hills*. Some translations of the Bible, in some contexts, render it *hill country*.

After most of the dramatic events involved with the Flood were finished, we find this: "Then the ark rested in the seventh month, the seventeenth day of the month, on the *mountains* of Ararat. And the waters decreased continually until the tenth month. In the tenth month, on the first day of the month, the tops of the *mountains* were seen." (Gen. 8:4, NKJV)

These are two valid translations of the same Hebrew word. What seems to have happened is that after the fifth month, and before the tenth month, the magmatic interior of Earth was pushed and pulled so drastically by the presence of the celestial intruder that mountainous uplift occurred. It happened just as stated in the Bible "The mountains rose, the valleys sank down to the place which thou didst appoint for them." (Psalm 104:8, RSV) In Genesis chapter seven, before the dramatic upheaval, there were high hills; in chapter eight, afterward, there were mountains.

Also lending support to the concept of mountain uplift during the Flood are other translations of Psalm 104:8, including the Modern Language ("The mountains sprang up…") and the Amplified ("The mountains rose, the valleys sank down to the place which You appointed for them.")

Besides giving a model of the Flood year showing two revolutions around the Earth by the celestial visitor that we have suggested was a comet, Donald W. Patten also presented a diagram of the world showing how the high mountains of the Earth were created during the same two revolutions. Patten called them "the two zones of recent orogenetic uplift."[7]

Since the two ranges were formed in directions that did not parallel each other, Patten concluded that during the time when the celestial visitor was in closest proximity to Earth and the gravitational interaction was extreme, the Earth was under so much stress that its axis was twisted and its rotational pattern was altered. This could have accounted for the differing arc angles of the two sets of mountain ranges tracing the path of the comet's revolutions around Earth.

The original biblical account of the Flood describes this tersely. We include only the pertinent phrases from a verse already cited: "And the waters decreased continually until...the tops of the mountains were seen." (Gen. 8:5) The mountains literally rose out of the depths of the Flood to the ascendant stature they hold today. And at the same time as the mountains rose, the floodwaters subsided into new depths being gouged out of the Earth simultaneously with the uplift. It was like a child squeezing a handful of clay. Some of it squirts out between fingers like mini-mountains; some of it is squeezed into depressed areas like valleys.

In *The Flood*, Alfred M. Rehwinkel described this process: "Think of the enormous volume of water rushing on with ever-increasing speed toward the new lower levels as the bottom of the sea slowly gave way and great land masses were forced up and new mountain ranges were being born. The eroding, transporting, and stratifying force of such masses of water in motion is beyond calculation...

"Volumes of water of such proportions, set into torrential motion, laden with rocks, gravel and other debris, rushing over the newly deposited materials not yet solidified and confined to places of narrow channels because of the rising mountains, could easily scoop out a Niagara Gorge, a Grand Canyon, and similar channels, or build up a Mississippi delta measured by thousands of square miles in a matter of days and weeks instead of the fantastic millions and billions of years commonly ascribed to that process."[8]

The First Volcanoes

If the ideas expressed so far in this chapter about the Flood are correct, they can be confirmed by finding evidence of massive volcanism at the time of the Flood. Ordinary volcanism, with an erupting volcano here and there, would not serve as confirmation for a theory that involves extraordinary seismic activity resulting in ruptures deep in the Earth that released enormous quantities of "new" water. If it cannot be established that massive lava bleeds also took place at the time of the Flood, we need to conceive another theory.

In *The World That Perished*, John C. Whitcomb discussed "the presence of enormous masses of igneous (volcanic) rock all over the world."[9] Whitcomb suggested that this may have occurred at the time of the Flood:

"The Columbia Plateau, of the northwestern United States, is a tremendous lava plateau of almost incredible thickness (several thousand feet) covering about 200,000 square miles. But the only modern process at all pertinent to these phenomena is that of volcanism, which in its present character could not possibly have produced these great igneous formations…The principal of uniformity breaks down completely at this important point of geologic interpretation. Some manifestation of catastrophic action alone (such as the breaking up of the fountains of the great deep during the Flood) is sufficient."[10]

The plateau described by Whitcomb covers two-thirds of Oregon, half of Washington and parts of three other states. Patten is more definite than Whitcomb in asserting that this plateau originated during the Flood: "In the intermontane plateau west of the Rockies and east of the Cascades there was a great outpouring of lava during the Flood catastrophe. In some places, the lava deposits exceed 8,000 feet in depth upon original bedrock. There are many successive layers of lava, anywhere from a few inches to hundreds of feet thick."[11]

The many layers could be attributed to the daily tidal effects of the interaction between Earth and the comet. The ice deposition area in Eastern Washington, to be discussed in the final part of this chapter, probably coincided with the lava flow. Patten states: "We contend that at this time of cataclysmic upheaval, lava flowed or bled out upon the Earth's surface in several parts of the world."[12] Here he mentions parts of Africa, India, Arabia and Brazil.

Rehwinkel concurs: "The devastating earthquakes accompanying the Flood were supplemented, or rather were produced either in part or entirely, by volcanic activities simultaneously occurring in every part of the earth."[13]

Rehwinkel mentions loess, a volcanic substance found in great quantities worldwide, and cites its universal presence as evidence for worldwide volcanism at the time of the Flood. He asserts: "My belief is that the loess is the product of subterranean volcanic eruptions...and that it is volcanic dust."[14]

He concludes that the source of the loess was the Flood: "The manner in which, and the places where it has been deposited, its ubiquity, the lateness of its deposition, its disregard for watershed, seems to postulate the action of water on a scale equal only to the great Flood described in Genesis."[15]

Whitcomb and Henry M. Morris, in *The Genesis Flood*, take note of the absence of geologic evidence for any volcanism before the Flood. They comment: "Great volcanic explosions and eruptions are clearly implied in the statement [in Gen. 7:11] that 'all the fountains of the great deep [were] broken up.' This must mean that great quantities of liquids, perhaps liquid rocks or magmas, as well as water (probably steam), had been confined under pressure below the surface rock structure of the earth since the time of its formation and that this mass now burst forth through great fountains, probably both on the lands and under the seas. By analogy with present phenomena associated with volcanism, there must also have been great earthquakes and tsunamis (popularly known as tidal waves) generated throughout the world. These eruptions and waves would have augmented the Flood waters as well as accomplished great amounts of geologic work directly."[16]

Indeed, there seems to have been worldwide volcanism during the Flood.

The First Freeze

We have discussed the idea that melting ice from a comet was the primary source of the vast quantities of rainfall during the Flood. But is it possible that after the forty days of rainfall some of the ice could have fallen to Earth without melting? Could it have launched what geologists refer to as the Ice Age?

The popular glacial theory is that most of North America, including all of Canada and portions of the United States, in addition to half of Europe and large parts of other continents, were covered at a time in the distant past with an enormous quantity of slowly moving ice comparable to but much larger than the glaciers found today in Greenland, the Antarctica and other parts of the Earth.

According to this theory, there were four or five glacial periods in world history, spanning millions of years.

During this time-span the climate changed very slowly until Earth was converted from a semitropical paradise into an icy wasteland. Then, for reasons unexplained, the world's climate changed again, the ice melted, the glaciers receded and again the planet bloomed, only to be turned into a glacial waste once more. And so the cycle was said to have repeated itself several times.

There are many problems with the glacial theory, including the basic one of failure to identify a cause of such radical climate vacillations. It needs to be understood that the theory of glaciation, like the theory of evolution, is just that—a *theory* developed by speculative human beings. It is said to have taken place so long ago that its truth or falsity cannot be ascertained by scientific experimentation.

After explaining some of the details of the theory of glaciation, including the blotting out of the sun over certain regions of Earth for millions of years while it continued to shine in other regions at the same latitude, Rehwinkel concluded:

"All of this is so utterly contrary to the process of the laws of nature, as we know them, that a miracle greater than the Flood would be required to account for such changes. It is folly therefore to assume that the glacial theory simplifies the problems of geology, or that it removes them beyond the sphere of the miraculous."[17]

And what about all of those fossils found in the so-called glaciated ice? There is a layer of them comparable to the layer found all over the world in water-laid clay that can be attributed to the Flood. Are we to believe that those mammoths stood there for long periods of time, while glaciers inched forward, covered and froze them? Or is it more reasonable that these creatures, found frozen in standing positions in Siberia, were trapped during a sudden, disastrous event? Writes Rehwinkel: "There they perished suddenly in some great catastrophe, and they have been preserved in cold storage to the present day."[18]

Rehwinkel, Patten and other geologists and archaeologists have produced evidence that there was a warmer climate, even in the polar regions, before the Flood than afterward. One of the clearest pieces of evidence for this is the finding of many fossils of tropical plants in polar territory.

Rehwinkel concluded that the animals drowned during the Flood, and those in polar regions were frozen as a result of a rapid period of climate change during the year of the Flood. It is likely that volcanism was involved with this change. Perhaps there were dramatic temperature drops for days or even weeks while volcanic emissions were polluting the skies and blocking the sun's rays throughout the globe.

A sudden cold snap occurred in Europe during 1783 and was attributed to emissions from an eruption of the Icelandic volcano, Skaptor Jokel. "It was coupled with the volcano Asamayo in Japan the same year, one of several combination eruptions throughout the world which at various times have joined forces to affect the atmosphere."[19]

We contend that, whenever two or more major volcanic eruptions occur simultaneously, it is wise to look for a common cause of the eruptions. First on that list would be the approach of a comet.

Or, as Patten postulated, a celestial visitor could be the direct cause of a sudden freeze. He thought the mammoths and other creatures in polar zones were victims of a sudden dump of ice from such an intruder onto the Earth.

Patten theorized that ice on the surface of an object roving the outer darkness of the solar system could become super-cooled to temperatures between minus-200 and minus-325 degrees Fahrenheit. At such low temperatures, a huge quantity of ice descending toward Earth in a polar region might not melt before striking the ground. On impact, it would splatter in all directions, leaving marks similar to those that have been identified as glacial movement. It might have quick-frozen millions of animals, including the mammoths. A comet, containing massive quantities of ice, would be the most likely source of such a sudden freeze, even one utilizing the intermediary participation of volcanoes.

Both Rehwinkel's and Patten's ideas have credibility. But there is a problem in explaining how ice from a comet's coma should fall to Earth as rain for forty days but then suddenly stop melting on the way down and descend intact as ice. By whatever means the comet produced the temperature change—and the most likely way appears to be volcanism—the Ice Age was associated with the Flood, and that is more reasonable than trying to make glaciers inch along for millions of years.

It makes sense that the mammoths would not have been discovered frozen in a standing position if they were crushed under tons of ice. They drowned during the Flood and then were quick-frozen just as they have been found more than 4,000 years later.

Summary

The Flood was a horrific global event that must have been as catastrophic for the comet as the Earth. Indeed, it is likely that the comet, with less mass than the Earth, did not survive. This would explain why there is no clear evidence of this comet returning to Earth at another time. Or, alteration of the comet's orbit may have resulted in its conversion to the planet Mercury. Whichever of these theories is correct, at the time the celestial intruder encountered Earth it was a comet.

We have then this summary of the aspects of the great Flood—the first seven pieces comprising the first segment of our big-picture jigsaw puzzle (All of these events were "firsts" for the Earth at that time.):

- An Earth-approaching comet's gravitational field interacted with Earth's to generate catastrophic seismic activity.

- Earthquakes rent the Earth so that the depths of the oceans were broken up releasing new torrents of water from pockets beneath.

- Blocks of ice broke off the coma of the comet, melted while falling through Earth's atmosphere and fell as sheets of rain.

- New mountains were formed by the continuing seismic action, including the highest ranges existing in the post-diluvial world.

- Worldwide volcanism accompanied the breaking up of the deeps and the mountainous uplift.

- In addition to rainfall, the comet may have dumped a huge amount of ice onto polar areas of the Earth, resulting in the Ice Age.

- Or there may have been a freeze resulting from volcanic air pollution. Either way, the Ice Age began during the year of the Flood.

Chapter Two

Sodom

AFTER THE FLOOD there is no mention in the Bible or other historical records of sudden natural catastrophes for more than three centuries. It's possible that there were none. It is probable that a 54-year cycle of disasters, known to be in effect in later centuries, did not begin with the comet that generated the global Flood. The Flood event devastated the Earth, and it seems unlikely that the comet could have survived it. Comets often are destroyed during clashes with planets, so it isn't surprising that we can't trace any more appearances of this comet.

It isn't necessary to establish with certainty which event launched the 54-year cycle of disasters. The comet that demolished the Tower of Babel and caused the "dividing" of the Earth into continents circa 1975 B.C. was timed so that it could have been the one, but it's more likely that it had a 2,000-year orbit (See Chapter Twelve). The next major event after that was the destruction of Sodom and Gomorrah, which happened when Abraham was 99 years old, circa 1923 B.C.

The event began with a warning from the Lord for Lot to take his wife and two daughters and flee the city of Sodom, which was about to be destroyed. Lot's sons-in-laws thought it was a joke and stayed in the city. While the four members of his family were fleeing there must have been preliminary rumblings because Lot feared imminent death. He pleaded with the Lord to be allowed to go to a small town nearby because he didn't think he and his family could make it as far as the mountains where they had been told to go. The Lord gave permission, and, while Lot and his family were leaving the danger area, the cataclysm occurred:

"Then the Lord rained brimstone and fire on Sodom and Gomorrah, from the Lord out of the heavens. So He overthrew those cities, all the plain, all the inhabitants of the cities, and what grew on the ground." (Gen. 19:24-25)

Like many other catastrophes discussed in this book, the biblical description of this one uses the Hebrew word usually translated *overthrow* or *overturn*. As we proceed with this study, we shall see that this verb was used often in the Bible to describe catastrophes resulting from overhead approaches of comets. The destruction of the Sodom area was so frightening that after it was over Lot's daughters got their father drunk and induced him to have sex with them because they thought it was the only way to sustain the human race on what appeared to them to be a desolate planet. Before suggesting the incestuous act, one of the young women said to the other: "Our father is old, and there is no man on the earth to come into us." (Gen. 19:31).

Archaeologists studying the area of the Dead Sea have found evidence of large quantities of soil and other surface materials being blasted out of the ground and hurled high into the air. They believe this happened at around the time when the Sodom event occurred. Here is a concise statement of their viewpoint:

"It was within God's power to produce an earthquake [in the Great Rift Valley] that would explode and throw immense supplies of petroleum into the air. When all the inflammable stuff was ignited, sheets of literal fire poured back to complete the destruction. Searing flames and black smoke must have covered every area of the city [Sodom], smothering and consuming every living thing."[1]

It was within God's power to produce an earthquake, especially in the volatile soil of the Rift Valley, but He had other options. The Bible suggests that the Sodom disaster was launched from above, not beneath. It pictures an angry God hurling down fire and brimstone "out of the heavens." Adam Clarke's analysis of what happened is more in line with the scriptural account:

"A shower of nitrous particles might have been precipitated from the atmosphere, here, as in many other places, called heaven, which by the action of fire would be immediately ignited, and so consume the cities; and, as we have already seen that the plains about Sodom and

Gomorrah abounded with asphaltus or bitumen pits, that what is particularly meant here in reference to the plain is the setting fire to this vast store of inflammable matter by the agency of lightning."[2]

Or, perhaps, there could have been another agency of ignition. The Clarke analysis falls short on two counts. First, it does not explain how the nitrous particles were precipitated from the atmosphere: What caused it to happen? How did they precipitate? Second, it does not explain how lightning can cause massive quantities of heavy earthen materials to be thrown high into the air. In fairness to Clarke, at the time he was working on his commentary two centuries ago, he did not have access to as much information as is available today.

We propose that there is but one explanation that fits all of the details of the Sodom event, based on the biblical description and archaeological discoveries: A comet approached Earth and its force fields interacted with those of Earth. There may have been seismic activity, but what happened to Sodom was that one or more incendiary pieces broke off the disintegrating comet and fell to Earth, like a bombardment of fire and brimstone, i.e., burning sulfur.

One aspect of the event may have been that when the incendiary elements landed, they ignited the bituminous, asphaltic, sulfurous and gaseous substances that abounded in the soil of that area. But it is more likely that it was the comet that deposited these elements there. The fires quickly consumed the entire area surrounding Sodom and Gomorrah, turning them into ashes (2 Peter 2:6). The name Sodom meant *burnt to ashes*. Ashes are the final remnants of very hot fires. They are susceptible to being blown away, and that is exactly what happened to Sodom and Gomorrah, as will be shown as we discuss other aspects of the event.

What Abraham Saw

The topography suggests that the city of Sodom could have been either at the northern end or the southern end of the Dead Sea. No remains have been found in the area suggesting that the two cities were anywhere outside the present boundaries of the sea, which stretches about forty miles in length, North to South, as an extension of the Jordan River. It is ten miles or less in width, but is much wider toward the northern than the southern end.

Because of the lack of discoveries suggesting otherwise, most archaeologists believe Sodom and Gomorrah were located in areas that are now buried beneath the sea. Most of them locate Sodom near the southern end, because it is shallow and Sodom was described as lying on a plain.

A comment in the Bible is important in establishing the site of the two cities. It says that when Abraham arose on the morning of the disaster, he went to the place where he had interceded for the Lord to spare Sodom and looked in the direction of the city. He saw "the smoke of the land which went up like the smoke of a furnace." (Gen. 19:28) Ashes were rising as we see them do after ascending through chimneys. And there was more than just smoke and ashes.

Abraham was living in Hebron, less than twenty miles west of the widest part of the Dead Sea, its northern half. Abraham had settled there after his nephew Lot had chosen the Sodom area for his residence. If Sodom was due East of Hebron as seems likely, it was situated within the northern boundaries of what would become the Dead Sea. If the city had been in the southern area of the sea, Abraham might not have been able to see the remnants of the disaster, over hill country, forty miles away.

Even if Abraham could have seen the southern end of the sea from where he was, it is more likely that Sodom was in the northern half. A key point is that Sodom was within a day's journey of Hebron. In Genesis chapter 18, angels appearing in the form of men leave Abraham's house in Hebron and journey to Sodom in a single day. The maximum day's journey in those times was twenty miles. Sodom probably was due east of Hebron, for that part of the Dead Sea is the only part within twenty miles of Hebron.

Furthermore, Sodom was the direct target the Lord was aiming at, and He doesn't miss. The southern sector of the sea shows little evidence of ground-surface damage. To this day it remains a plain of shallow depth, nowhere deeper than fifteen feet and in many places less than ten feet deep.

The northern half of the sea covers an area, which, if not filled with water, would be seen as a catastrophic crater. It likely was gouged during the event that destroyed Sodom. Josephus wrote, "God cast a thunderbolt upon the city and set it on fire with its inhabitants; and laid waste the country with the like burning."[3]

This was not a case of an underground explosion blowing debris into the air, but of an aerial assault. A "thunderbolt" was a bolide, a large explosive rock descending from the sky and blowing up noisily like a bomb. A disintegrating comet can produce a dozen or more large bolides. A bolide is a rock containing a variety of explosive and incendiary chemicals, including sulfur and methane, and possibly their deadly derivatives sulfuric acid and methanol.

Sulfur is so explosive that it is used in the manufacture of black gunpowder. A comet may contain thousands of times as much sulfur as a single charge of gunpowder. A sulfurous stench is present and prevalent during many comet events. A bolide explodes upon hitting the ground or shortly before impact. Whether it is an air blast or a contact explosion, its force can be of nuclear proportions.

In July of 1994, Comet Shoemaker-Levy 9 approached Jupiter and was torn apart by the planet's powerful gravitational field. The comet broke into 21 pieces, most of them bigger than the largest known asteroid. Some of the pieces generated explosions leaving enormous scars on the surface of the planet.

Comets cause events with many ramifications, celestial and terrestrial. A single comet can produce a dozen or more bolides. A bolide is a rock containing a variety of explosive and incendiary chemicals. During descent or upon hitting the ground, a bolide explodes. Whether it is an air blast or a contact explosion, its force can be much greater than that of a nuclear bomb. So, along with the other debris raining from the sky, there was a nuclear-level blast.

Bolidic explosions can do immense damage, as did the one that destroyed the Tower of Babel (See Chapter Twelve). But in the case of Sodom, the explosion was not an aerial blast, like the one at Ur. The bolide—an enormous piece of the comet's shattering coma, or perhaps the entire piece of rock that made up the core of the coma—exploded on contact with the ground. The result was a gigantic crater at the northern end of the lake, directly opposite the viewing position of Abraham, who saw a cloud of smoke rising "like the smoke of a furnace" (Gen. 19:28).

The Sodom crater has been measured in depth up to 1,000 feet, which is not surprising: "The impact of even a small comet fragment (bolide) over Sodom and Gomorrah could release energy equivalent to the explosion of many hydrogen bombs and raise a mushroom cloud like that in nuclear explosions."[4]

We have mentioned the idea that the Sodom event could have been one in which an intact comet's coma fell and exploded. If the coma had broken to pieces there would be evidence in recorded annals elsewhere in the world of other regions of the globe being blown up at about the same time. So, it is the opinion here that Sodom was destroyed, not by one of numerous pieces of a large comet, such as the ones that assailed Jupiter in 1994, but by a single bolide—the rocky core of a medium-sized comet—like the isolated Tunguska blast in 1908.

The comet that assaulted Jupiter dropped 21 bolides onto the surface of the planet and left earth-sized scars. The one that blew away Sodom had just one missile, but it had a specific target and was guided by the hand of God.

Concerning the idea that Sodom was wiped out by an earthquake, neither the biblical account nor that of Josephus give credence to it. The vast crater at the bottom of the Dead Sea and the huge cloud of smoke rising from the site of the explosion in full view of Abraham, nearly twenty miles away, support the premise that this was a bolide. One instant, Sodom was there. The next, it was gone.

Before God's judgmental assault on Sodom, it lay upon a beautiful plain near the west bank of the Jordan River, which then probably extended the full length of the Rift Valley and emptied into the Gulf of Aqaba. The explosion that destroyed Sodom was even more dramatic than the massive volcanic blast of Thera that blew away an entire island civilization, perhaps the legendary Atlantis, and left a caldera in the Aegean Sea. The Sodom blast did indeed eject massive amounts of earthen materials out of the ground, as archaeologists have surmised, and left a hole in the ground larger than the Thera caldera. Archaeologists aren't likely to find remains of Sodom anywhere in the Dead Sea area, even at the bottom of the crater, because no traces remain of that wicked city or its evil neighbor Gomorrah.

After the explosion, the river filled in the crater and, like all moving waters, began to erode away soil in its direction of flow, forming the shallow southern end of the sea as it exists today. If it continues to erode, perhaps at some future time it will resume flowing all the way to the Gulf of Aqaba.

The Salt Sea

Alternative names of the Dead Sea are Lake Asphaltitis (Greek) and the Sea of Salt. There is much salt in the sea and the soil of the area. It has been associated with Lot's wife, whom the Bible says was turned into a pillar of salt. (Gen. 19:26)

Near the southern part of the sea there are large salt deposits. One of them was measured to a depth of 150 feet. There are also many pillars of salt. It has been speculated that one of them fell from the sky and buried Lot's wife during the destruction of Sodom and Gomorrah.

What may have happened was this: Lot and his family fled the city heading in a southerly direction along the river, where their progress was swift because they remained on the plain. Knowing that the entire river valley area would be affected by the blast that destroyed Sodom, the Lord warned Lot to go instead into the nearby mountains, but agreed to a first destination of tiny Zoar, on the plain.

While fleeing, Lot's wife turned continually, casting frequent inquisitive looks in the direction of the city. She fell behind her husband and daughters and was buried under a heap of salt that fell from the sky.

It is possible that this was fallout from the blast that blew up the city, but that would have made it a part of the latter portion of the event, hours or possibly even days after the big blast. More likely, it was a preliminary part, occurring in conjunction with the biblical account describing the fire and brimstone raining on the city from the hand of God.

Along with fire and brimstone, there apparently was a lot of salt falling from the comet. Recent studies of comets have shown that they contain large quantities of many kinds of substances, including sodium. For instance, the observable surface of the coma of Kohoutek was found to be covered with salt. Hale-Bopp had a long tail of sodium. The Deep Impact Mission probing the coma of Tempel 1 in 2005 revealed the presence of sodium.

During interaction with Earth, a comet in an early phase of conflict could dump large piles of salt onto the planet. Some of the salt falling from the Sodom comet fell on Lot's wife, like sand being unloaded from a celestial dump truck.

But the presence of salt piles near the southern end of the Dead Sea doesn't necessarily mean Sodom was situated there. The family of Lot already had left the Sodom area and might have been headed south, where the salt piles have been found. Or, equally likely, they weren't far from the area that is now buried beneath the northern end of the sea.

In ancient times there was so much salt in that area that a settlement adjacent to the northern extremity of the sea was named the City of Salt.[5] Today, the same location is identified as Qumran, site of the discovery of the Dead Sea Scrolls, which have provided confirmatory evidence for the authenticity of the Bible.

Since there seems to have been a large amount of sodium on the Sodom comet, this helps explain other aspects of the event. While sodium-chloride (salt) is a stable substance, natural sodium is not. Both natural sodium and salt have been found in large quantities on comets. If both were involved in the Sodom event, it could account for the fire falling from heaven. When brought into contact with water, elemental sodium ignites. If while falling to earth sodium passed through a rain cloud, some of it would have burst into flames on the way down.

This would be even more likely if, in addition to sodium, some ice broke off the head of the comet. Ice would melt while falling through Earth's atmosphere and the water, falling as rain, would react with the falling sodium to generate a fiery precipitation, exactly as described in the Bible (Gen. 19:24).

The explosive blast that followed as a bolide struck the ground would have been augmented by the sodium falling along with it. As the sodium fell into the river, it would have generated a series of fire-bursts. *Brimstone* is a descriptive word meaning an extremely flammable, sulfurous substance. It was burned in antiquity as a purifying agent. How appropriate that God should use a purifying agent in the fiery purging of sinful Sodom!

The resultant crater from the blast is so deep that it has become a slowing-down point for the river that flows into it. Some of the flowing waters make it through the deep northern end of the sea, but they are sluggish and terminate in the shallow southern end.

The blast was so terrible that the Earth may have trembled all the way to Athens, Greece, about 700 miles away. The ancient Greeks gave the sea a Greek name—Lake Asphaltitis.

While the ashes rising from the charred remains of Sodom and Gomorrah were being dispersed, other smoldering particles that had been blasted out of the crater continued to fall back to earth. This fallout may have been one of the reasons that Lot and his daughters left Zoar and took refuge in a mountain cave, where they should have gone in the first place: It was dangerous to dwell in the open with fiery debris falling all around them.

Another reason they stayed in the mountain cave was that they feared being close to the desolate plain where the cataclysm had taken place. (Gen. 19:30). "[The Lord] overthrew the cities in which Lot had dwelt." (Gen. 19:29) The cave probably was northeast of the sea. The descendants of Lot were the Ammonites (Deut. 2:19). The Ammonites settled in the area east and northeast of the sea, perhaps not far from the original site of Sodom.

What an awesome picture of the judgment of God upon sin! It happened first in Eden, and then the Flood and the Tower of Babel, Sodom and the plagues of Egypt, all discussed in this book. These are but preliminaries to the grand finale on the Day of the Lord analyzed in the closing chapters of this work. Describing both Sodom and the Day of the Lord, Jesus said: "On the day that Lot went out of Sodom it rained fire and brimstone from heaven and destroyed them all. Even so will it be in the day when the Son of Man is revealed." (Luke 17:29-30).

Most of the inhabitants of Sodom were "dead" in sin before the purgative fire-fall and deadly explosion, so it seems appropriate that water filling in the new crater is known as the Dead Sea and that the sea is devoid of living things.

Abraham's Astronomy

Josephus wrote that while Abraham was sojourning in Egypt he shared his astronomical knowledge with the Egyptians, "for, before Abram came into Egypt, they were unacquainted with those parts of learning; for that science came from the Chaldeans into Egypt, and from thence to the Greeks also."[6]

One of the themes of the twelfth chapter of this book is that Abraham and his family were living in Ur of the Chaldees, site of the Tower of Babel, when God destroyed the tower by means of a comet-generated bolide exploding in air directly above it. Abraham's youngest brother Haran may have been killed in the Babel blast, and it seems as if the impressionable Abraham, then known as Abram, began taking interest in sky-watching at that time.

The Bible states that the people living in Ur, including Abram's father Terah, were disobedient in remaining there after God had instructed them to disperse throughout the Earth (Gen. 9:1, 11:4). These were mostly the descendants of Noah's son Shem. However, apparently, the descendants of another son of Noah, Ham, already had migrated to the southwest into Africa, and had settled in Egypt. The Hamites did not know as much as Abram and the other Chaldeans knew about the Babel event, which had led them into astronomical studies.

Abram's next astronomical experience was seeing the smoldering remains of Sodom after it was destroyed during a comet event. No doubt he also saw the comet in the sky on that occasion, as he had in Ur.

It is possible that Abraham witnessed one more comet event for, upon the occasion of his visit to Egypt, the Bible says there was a famine (Gen. 12:10). Not all famines are caused by comets. But there is evidence that this one was.

It occurred 430 years before the Exodus (Exo. 12:40). At this time, according to one source, there was a comet event that fit into the cyclical pattern of the comet with a 54-year orbit.[7] We have no details of the event that caused this famine, but another famine, again within the 54-year cycle, occurred 215 years later—four times 54 equals 216—and forced Jacob's family into Egypt in search of food. Finally, after another cyclical period of 215 years there was another famine, this time in Egypt, turning that once-fertile land into desert. The ten plagues that decimated Egypt and their source are to be discussed in Chapter Three.

Moreover, unless you believe in coincidence, during Abram's stay in Egypt, the topic of astronomy probably didn't come up casually. If there had been, indeed, a comet event that caused famine in some lands, it would have been a major topic of conversation for the Egyptians and all of the peoples who had migrated there to find food. Abram's experiences would have made him an expert on the subject, as were other Chaldeans who had witnessed the fall of the Tower of Babel. Thus, the words of Josephus are significant that not only Abraham but other Chaldeans arriving in Egypt were knowledgeable in astronomy.

Job's Afflictions

There is no timeframe in the book of Job, but most biblical scholars believe he lived contemporary with one or more of the patriarchs Abraham, Isaac and/or Jacob. Jacob lived to age 147, Isaac to 180 and Abraham to 175. Job had ten children before the events that killed them all, afflicted their father with painful boils, and left him desolate. He lived 140 years after that, so his full lifespan may have been between 180 and 200 years. This longevity made it likely that he was a contemporary of Abraham and his father, Terah, who lived to the age of 205. This was during the period after the flood when the age expectancy of human beings declined because of changing atmospheric and geologic conditions, so it was for only two or three generations that this was the normal lifespan.

If Job, a Hebrew, was indeed a contemporary of Terah and Abraham, he would have known about the destruction of Sodom and perhaps was directly affected by it. Job lived in Uz, a land that was near Edom or perhaps was another name for Edom (Lam. 4:21).

The land of Edom lay southeast of the Dead Sea, so it is possible that the home of Job was not far from ground zero of the celestial barrage that destroyed Sodom. Some of the fallout from the comet could have been "the fire from God [that] fell from heaven and burned up" Job's sheep and shepherds (Job 1:16).

Comets can place stress on Earth's atmosphere and generate terrible storms, including tornadoes more powerful than the ones that have flattened Midwestern towns in the United States. It might have been a comet-created tornado that blew "across the wilderness and struck the four corners of the house" in which Job's children were gathered, killing all ten of them (Job 1:19).

The biblical description of a "great wind" simultaneously striking the four corners of a house refers to a tornado that passed directly over and/or through the house. Its circulating winds engulfed the house from all directions—the four corners of the house—and destroyed it.

Tornadoes are generated when radically different airstreams collide. The colder air in one stream descends while the warmer air in the other rises and forms a persistently rotating updraft known as a supercell. Supercells can spawn tornadoes. The most powerful tornado on record in the United States had wind velocities higher than 300 miles per hour.

Upon the approach of a comet to Earth, the potential would exist for clashes of extraordinarily hot and cold airstreams. There would be fires set by methane, sulfur and other flammable elements ejected by the comet onto the Earth. The hot air generated by the flames, and also by volcanism associated with the comet, would clash with cold air produced by icy discharges from the comet's head. Tornadoes generated by supercells formed under such extreme conditions might produce winds twice as strong as those from non-comet sources.

In the biblical story of Job the next thing that happened was an outbreak of painful boils on his body. The above-cited Job 1:16 identified the fire-fall as an act of God, as are all events that happen within the province of the natural universe God created. But Satan also was a participant in this process (Job 1:6-12, 2:1-6). It was he who incited the Sabeans and Chaldeans to raid Job's property, killing many of his servants and stealing his oxen, donkeys and camels (Job 1:15, 17).

The only aspect of the series of events left in doubt was the source of sore boils that broke out on Job's body. The Bible says Satan received permission from God to do physical harm to Job, short of killing him, so it is often assumed that Satan caused the boils. But God was directing this event and the Bible states that God was the source of the "fire that fell from heaven." The breakout on Job's skin occurred immediately after the fire-fall, and inflammation of the skin of human beings and animals can be a result of such a fiery comet event. Job, in talking with his friends after the terrible event, said "the hand of God struck me." (Job 19:21) This is common phraseology for the destructive action of a comet.

Sulfuric acid, burning methane and/or flaming sodium falling to earth from a comet can produce painful inflammations on human skin, and we know sulfur and sodium were present during the Sodom event. The Hebrew word translated *sore boil* meant a burn, inflammation or ulcerous sore. It seems as if Job may have done what we all have done at some time or other—got caught in the rain. Heavy rainfall apparently was a byproduct of the Sodom comet event, and the combination of raindrops and burning sulfur falling from a comet could produce a deadly precipitation of sulfuric acid and/or a corrosive aerosol. The only other element necessarily present to complete the process would be carbon dioxide.

In fact, sulfuric acid is known to exist naturally, in vast amounts in vaporous form, in the atmosphere of the planet Venus. The mysterious thick clouds enshrouding Venus consist mostly of sulfuric acid.

The Bible's description of Job scraping away his blackened skin indicates that sulfuric acid was the probable cause (Job 2:8, 30:30). If you want to survive, you won't scrape away skin that has been severely burned, as by flaming sodium or methane. But a person with acid-damaged skin might use a scraper to remove remnants of the corrosive acid. Sulfuric-acid-damaged skin would be blackened. It would look and smell awful (2:12).

The description of Job sitting in ashes could refer to the scrapings of his skin, but more likely makes reference to the completion of fallout a few days after the event. By that time the smoking remains of Sodom that Abraham saw rising into the sky would have settled back to earth and left a layer of ash on the surface of the ground (Job 2:8, 2 Peter 2:6).

We shall discuss this subject further in Chapter Three in connection with the plagues God sent upon Egypt while Pharaoh was refusing to let the Israelites leave. The biblical and Josephus descriptions of the sixth plague give more detail about boils resulting from cosmic fallout than does the book of Job.

Even if the skin-blackening was directly caused by Satan, it does not mean that God and His celestial agent, the comet, were not involved. Just as God uses comets, he employs Satan and his evil minions to accomplish His purposes (see 1 Sam. 16:14-23, 18:10, 19:9; 1 Kings 22:21-23). Satan could not have done anything to Job without God's authorization (Job 1:6-12, 2:1-6).

One of Job's post-calamity speeches, quoted in the Bible, mentions four things that can be associated with comet events: Mountains flattened, stars obscured from view, a sun failing to rise at the usual time, and seismic activity so violent that Earth's normal axis of rotation was disturbed (Job 9:5-8). Job seems to have been describing repercussions of the comet event he witnessed as it zeroed in on Sodom near his home in Edom—even the axial disturbance that, if his language is to be taken literally, delayed a sunrise and created a long night as an obverse of the long day of Joshua ten orbital cycles later.

The apostle Peter wrote that Sodom was a type of the judgmental event described in Chapter Thirteen of this book that will terminate world history: "And turning the cities of Sodom and Gomorrah into ashes, [God] condemned them to destruction, making them an example of those who afterward would live ungodly; and delivered righteous Lot, who was oppressed by the filthy conduct of the wicked." (2 Pet. 2:6-7)

Here's a ten-piece summation of the Sodom puzzle segment:

- The Lord directed a comet into a position from which it could assault Sodom and Gomorrah.

- The comet ejected incendiary materials, including sodium and sulfurous rock that is identifiable as brimstone.

- The sodium combined with moisture to create fiery rainfall, and touched off a series of explosions on the surface of the Jordan River.

- A pile of salt falling from the comet buried Lot's wife as she dallied and looked back inquisitively.

- A large bolide landed directly on Sodom and exploded, blowing away the city and its surrounding area.

- The explosion left a thousand-foot-deep crater where Sodom, Gomorrah and a portion of the Jordan River had been.

- From his home in Hebron, Abraham saw the smoke and ashes of Sodom rising into the sky as a mushroom cloud.

- Job's home was so close to Sodom that fiery fallout from the comet killed his sheep and shepherds and caused his skin to blister.

- A tornado generated by the comet demolished a house, killing all ten of Job's children.

- The sore boils that broke out on Job's skin were caused by acidic fallout from the comet.

Chapter Three

The Exodus

THE SEVEN-YEAR FAMINE during which Jacob took his family to Egypt happened 215 years before the Exodus, a time frame that represented almost exactly four orbital cycles of 54 years. The Bible gives no details of the cause of the famine, but it may have been a similar event to the plagues that converted Egypt into a wasteland. The Bible's description of the ten plagues makes clear that they desolated Egypt, resulting in famine, which was ironic in a land that on at least two prior occasions had been a place of plenty during famines in other lands.

The first issue that faces us with regard to the Egyptian plagues is the underlying cause: Was it indeed a comet? Or was it something else?

Early during the author's study of the plagues the conclusion was reached that they were caused by volcanism. A lot of the details seemed to fit a volcanic event, and this premise seemed confirmed by the discovery that the eruption of Santorini (then known as Thera) in the Mediterranean Sea happened during the same time frame as the Exodus, circa 1450 B.C. This theory gained support from the dating of pottery found in the rubble.

Subsequent studies raised difficult questions, but it still seemed that Thera's timing was not coincidental with respect to the ten plagues. The volcanic event may have been partly responsible for some of them.

It was a great explosion—six times as powerful as the infamous Krakatoa—so that some red dust ejected into the air could have drifted all the way to the heartland of Egypt, between 400 and 600 miles away. But it is unlikely that enough dust traveled that far to pollute all of that land's surface waters and kill thousands upon thousands of frogs.

Thera's explosive effects, though destructive, seem to have been confined primarily to a radius of 100 miles at the southern end of the Aegean Sea. A tidal wave generated by the eruption overwhelmed Crete, but it is scientifically demonstrable that the same wave could not have been the source of events that occurred at the Red Sea.

Volcanism can generate fire that runs along the ground (Exodus 9:23). Volcanic lava fits this description of one aspect of the seventh plague. There are lava remains from the Thera eruption still extant in the area of the original caldera. However, lava is heavy. It cannot be blown hundreds of miles across a large body of water like dust and then splattered upon the ground in quantities large enough to be described as fire running along the ground.

Nor can the rocks and other heavy objects, including lava bombs, ejected from an erupting volcano, fly through the air for hundreds of miles before falling to earth. They can be launched several miles, but not several hundred miles. This was the other half of the seventh plague.

In the eighth plague, a powerful wind blew a cloud of locusts into Egypt, which Pharaoh described as a "deadly plague." (Ex. 10:17). Volcanic explosions can generate powerful winds, but these winds do not blow with furious velocity across hundreds of miles. And even if they could, this was not the wind that brought the locusts. It was a wind blowing from the East (Exodus 10:13).

Thera was northwest of Egypt. An East wind blowing from Thera would have carried over the Mediterranean Sea in the direction of Spain. Also, the directional question must be considered from another perspective. The explosion of Thera was all-encompassing. The caldera left by the blast showed that it burst forth in every direction, not just one. There is no possibility that the eighth plague could have been generated by the eruption of Thera.

Phase One

If the eruption of Thera could not have accounted for the ten plagues, is there a single event that could? Let's put this in another way: Is it possible that the eruption of Thera was one aspect of a larger event that generated the plagues?

It is here proposed that Thera's eruption was one of the consequences of the approach to Earth of the comet having an orbital cycle of about 54 years. Let's discuss the three phases of the plagues, with the understanding that they would have become worse as the comet drew closer. The fact that the Egyptian magicians would emulate the first two showed that they were the least severe of the ten. It also showed how foolish the Egyptian magicians were, to add to the plagues that had begun to destroy their land. The first phase of the plagues consisted of the first four of the ten.

Advocates of the theory that Thera generated the plagues have pointed out that before a volcano erupts it can eject a lot of red dust into the air, which may be blown a long way before falling to Earth. But could the dust be blown more than 600 miles—far enough to cover all of the inhabited area of Egypt west of the Nile River? Could it be blown so far and in such volume that the land's surface waters were polluted enough to become undrinkable?

Since the only wind referenced in the story of the plagues was an East wind, which would have carried the dust in a different direction, this appears to be impossible. Indeed, even if there had been a wind from the Northwest instead of the East, and this wind blew dust all the way into Egypt, it follows that all of the surface water at the eastern end of the Mediterranean Sea between Greece and Egypt would have been tinted red, and there is no record of this having happened.

A comet, especially one sent by the Lord to rain destruction upon Egypt, could have accomplished everything that happened during the first four plagues. This, like the great Flood, was a spring event, for we know that its duration included the first Passover (Exod. 12:11). If this event involved an inside approach of the comet, which had rounded the sun and moved into position between the Earth and the sun, near the vernal solstice, the comet's tail would have swiped across the Earth and dumped a lot of polluting red dust.

The second plague was a direct consequence of the first. The dust of this particular comet contained such virulent pollutants that, not only did the water of the Nile become undrinkable, but the frogs were poisoned, fled the waters, died and stank in houses, in food supplies and wherever else they wound up after leaving the waters.

Comet contents include methane, ammonia, sulfur, methanol, formaldehyde, ethanol, carbon monoxide and hydrogen cyanide. These things, present in significant quantities in the dust that landed upon Egyptian surface waters, would have killed the frogs and thousands of fish, too (Psalm 105:29). Sulfur, the substance found in greatest quantity in many comets, would have sufficed for this by itself because, in its common form of sulfur trioxide, it converts upon contact with water into a corrosive aerosol akin to sulfuric acid.

The third plague has been identified by some translators as lice, by others as gnats. The Hebrew word *ken* is used in the Bible only to identify the insects that generated this plague, nowhere else. The word refers to an insect that fastens onto a host, probably a stinging insect. The text describing this plague states that these insects emerged from "the dust of the land." (Ex. 8:17) If this dust was introduced into Egypt by the tail of a comet, the insects emerging from it would have been unknown to the Egyptians. Had they been lice or gnats, the healing ointments of the Egyptians would have been effective. But these ointments had no effect on the insects that emerged from the dust, and some Egyptians died after being stung.[1] These deadly insects were unfamiliar to the Egyptians as should be expected of creatures with extraterrestrial origin.

During the second plague, so many frogs perished that the Egyptians stacked them into piles and left them to rot and stink. (Ex. 8:13-14) The fourth plague may have been a consequence of the second, because a stinking pile of frogs is going to attract a lot of flies, and the flies, feeding on the dead frogs, will breed quickly in such a favorable environment. "Thick swarms of flies came into the house of Pharaoh, into his servants' houses, and into all the land of Egypt. The land was corrupted because of the swarms of flies." (Ex. 8:24)

Phase Two

During the time period covered by the first four plagues, probably at least two weeks, the comet was moving closer and closer to Earth. By this time it was near enough to do some extreme damage, especially in Egypt, under the guidance of the hand of the Lord.

While this study of the plagues was going on the question came up: "What the heck is *grievous murrain*?" This is King James language (Ex. 9:3). It is an antiquated translation of the Hebrew word *deber*, which means literally *destroyer* and is sometimes in the Bible translated *pestilence* or *plague:* "It describes meteoric fallout as contrasted to volcanic fallout. It describes fire and brimstone."[2]

The ninth chapter of Exodus is the only place in the KJV Bible where *deber* is translated *murrain*, but it is not the only place where it describes the effect of a comet. We shall discuss other such occasions in this book. In this case, fallout from the comet was so intense that it killed all of the cattle in the fields of the Egyptians without harming anything in Goshen, east of the Nile (Ex. 9:6).

The sixth plague is described in the Bible as soot from a furnace falling on man and beast throughout Egypt and causing painful boils to break out on their skin. An erupting volcano can be described as a furnace. Its ashy emissions are acidic, can be dispersed for hundreds of miles through the atmosphere, and can cause festering boils when they touch human skin. It is possible that this could have been a direct repercussion of Thera's eruption, that eruption being a part of worldwide seismic activity instigated by the clashing gravitational fields of the comet and the Earth.

Some of the volcanic mountains on the Sinai Peninsula, closer to Egypt, may have been active also at that time. But it is doubtful if one of them was the source of this plague because, if it was, the Hebrews in Goshen, east of the Nile River, would have been more seriously affected than the Egyptians, west of the Nile.

Whatever geographic location it sprang from, this event probably also was caused directly by the comet. A comet's contents, both in the coma and in the tail, can be even more consumptive of a human body than a volcano's, and there remains the question of how a volcano could have generated such a severe plague as far as 600 miles from the source. The Bible says even Pharaoh's magicians broke out in these awful boils and could not remain standing in the presence of Moses (Ex. 9:11).

Josephus describes this as a deadly plague: "[The Egyptians'] bodies had terrible boils, breaking forth with blains, while they were already inwardly consumed; and a great part of the Egyptians perished in this manner."[3]

This is the second time we have discussed a comet event that caused boils to break out on a human body. The first was Job, who was too close to the sulfurous discharge from the comet that blew up Sodom. And we shall encounter it three more times, with reference to kings Hezekiah and Uzziah and in connection with Day of the Lord prophecies about Jesus' return. Inflammation of human skin seems to be an expectable consequence of a severe comet event, especially one involving sulfurous rock (brimstone), which, combined with water, can become a corrosive aerosol or even sulfuric acid.

The Exodus event was one of the worst. Since it probably was caused by a later arrival of the same comet that demolished Sodom, we should expect to find similar happenings in both events. In the case of Sodom, we have seen that the comet caused inflammations described as boils, which actually were acidic burns, to break out on Job's body.

The boils most commonly seen on human skin develop from staph infections. The ones that broke out on Job and on the Egyptians happened all of a sudden. Like Job, the Egyptians were struck by fallout—possibly containing sulfuric acid—and received pernicious burns on exposed portions of their bodies. They likely had scars for the rest of their lives.

Pharaoh, of course, was refusing to repent through it all, and after plague No. 6 it got worse. Here is the NKJV translation of the seventh plague: "Moses stretched out his rod toward heaven; and the Lord sent thunder and hail, and fire darted to the ground. And the Lord rained hail on the land of Egypt. So there was hail, and fire mingled with the hail, so very heavy that there was none like it in all the land of Egypt, since it became a nation. And the hail struck throughout the whole land of Egypt, all that was in the field, both man and beast; and the hail struck every herb of the field and broke every tree of the field. Only in the land of Goshen, where the children of Israel were, there was no hail." (Ex. 9:23-26)

Comets contain ice, but it was not ordinary icy hail that demolished trees. The word translated *hail* was *barad*. These were hailstones, that is, a hail of *very heavy* stones, falling from the comet. Like most comet fallout, it was mixed with fire. NKJV says fire "darted to the ground" but in this case the KJV translation gave a clearer picture of what was actually happening. According to KJV, mixed with the fall of heavy stones was fire that "ran along upon the ground."

The first inclination may be to identify the fire running along the ground as lava from a volcano. Lava does indeed move along the ground, but, as mentioned earlier in this chapter, it is so heavy that it cannot be blown hundreds of miles through space, even from an explosive blast as violent as Thera's, or from one that could have been erupting on the Sinai Peninsula. Lava generally slops over the edges of a volcanic crater and flows down from there or is blown in the form of lava-bombs a few miles through the air before splattering on the ground.

The actual meaning of this text is related to an aspect of a comet plague that we have not yet discussed: a firestorm. Some elements from the coma and tail of a comet may generate atmospheric fire as they fall to earth. When they strike the ground, they can move in any direction bringing fiery devastation to whatever they touch. A firestorm or fire whirl is, literally, a storm of fire whirling along the ground like a small tornado. Like any other storm, a firestorm generates wind. It can race along at high speed. Its heat is so intense that it sets ablaze everything in its path.

The *thunder* probably referred to the loud noises made by exploding bolides in the lower atmosphere, for the word *barad* can refer to one or more bolides, like the ones that demolished Sodom and the Tower of Babel (see Chapter Twelve). The seventh plague was a real killer, and one of the worst things about it was the firestorms.

The Chicago Firestorm

In 1846, Biela's comet was seen breaking apart. Biela's had one of the shortest orbital periods of any comet observable from Earth. It completed a full revolution around the sun in six to seven years. At the time of its scheduled reappearance four cycles later, early in 1872, a meteor shower radiated from the section of the sky where it was expected to be. This happened shortly after a series of fires ravaged the Midwestern United States, including the city of Chicago.[4]

According to tradition, Mrs. O'Leary left her lantern too near her cow, which kicked it over, starting the great Chicago fire in October of 1871. In 2004, physicist Robert Wood disclosed his theory that the wind-driven Chicago fire was ignited not by a cow but by a fragment of Biela's comet:

"The main body of the [comet] fragment crashed into one of the Great Lakes on October 7, 1871, and peripheral fragments and debris, including small pieces of frozen methane, acetylene, and other highly combustible chemicals, exploded from the friction of entering the earth's atmosphere and ignited the Chicago fire and dozens of other fires that burned simultaneously in Wisconsin and Michigan."[5]

All of the fires were exceedingly hot and, driven by high winds, raged quickly out of control. Millions of acres of forest, prairies, and farmland were razed. About two hundred fifty people died in the Chicago fire.

In less notorious blazes in a dozen Wisconsin villages on the same night, two thousand people died. The Wisconsin fires were the deadliest in the history of the United States. The town of Holland, Michigan, burned to the ground.[6] Parts of Ohio and Minnesota also were charred by the fires, which consumed an area the size of the state of Connecticut.[7] The destruction may have been comparable to that felt in Egypt from the comet-generated firestorms during the seventh plague.

In regard to the Chicago fire, public opinion, abetted by shallow journalism, had already condemned Mrs. O'Leary. The comet theory was received with snickers when it was first suggested in 1882. But Wood developed a persuasive case for it more than a century later:

"[Wood] cites eyewitness reports of spontaneous ignitions, lack of smoke, and 'great balls of fire' or 'fire balloons' that fell from the sky and exploded over the trees. He believes that reports by Chicago firemen that buildings 'burned blue' may be evidence that the Chicago fire was caused by the methane that is commonly found in comets."[8]

Systems design engineer Ken Rieli offered confirmatory evidence. Rieli discovered a fifty-eight-pound meteorite near the shores of Lake Huron. Geologists found a large impact crater at the same site from which Rieli removed the meteorite. Crews drilling a water pipeline in the area found other meteorite-like rocks.[9] These discoveries provided enough supporting evidence for serious consideration to be given to Wood's theory that one or more fragments of a comet started the Midwestern fires in 1871.

The Comet Venus

A firestorm is not the only kind of storm that can be produced by a comet. A comet interacting with Earth from close range can cause upheaval within Earth's atmosphere producing dangerous cyclonic and tornadic storms. The worst of these are tornadoes of vastly greater size and wind velocity than the ones that have been known to destroy entire communities in the Midwestern United States.

In ancient times, imaginative human beings observing the consequences of approaching comets tended to personify the comets as dangerous enemies. A comet, in the vertical position, can appear to be a human being wearing a long flowing robe (the comet's tail); the coma of the comet is seen as the human head. The emissions of a comet in dangerous proximity to Earth can look like the outstretched arms of a man, horns of a bull, or wings of a bird.

If the comet generated storms in Earth's atmosphere, descending from supercell clouds, as tornadic appendages are commonly seen to do, these storms could be identified as the "legs" and "feet" of the "person" or "animal" in the sky. Witnesses of these events could record them as an attack of a goring, trampling bull or some other vicious animal. The animals would then be deified, just as bulls were in Egypt.

Could it have been mere coincidence that shortly after the Exodus the Israelites persuaded Aaron to make the image of a young bull for them to worship? (Exodus 32) The Hebrew word *egel* used to describe this idol did not mean calf, as it is often translated, but a nearly full grown bull, probably with horns.

Immanuel Velikovsky did much research before publishing his views that this idol depicted the celestial object the Israelites had seen over Egypt during the ten plagues. Velikovsky thought at that time Venus was a comet and caused the plagues. Whether or not Venus was originally a comet is insignificant to our study. We propose merely that the cause of the plagues was a God-directed comet.

Velikovsky wrote: "The worship of a bullock was introduced by Aaron at the foot of Mount Sinai. The cult of Apis originated in Egypt in the days of the Hyksos, after the end of the Middle Kingdom, shortly after the Exodus. Apis, or the sacred bull, was very much venerated in Egypt; when a sacred bull died, its body was mummified and placed in a sarcophagus with royal honors, and memorial services were held."[10]

Regarding the destructive activity attributed to the then-comet Venus, Velikovsky wrote: "The [Morning] Star shattered mountains, shook the globe with such a violence that it looked as if the heavens were shaking, was a storm, a cloud, a fire, a heavenly dragon, a torch, and a blazing star, and it rained naphtha on the earth...In the attributes and in the deeds ascribed to the planet Venus—Isis, Ishtar, Athene—we recognize the attributes and deeds of the comet described in the earlier sections of [Worlds in Collision]."[11]

Velikovsky concluded: "Isis, the planet Venus, was represented as a human figure with two horns, like Astarte (Ishtar) of the horns; and sometimes it was fashioned in the likeness of a cow. In time Ishtar changed from male to female, and in many places worship of the bull changed to worship of the cow. The main reason for this seems to have been the fall of manna which turned the rivers into streams of honey and milk. A horned planet that produced milk most closely resembled a cow."[12]

But planets do not grow "horns" as comets may appear to do.

Phase Three

The image of a young bull fashioned by Aaron is basic to our discussion of what happened during the eighth plague of the Exodus. During this plague, the first of the event's third and final phase, the biblical account states that an east wind carried a cloud of locusts into the part of the land, west of the Nile River, where the Egyptians lived (Ex. 10:12).

But how could the locusts have bypassed Goshen? If the locusts had originated in Goshen, they would have devoured the crops of the Israelites. If they had originated east of the Red Sea, as probably was the case, they miraculously bypassed Goshen on their way to the heart of Egypt. Of course, God could have prevented them from eating while they were moving through Goshen, but there is a more natural way this could have happened during a comet event.

A "leg" of the "bull" could have set down near the Red Sea where the locusts were at the time. If that "leg" was a tornado generated by the comet, the circulation at its base or "foot" could have raised the entire cloud of locusts into the sky. Then the tornado perhaps did one of the maneuvers tornadoes are noted for and suddenly lifted off the earth. It did no damage to Goshen but, like the giant leg it appeared to be, stepped right over Goshen and came down in Egypt, spraying the locusts all over that land, like sparks flying from a spinning wheel.

A tornado is the most violent of all spinning wheels, and a tornado generated by a comet could produce winds of such extreme velocity that they were capable of blowing the locusts many miles in all directions even as it carved a destructive path through Egypt. The locusts feasted on whatever greenery and seed were left from earlier plagues generated by the comet.

Neither the wind from the storm nor the locusts carried by the wind damaged Goshen. A tornado is unique among storms in its ability to advance like a pogo stick, which would have produced this "stepping" effect. It could have been similar in destructive power to the comet-produced tornado that demolished the house where Job's children were having a party, killing them all. (Job 1:19)

This plague ended with the locusts being blown by a strong west wind into the Red Sea, perhaps not far from the area where they had originated. Once again they miraculously bypassed Goshen, and again it may have happened in the same pogo-stick way, under the orchestration of God.

The three days of oppressive darkness identified as the ninth plague could have been caused by comet fallout or by a stifling cloud of material from a volcanic eruption instigated by the comet. Erupting volcanoes can eject clouds of debris capable of producing oppressive air pollutants that can cause serious breathing problems (Ex. 10:21).

Josephus described this plague: "A thick darkness, without the least light, spread itself over the Egyptians, whereby their sight being obstructed, and their breathing hindered by the thickness of the air, they died miserably, and under a terror lest they should be swallowed up by the dark cloud."[13]

There are no known volcanoes in Egypt that erupted at this time, though there is evidence that, in addition to Thera, there may have been other active volcanoes in the Aegean Sea, and also on the Sinai Peninsula.

However, ash from an erupting Mount Sinai or another volcano in that neighborhood would have spread out over Goshen east of the Nile before reaching the Egyptians' cities on the west bank of the river. Ash from Thera might have been the cause of this darkness, and possibly could have avoided Goshen. But the stifling cloud that killed many Egyptians was exceedingly dense and dark. If it came from Thera, by the time it drifted hundreds of miles to Egypt it would not have been dense enough to cause such oppressive air pollution (Ex. 10:22).

A comet event, with or without volcanic accompaniment, can create oppressive clouds of debris from bolidic explosions and residual ash from firestorms. These could have accumulated over God's target zone of Egypt during the plagues. The effects of these clouds may be likened to nuclear fallout from a mushroom cloud after an A-bomb blast.

The biblical text makes clear there was pitch darkness for three days, an unlikely consequence of volcanic air pollution emanating from hundreds of miles distance. But it could have been produced by the intense fallout from a comet and the explosions produced by that fallout.

We don't have any descriptive details of the tenth plague, which killed the firstborn of every household in Egypt that did not have lamb's blood on the doorframe. The Bible simply states that the Lord "smote" or "struck" or "struck down" the firstborn in every uncovered Egyptian household (Ex. 12:29, various translations). This was the Hebrew verb *nakah*, which meant to strike, kill, slay or slaughter. God could have done this directly by His own hand, or He could have used the object in the sky. In the next chapter we shall discuss the propensity of God for identifying with the objects He uses to accomplish His purposes.

A key text indicating that the final plague may have been instituted by the same comet as the other plagues states: "For the Lord will pass through to strike the Egyptians; and when He sees the blood on the lintel and on the two doorposts, the Lord will pass over the door and not allow the destroyer to come into your houses to strike you." (Ex. 12:23) This is the second time we've seen the unusual word *destroyer* associated with the ten plagues.

The book *The Long Day of Joshua and Six Other Catastrophes* has an intriguing explanation of the word *firstborn* used in the biblical description of this plague: "The word 'firstborn' in Hebrew is *bekowr* meaning elder, chief or first-born and comes from the prime verb *bakar*, to burst from the womb. We suspect the death toll throughout Egypt that cataclysmic night was 15% to 25% and that, on the average, 'one born' of most families perished."[14]

The New International Version translation of Exodus 12:29-30 supports this idea: "At midnight the Lord struck down all the firstborn in Egypt, from the firstborn of Pharaoh, who sat on the throne, to the firstborn of the prisoner, who was in the dungeon, and the firstborn of all the livestock as well. Pharaoh and all his officials and all the Egyptians got up during the night, and there was loud wailing in Egypt, for *there was not a house without someone dead*." (italics added)

This event is known as the Passover "because on that day God passed us [the Israelites] over."[15] God seems to have been consistent to the end in using the comet as his agent of judgment. The ten plagues consumed a recognizably judgmental period of time, forty days. They began and concluded as the divinely-sent comet carried out the will of the Lord in minutest detail.

The word *passover* may have two meanings in this context. It did mean that the Lord, or His "angel" (Hebrew, *messenger* or *agent*) of destruction, the comet, bypassed the Israelites who dwelt behind doorframes covered with lamb's blood (Ex. 14:19). And it could also have referred to the fact that God used the object in the sky as a whip or a scourge or a rod of punishment—traditional depictions of comets—to strike lethal blows on the Egyptians one final time as it passed visibly overhead.

A reason to suspect it had the latter meaning is drawn from a comparison with a prophecy that God would come down to defend Jerusalem against the Assyrians: "Like birds flying about, so will the Lord of hosts defend Jerusalem.

Defending, He will also deliver it. Passing over, He will preserve it." (Isaiah 31:5) Use of the phrase *passing over* here refers to a lofty presence. The same Hebrew word was used by Isaiah to describe God passing over the Assyrians as was used by Moses to describe the Passover in Egypt (Exodus 12:13, 23).

Conclusion

If the interpretation is correct that a comet was the primary agent of destruction during the ten plagues, it demonstrates not only the awesome power but also the versatility of this particular comet. And we have not yet exhausted the amazing facts that are known about this comet and its aftermath.

A pharaoh whose Jewish mother witnessed this victory of Jehovah over all of the Egyptian gods raised a son, Akhenaton, who became the only monotheistic pharaoh in the history of Egypt. Several artistic images of the god Aton, worshipped by Akhenaton, looked remarkably like a comet, not the sun, which some have said Akhenaton worshipped. All of these images depict the Aton as a shining round head with a broad tail descending from it. Unless the sun once had a tail, these are depictions of a comet.[16]

Furthermore, the name Aton ascribed to this deity was almost identical to the name Adon, or Adonai, sometimes ascribed to the God of Israel. The two names were so similar that it seems likely that the slight difference in spelling was a linguistic one. A surviving poem of Akhenaton describes the grandeur of his god Aton in words and phrases that could have been written by an Old Testament psalmist in praise of Jehovah/Adonai.

Moreover, the memory of this event so affected the Egyptians that their land still shows evidence of it. The forty days of plagues caused by this comet were so devastating that Egypt has been a desolate land ever since. We know that the Israelites dwelt on the east side of the Nile, in Goshen, while the Egyptians occupied territory along the west bank of the river. The river was and still is so important to the Egyptian economy that a majority of Egyptians have continued to live near its banks.

A recent map of Egypt identifies many cities in the Nile Delta, which have been Egyptian since ancient times. South of the capital city Cairo, and extending as far south as what is believed to have been Goshen's southern limits, there are dozens of Egyptian settlements on the west bank but only a few on the east bank. On one map, where the most significant contemporary Egyptian cities are identified, it appears that *all* of them are on the west bank.

There are a few Egyptians living on the east bank of the river, but less than should be expected. Why didn't the Egyptians establish larger settlements on the east bank after the Israelites left? Land on the east side of the river was left in better condition than the west side, which bore the brunt of the plagues.

A possible answer to this question is that descendants of the Egyptians who witnessed these plagues have dwelt in fear of the God of the Israelites to the present day, or at least in superstition strong enough to prevent them from fully occupying the area where the Israelites used to live. This land of Goshen was blessed by the God of the Israelites even while He was raining destruction upon the Egyptians and their gods.

The premise of this chapter is that a comet generated all of the ten plagues, including one or two that may have had a secondary cause, an eruption of the volcano Thera. During a major comet event, such as the Flood, the earthquake and volcanic activity are widespread owing to the clashing gravitational forces of the Earth and the comet. Therefore, if the Exodus involved a major comet event, there should have been a lot more seismic activity going on than a single volcanic blast.

There is evidence of other volcanic activity at this time, but because of questionable dating methods some of it is not provably concurrent with the Exodus. It is known that severe cooling occurred in the middle of the 15th century B.C., probably because of dense cloud cover after eruptions of many volcanoes. Two volcanoes known to have blown their tops at this time were El Misti and Arequipa in Peru. And, as we shall see in the next chapter of this book, the Sinai Peninsula into which the Israelites wandered after leaving Egypt was shaking with seismic activity and ablaze with volcanism.

Summary/Analogy

There is a strong strain of spiritual analogy in the story of the Exodus. Pharaoh represents Satan (Ezek. 29:1-7). Ever since Adam and Eve gave in to Satan's temptation, he has enslaved people and kept them in bondage to sin for as long as they remained living in his kingdom, the "Egypt" of wickedness.

But when the deliverer came, not Moses but Jesus Christ, He became the Passover for us, the Lamb of God who took away the sin of the world (1 Cor. 5:7, John 1:29, 36). He who knew no sin became sin for us so that in Him we could become the righteousness of God (2 Cor. 5:21).

He removed us from the realm of the wicked one and promised to us a dwelling place in the highest heaven, there to dwell with Him and His Father not just for 215 years—the duration of time the children of Israel spent in Egypt after their father Jacob (Israel) arrived there—but for all eternity.

Here is a summary of the Exodus plagues, the next ten pieces of our puzzle:

- ONE: Red dust from the comet's tail fell into Egyptian surface waters, polluting them and turning them a blood-red color.

- TWO: Frogs, poisoned by the pollution, left the waters and died, creating a terrible stench.

- THREE: Insects unknown to the Egyptians flew out of the newly deposited dust, stung and killed some of them.

- FOUR: Flies bred upon piles of dead frogs and got into Egyptian homes, spoiling food supplies.

- FIVE: Meteoric fallout from the comet killed cattle in fields owned by the Egyptians, but not the Israelites.

- SIX: Caustic elements fell from the comet's coma and tail, causing virulent boils to break out on the skin of the Egyptians.

- SEVEN: Incendiary stones broke off the comet's head, exploded and blew up large areas of earth, and ignited deadly firestorms.

- EIGHT: A cometic tornado lifted a cloud of locusts high into the air and distributed the ravenous creatures throughout western Egypt.

- NINE: Thick air pollution generated by comet fallout and firestorms suffocated the Egyptians.

- TEN: The Lord's destroyer "struck down" and killed at least one person in every Egyptian household.

Chapter Four

Sinai

THE BIBLE'S CATASTROPHIC events come from the hand of God in response to human sin. During the Passover, for example, the Bible says the Lord struck down the Egyptians, thereby identifying Him with the devastation wrought by a comet. But there is probably no more picturesque phrase in the scriptures describing such an event's Initiator than the one used in connection with the Red Sea pass-through: It was the *arm of the Lord*, also described as His *outstretched arm* that led the Israelites safely through the sea before releasing the sea waters to drown the Egyptian armed forces: God saved the Israelites with His outstretched arm.

Nearly always, when the Bible mentions the arm of the Lord, or the Lord's outstretched arm, it refers to the Red Sea event. These phrases were used fifteen times in Scriptures about the Red Sea, twice with respect to creation, and no more than once concerning anything else. What was unique about the Red Sea event that associated it so closely with the arm of the Lord? Wasn't the Lord's presence equally felt in connection with the Flood, the destruction of Sodom, the Exodus, and every other cataclysmic event discussed in this book?

When the Egyptian army showed up while the Israelites were encamped on the west side of the sea, it appeared that they were trapped between the sea and a range of mountains. The Israelites complained to Moses about their plight, and he said to them: "Do not be afraid. Stand still and see the salvation of the Lord, which He will accomplish for you today. For the Egyptians whom you see today, you shall see again no more forever. The Lord will fight for you, and you shall hold your peace." (Exodus 14:13-14)

Then the Lord said to Moses: "Why do you cry to me?"

It's implied by this that after speaking to the people Moses prayed. Here is part of that prayer from Josephus' account: "We are in a helpless place that thou possessest; still the sea is thine, the mountains also that enclose us are thine; so that these mountains will open themselves if thou commandest them, and the sea also, if thou commandest it, will become dry land."[1]

The Lord replied: "Tell the children of Israel to go forward. But lift up your rod, and stretch out your hand over the sea and divide it. And the children of Israel shall go on dry ground through the midst of the sea." (Ex. 14:15-16)

Moses obeyed. We can picture him with his hand, holding his rod, stretched out toward the sea. At the same time, in the sky above Moses, we see a similar picture, only much larger, so that the hand and rod of Moses appear to be a tiny representation of it: It is a dangerously close comet in a horizontal position with the coma, its "hand," attached to an outstretched "arm" or "rod" (the comet's tail), above the Red Sea. This celestial vision is described in scriptural accounts and recounts of the Red Sea event as the mighty hand and outstretched arm of the Lord. (Ex. 6:6, 15:16; Psalm 77:15; Deut. 4:34, 5:15, 7:19, 9:29, 11:2, 26:8, et al.)

Moses and the rest of the Israelites recognized the Lord as the instigating force behind the judgmental comet and identified it as His. The horizontal position is an unusual one for a comet, which may be seen with the coma and tail pointing in any direction, depending on the comet's position in relation to the sun. This perhaps is the reason that the Red Sea event is uniquely identified as the mighty hand and outstretched arm of the Lord: It was a rare occasion when a comet appeared in this distinctive position.

The East Wind

Next, "The Lord caused the sea to go back by a strong east wind all that night, and made the sea into dry land, and the waters were divided." (Ex. 14:21)

This was three days after the Passover and less than two weeks after a similar event, an east wind from a comet-generated tornado, blew locusts into Egypt from the vicinity of the Red Sea. Since it originated in almost the same place, and with the same comet still in the sky, it makes sense to study this east wind in comparison with the one that brought the locusts.

The first east wind was an immense tornado generated by the comet, and this is another, from the same comet. But this time, late at night, with the ice-laden object from outer space in close proximity to the Earth, there was a sudden freeze.

The gigantic tornado, touching the ground for an area probably two or three miles wide, moved along from east to west, sucking the contents of the sea into the air like a gigantic vacuum cleaner. It was so huge and generated such intense winds that it produced a scary thunderous noise (Psalm 77:18). It moved all the way through the shallow sea before, responding to the guiding hand of the Lord, it rose from the ground and passed over the camps of the Israelites and Egyptians.

After the tornado passed there was a gap in the sea wide enough for three or four-million Israelites to pass through before sunrise. As Moses led them into the seabed, they discovered the bottom to be unexpectedly dry and hard, easy to walk upon, for it had frozen. On both sides as they hurried forward, they saw walls of what the Scripture described as "congealed" water (Ex. 15:8).

"Congealed" water is an archaic way of describing ice. Icy winds from the cold tornado had frozen in place thick walls of ice capable of restraining the sea waters for as long as God wanted them to be restrained. God's timing, as always, was perfect. He sustained the icy walls through the night, until every one of the Israelites made it through and climbed onto the eastern shore of the sea.

The Egyptians, who had decided to wait until morning to pursue the Israelites, were not prepared for this sudden turn of events. The Israelites advanced far into the sea while the Egyptians were still "putting on their armour (sic), and therein spending their time."[2]

After getting a slow start, the Egyptians' visibility was inhibited by the oppression of a "dark and dismal night," an occurrence not uncommon during a comet event with its dense fallout.[3] Day broke, and the temperature climbed just enough to begin melting the ice. While the Egyptians all were within the seabed, the warming temperature converted the sea bottom from ice to mud, and their chariot wheels became mired.

Then the walls of ice crumbled with a terrible cracking sound (Psalm 77:18). At the same time as the icy walls crumbled, and the waters began pouring back into the seabed, there was also a deluge from above, a fierce storm combining high winds and torrents of rain mixed with fire, as only a comet discharge could produce. The fire, of course, expedited the melting of the ice.

The celestial aspect of the event was described by the Bible: "The clouds poured out water. The skies sent out a sound. Your [God's] arrows also flashed about. The voice of Your thunder was in the whirlwind [tornado]. The lightnings lit up the whole world. The earth trembled and shook." (Psalm 77:17-18)

The Hebrew wording is important here. It was not an ordinary earthquake, but a quaking (trembling, shaking) Earth. We shall encounter the phenomenon of a quaking Earth three times more in association with severe comet events. The Hebrew word translated *lightnings* was *baraq*, which often was associated with comet events. It meant *gleaming* or *glittering* or *flashing*, or, more specifically, *flashing sword*—a common image of a comet.

Josephus described the culmination of the Red Sea event in this way: "As soon, therefore, as ever the whole Egyptian army was within it, the sea flowed to its own place, and came down with a torrent raised by storms of wind and encompassed the Egyptians. Showers of rain also came down from the sky, and dreadful thunders and lightning, with flashes of fire. Thunderbolts also were darted upon [the Egyptians]."[4]

The thunderbolts may have been explosive meteorites or bolides. Guided by God's hand, they landed only among the Egyptians within the sea, without harming the Israelites on the shore. The Israelites, standing safely on the shore, saw the dead Egyptians with their chariots floundering in the water.

All of the aspects of this event—gigantic tornado generating freezing winds, rainfall mixed with sodium, sulfur and/or methane producing fiery precipitation, bolides, terrible noises and a sudden freeze—are explainable by the premise that the same God-guided comet generated the Red Sea event as did the ten plagues. It would be difficult to explain all aspects of the event in any other way.

Two areas of doubt may be suggested. First, how is it possible for the winds from a tornado, not only to suck up waters out of a sea but then, before the remaining waters can flow back, to freeze them in place instantaneously?

Let's simplify the issue with another question: How cold is a comet? In 1986, when Halley's Comet was visible, astronomers turned their instrumentation in its direction to learn as much as they could about it. One thing they discovered was that the solid ice within the comet's core was 35 degrees Kelvin. The equivalent Fahrenheit temperature is about 60 degrees above absolute zero. Since absolute zero is about minus-460 degrees Fahrenheit, this meant that the temperature of the ice was in the vicinity of 400 degrees below zero Fahrenheit.

The Red Sea comet was in closer proximity to Earth than Halley's. The temperature of the downdraft from the comet that produced the tornado probably wasn't quite as cold as minus-400 degrees Fahrenheit. But it is important to understand that the frictional forces of Earth's atmosphere that heat up comet fallout to very high temperatures would not have the same effect on a downdraft.

A downdraft of cold air from the comet would not be warmed by frictional contact with Earth's atmosphere, but would simply supplant the warm air while churning into tornadic form on its way down. Cold air always descends beneath rising warm air: It's the hot air balloon effect. The descending cold air would warm minimally due to some intermingling with the warmer air, but would remain very cold until making contact with the ground. The contrast between the extreme cold of the downdraft and the much warmer air surrounding it would produce an exceedingly violent tornado.

Let's estimate generously that the downdraft from the Red Sea comet warmed between 100 and 150 degrees before it reached the Earth's surface. Let's say the temperature rose all the way from minus-400 degrees to minus-300 degrees or even minus-250 degrees: Then, what would happen? Answer: an instant freeze. It still would have been cold enough to generate a tornado "leg" that would instantly freeze anything it touched. The miracle was not that the tornado caused a fast-freeze of part of the Red Sea and its bed, but that God mercifully lifted it over millions of Israelites standing on the shore. They would have been frozen and blown away by the tornado, if it had remained in contact with the ground.[5]

A second and related question is this: How could such a cold object as a comet generate terrible fires upon the Earth? As long as a comet remains orbiting through space, it is so cold that its elements remain frozen. Even incendiary gases, such as methane, will remain in a frozen state as long as the comet is roaming through space.

But upon contact with atmospheric conditions such as are present around the Earth, the situation changes. All solid parts of a comet, if they break away and begin plummeting through Earth's atmosphere, will heat up owing to the friction generated by their freefall. Sodium will explode into flames, if it contacts water or water vapor. Sulfur will burn furiously hot and with deadly persistence. Methane will change to a liquid state, heat up and generate deadly fires and firestorms upon contact with the ground. Water-based ice will simply melt and fall as rain but, if it contacts sodium or methane on the way down, will change to a fluid fire-fall.

Sea of Termination

One of the points of controversy regarding the sea is whether its actual name was Red Sea or Sea of Reeds. It is a petty controversy, one that is off the mark.

There is a basis for both names, linguistically and logically. The sea was shallow near the Mediterranean Sea where the Israelites passed through, so that it would have been possible for reeds to grow from the bottom all the way to the surface in some areas, even when the sea's bed was filled to capacity.

It also would have been appropriate for it to have been called Red Sea in conjunction with these events because the comet's tail dumped red dust, not only on Egypt but on lands and seas in other parts of the world, especially the neighboring seas.

Two of the three Hebrew adjectives translated *red* meant *reed* and/or *red*. The third, *cuwphah*, was different. From the root word *cuwph*, meaning terminate, consume or perish, *cuwphah* meant hurricane, tempest or whirlwind (tornado).

The words *cuwph* and *cuwphah* were more pertinent to the story of the sea than were the other two words that were spelled similarly in Hebrew but had different meanings. Under assault from the terrible object in the sky, it became, for the Israelites, a sea of salvation, but for the Egyptians, a sea of tempest or termination.

Song of Moses

After seeing the Egyptians drown, Moses and his sister Miriam led the Israelites in a song of praise to God for the victory. This song contained vivid language describing events the Israelites had just witnessed. Here are excerpts:

> "I will sing to the Lord, for He has triumphed gloriously!
> The horse and its rider He has thrown into the sea!
> Pharaoh's chariots and his army He has cast into the sea;
> His chosen captains also are drowned in the Red Sea.
> Your right hand, O Lord, has become glorious in power.
>> Your right hand, O Lord, has dashed the enemy in pieces.

And with the blast of Your nostrils
  The waters were gathered together;
The floods stood upright like a heap;
  The depths congealed in the heart of the sea.
You blew with Your wind, the sea covered them;
  They sank like lead in the mighty waters.
You stretched out Your right hand;
  The earth swallowed them.
You in Your mercy have led forth
  the people whom You have redeemed;
You have guided them in Your strength
  to Your holy habitation."

(Ex. 15:1, 4, 6, 8, 10, 12-13)

Notice the picturesque reference to the stretched out right hand of God dashing the enemy to pieces. It is also intriguing that the tornado that parted the sea was described as "the blast" of God's "nostrils." It was more than imagination that produced these images. The Israelites were cognizant of the vital presence of a God so mighty that if He merely sneezed it would generate wind of such velocity that it could wipe out an entire army.

The final verse is a good one for us to meditate upon. God, in His mercy, redeems His people and guides them in His strength all the way to His heavenly habitation. The human part of the process is merely to accept His free offer of forgiveness for sins, and to follow His "pillar of cloud" (Holy Spirit) to the lofty destination.

Rephidim

Three days later the Israelites complained to Moses for lack of drinking water. Many a preacher has delivered a sermon making the Israelites seem faithless for complaining so soon after experiencing God's deliverance. However, under desert conditions, such as prevailed on the Sinai Peninsula, a person without water could die within three or four days. This was a crisis as real as when the Israelites seemed entrapped beside the Sea of Termination at the mercy of well-armed Egyptians.

The Israelites named the place of their encampment Marah, meaning bitter, because the water they found there was too bitter (polluted) to drink. On this occasion, God told Moses to throw a piece of wood into the water and, when he did so, the water miraculously turned potable.

But as their journey drew them closer to their next destination, Mount Sinai, they had to traverse some more difficult terrain. At Rephidim, within view of Mount Sinai, they found no water at all. This time, when the thirsty people complained, Moses prayed and the Lord instructed him to take some elders with him, walk to a large rock in the shadow of the mountain, and strike the rock with his rod. When Moses did so, water began pouring out of the rock.

The Bible often omits intermediate details between a commandment or instigation of God and the conclusion of a matter. In this case, it says nothing about what happened to the rock to cause it to begin gushing water. But, as we shall see, in the next section of this chapter, Mount Sinai was an active volcano at this time, having been primed by the comet, just as Thera had been. There was a lot of seismic activity in the area around the mountain, and it seems that an earthquake may have been the intermediate cause of the rock-splitting outpour.

Josephus mentions that when Moses struck the rock with his rod that it "opened a passage" so that "a river should run for their sakes out of the rock." This amazed the Israelites, who believed they would have to break the rock in order to uncover the spring of water beneath it.[6]

The statement that a passage was opened in the rock shows that a physical break had occurred, and Moses could not have made this cleavage by striking the rock with his rod. In a clash between a rock and a piece of wood, the rock will win every time, unless other forces are at work, natural and/or supernatural.

At Rephidim, both the supernatural (God) and the natural (a rock-splitting earthquake caused by a comet) were involved. A comparable event was the splitting of rocks by an earthquake at the time of Jesus' death (Mat. 27:51).

Mount Sinai

Josephus, citing ancient writings, described the challenge of Moses' mountain climb: "[Sinai] is the highest of all the mountains that are in that country, and is not only very difficult to be ascended by men on account of its vast altitude, but because of the sharpness of its precipices also; nay, indeed, it cannot be looked at without pain of the eyes: and besides this, it was terrible and inaccessible, on account of the rumour (sic) that passed about, that God dwelt there."[7]

Those who enjoy diversionary details have pointed out that Mount Sinai (Horeb) is not the tallest mountain on the peninsula. St. Katherine's is taller. However, a study of photographs of the two peaks explains the discrepancy. St. Katherine's rises to a single pristine peak. Mount Sinai is truncated in the manner of a volcano that has literally blown its top. This evidently is what it did during the seismic repercussions of the Exodus/Red Sea comet event. Before that time, it was the highest mountain on the peninsula. Afterward, it was not.

It is known by archaeologists that Mount Sinai is a volcano and that it was active during the 15th century B.C. Its slopes are covered with thick lava deposits. Even if there were no archaeological evidence of the volcano's activity, it is clearly depicted on the pages of Moses' historical account of his ascent to meet with God and receive the Ten Commandments:

"Then it came to pass on the third day that there were thunderings and lightnings, and a thick cloud on the mountain; and the sound of the trumpet was very loud, so that all the people who were in the camp trembled.

And Moses brought the people out of the camp to meet with God, and they stood at the foot of the mountain. Now Mount Sinai was completely in smoke, because the Lord descended upon it in fire. Its smoke ascended like the smoke of a furnace, and the whole mountain quaked greatly." (Ex. 19:16-18)

Mount Sinai was in full eruption. The loud noises, the thick clouds of smoke, the fire at the peak of the mountain and the specific statement that the entire mountain was quaking all give evidence of an eruption. The statement that the Lord descended to the mountain "in fire" may indicate that the comet had not finished with its flaming discharges. Fire erupts from a volcano in an upward direction. A comet's discharges descend. A trumpet is a traditional image for a comet because of its shape and its loud resonant sounds.

Josephus' account is similar to Moses': "On the third day, before the sun was up, a cloud spread itself over the whole camp of the Hebrews, such a one as none had before seen, and encompassed the place where they had pitched their tents; and while all the rest of the air was clear, there came strong winds, that raised up large showers of rain, which became a mighty tempest. There was also such lightning, as was terrible to those that saw it; and thunder with its thunderbolts, were sent down, and declared God to be there present."[8]

A tempestuous rainstorm accompanied by falling thunderbolts (bolides) describes comet activity. The combination of a comet still in discharge phase while a volcano was in full eruption must have been terrifying to the Israelites. It took great faith in God, and the courage engendered by that faith, for Moses to challenge such a dangerous mountain.

Deuteronomy chapter five describes the scene when Moses was atop the mountain while the commandments were being delivered: The Lord spoke from within the flames atop the mountain; all the people heard His voice; they identified His glory with the fire but feared being consumed by the flames; it was His intention that they should fear Him so that they would keep the commandments and live long and full lives.

Moses wrote that as he was descending from Sinai after spending forty days on the peak in God's presence, "The mountain burned with fire." (Deut. 9:15)

Aaron's Sons

The Israelites spent two months journeying from Egypt to Mount Sinai and eleven months encamped beside the mountain. Since this period of time was comparable to the duration of the Great Flood, it is not surprising that the Earth was still in an unstable condition after such a dreadful encounter with a comet.

The book of Leviticus was written by Moses during this period and describes two successive incidents that seem relevant to our theme. After being instructed how to worship God at the newly-constructed tabernacle, Moses and Aaron entered the ornate tent, performed their duties, and emerged to bless the people. "Then the glory of the Lord appeared to all the people and fire came out from before the Lord and consumed the burnt offering and the fat on the altar. When all the people saw it, they shouted and fell on their faces." (Lev. 9:23-24)

The Hebrew word here translated *glory* meant *weightiness, splendor* or *copiousness*. The meaning that seems most apropos in this context is *splendor*, because splendor is a visible thing and it is twice said by Moses that this was visible to all the people. After this flash of brilliance, "fire came out from before the Lord." (Lev. 9:24)

The Lord's glory appeared atop Mount Sinai. This fire probably emerged from the belly of the volcano. It was not a major eruption, because none of the people were killed.

While this awesome event was taking place the people fell on their faces in a position of humble worship. That is, all of them except Aaron's sons Nadab and Abihu. These two youthful priests behaved insolently: "[They] took their censers, put fire in them and added incense; and they offered unauthorized fire before the Lord, contrary to His command. So fire came out from the presence of the Lord and consumed them, and they died before the Lord." (Lev. 10:1-2)

The eruption which had begun for demonstrative purposes now became deadly, but only for the two disobedient young men. God directed some of the fiery discharge so that it fell directly on the two young men and killed them.

He explained to Moses, who told the grieving Aaron: "This is what the Lord spoke of when he said: 'Among those who approach me I will show myself holy; in the sight of all the people I will be honored.'" (Lev. 10:3)

Taberah

After the Israelites decamped from Mount Sinai, it was about a three-day journey to their next encampment, where another deadly event occurred. The comet by this time had faded into the distance. But the peninsula was still smoldering with seismic activity.

The new encampment was in a range of mountains west of the Gulf of Aqaba. After arriving there the Israelites began complaining to Moses that they wanted meat to eat, not monotonous manna. "It displeased the Lord, for the Lord heard it, and His anger was aroused. So the fire of the Lord burned among them, and consumed some in the outskirts of the camp." (Num. 11:1)

The people ran to Moses in desperation, Moses prayed, and the fire was extinguished. Moses named the place Taberah, which meant *burning.*

While still encamped at Taberah, the people continued to demand meat as part of their diet. Finally, God sent so many quail that they experienced extreme indigestion. He also sent "a very great plague" that killed many of them.

The word *plague* often was used in connection with a comet event, and such events almost always included a fiery discharge, directly from the comet or from a volcano activated in the stressful presence of the comet. It is likely that volcanism was involved with one or both of the events at Taberah, but we cannot be as certain about this as about events that have been described by the Bible in more detail.

Paran

The next major encampment of the Israelites was in the desert of Paran near the Gulf of Aqaba in the northern segment of the Sinai Peninsula. It was there that an Israelite named Korah led a rebellion involving 250 men with the intention of replacing Moses and Aaron in positions of leadership. Dathan and Abiram also took part in the rebellion described in the sixteenth chapter of Numbers.

The rebels offered incense before the Lord, as did Aaron, in a test of who the Lord would choose. While this was going on the Lord told Moses: "Speak to the congregation, saying, 'Get away from the tents of Korah, Dathan and Abiram.'"

Moses said to the people: "Depart now from the tents of these wicked men! Touch nothing of theirs, lest you be consumed in all their sins."

After the others had left, Moses summoned Dathan and Abiram, but they refused to come. They stood defiantly in front of their tents with their families.

Moses said: "If the Lord creates a new thing and the earth opens its mouth and swallows them up with all that belongs to them, and they go down alive into the pit, then you will understand that these men have rejected the Lord."

And then, according to Josephus, there was an earthquake: "The ground moved on a sudden; and the agitation that set it in motion was like that which the wind produces in waves of the sea."[9]

The movement of earth, like waves of the sea, often has been described by witnesses of earthquakes. Seismic fissures appeared in the ground beneath the tents of Dathan and Abiram and they fell, along with every member of their families, into these clefts, which then closed over their heads, burying them alive.

The next day Moses faced the remaining rebels, who were contending, along with Korah, against Aaron, for the high priesthood. Siding with the wealthy and popular Korah, a spokesman for the rebellious congregation pointed his finger accusingly at Moses and Aaron: "You have killed the people of the Lord."

This accusation incurred the wrath of the Lord and He said to Moses: "Get away from among this congregation, that I may consume them in a moment."

Moses and Aaron interceded for the rebels, but before the ensuing plague was stopped, 14,700 Israelites had perished, including Korah and the rest of the rebels who were offering incense. Josephus described the plague:

"So great a fire shone out as no one ever saw in any that is made by the hand of man, neither in those eruptions out of the earth that are caused by subterraneous burnings… but this fire was very bright, and had a terrible flame, such as is kindled at the command of God; by whose eruption on them, all the company, and Corah himself, were destroyed, and this so entirely that their very bodies left no remains behind them. Aaron alone was preserved…and thus Aaron was now no longer esteemed to have the priesthood by the favour (sic) of Moses, but by the public judgment of God."[10]

This could not have been a volcanic eruption because of the statement that it was unrelated to the "eruptions out of the earth that are caused by subterraneous burnings." The incinerating fury of the fiery plague indicated it was similar to the methane-ignited firestorms, emanating from comet fallout, which in 1871 killed hundreds of people in Chicago and elsewhere in the American Midwest.

The prophet Habakkuk described these events from God's perspective: "God came from Teman, the Holy One from Mount Paran. His glory covered the heavens and the earth was full of his praise. His brightness was like the light (sunrise, NIV); He had rays flashing from his hand, and there his power was hidden" (Hab. 3:3–4). Completing the vision, God sent plague and pestilence. He stood and shook the earth. Nations trembled. Mountains crumbled (Hab. 2:5–6).

There are figurative aspects to this vision. Attributing to God the glory of His chosen object of judgment, how would we describe it if we looked up and saw a God-sent comet in near proximity to the Earth?

We might describe the Lord's "glory covering the heavens." We might compare the brightness of His splendor with the sunrise. A word picture we could use to portray what we saw would be His hand (the coma) with rays emanating from it and flashing across the sky (the tail). Plague, pestilence, trembling, and crumbling would be consequential.

The comet that accounted for the worldwide flood stayed in proximity to Earth for eight months, so it seems unlikely that the Sinai comet was still around after more than a year. But it could have been the same comet, making a second contact with Earth after circling the sun. This means it also could have been a comet event that took the lives of Aaron's sons. A confirmed instance of a comet making a second approach to Earth a year later is described in Chapter Ten of this book.

Summary

Another fiery incident happened 38 years later as the Israelites marched through the Ammonite city of Heshbon on their way to crossing the Jordan River and entering Canaan. Indeed, there were so many fiery incidents that the sum of them, including those directly from a comet and indirectly from volcanoes stirred by the comet, established a pattern.

A comet guided by the hand of the Lord is a deadly judgmental agent. Indeed, it is an agent we could expect

God so to use, "For the Lord your God is a consuming fire, a jealous God." (Deut. 4:24) If fire has become the chosen method of God for rendering judgment against sinful human beings, it fulfills His promise not to destroy the Earth a second time with floodwaters (Genesis 9:11).

There was fire present during nearly every Sinai event for more than a year. That it is possible for a single comet event to sustain such activity for so long was proven by the comet that generated the Great Flood. However, the Lord withheld fire from the Red Sea event long enough for the freeze to take effect and save the lives of the Israelites. As soon as the Israelites had safely emerged from the sea, fire began accompanying the fallout from the comet in order to expedite the melting of the ice and drown the Egyptians. This is an example of the precise control God is able to exercise even during the most dreadfully catastrophic event.

Here is a summary of the major themes of this chapter:

- The rod Moses stretched out toward the Red Sea was a mirror image of the "arm of the Lord" in the sky above his head.

- A comet-generated tornado parted the sea and froze it in place long enough for three-million or more Israelites to pass through.

- A comet-produced earthquake cracked the frozen walls, releasing the sea waters to flow back over the Egyptians.

- Fiery rain and explosive bolides from the comet fell upon the Egyptians at the same time as the sea was overwhelming them.

- At Rephidim, a rock-splitting earthquake caused by the comet provided drinking water for the Israelites.

- Moses climbed Mount Sinai during a major eruption by the volcano while fiery debris and bolides were falling from the comet.

- Another eruption by the same volcano killed Aaron's insolent sons Nadab and Abihu.

- A volcanic plague at Taberah ("burning") killed many Israelites who had been complaining that they wanted meat, not manna.

- An earthquake buried the Israeli rebel leaders Dathan and Abiram with their entire families at Paran.

- The next day a deadly comet event incinerated 14,700 rebels, including their ringleader, Korah.

Chapter Five

The Longest Day

THE MYSTERY OF the Israelites' Jordan River crossover may have been solved when, in A.D. 1927, an earthquake caused a landslide that dammed the river in the same area, north of the crossover point near Jericho. The landslide blocked the river's flow for hours before pressure from the rising waters broke through the blockage and resumed the normal flow. Earthquakes occur often along the river because it is in a seismic rift zone. There is no biblical or historical evidence that the blockage that happened, circa 1407 B.C., was part of a comet event, but it may have been associated with the quake that a week later flattened Jericho.

The Bible does not specify that an earthquake was involved as the secondary cause, with God the providing the instigation. However, archaeologists have found the location of Jericho and have discovered evidence that the original settlement was destroyed by an earthquake and that the walls fell outward, giving the Israelite soldiers easy access after they had marched around the city seven times.

It is likely that the cadence of the marching, trumpeting and shouting of hundreds of thousands of Israelites contributed to the instability of the ground, for it is demonstrable that a stadium containing many fewer people may be set in vibration when the spectators shout in unison. There is no evidence that the Jericho event, either, was associated with a comet. However, both the Jordan and Jericho incidents add to the accumulating evidence of frequent catastrophism that contradicts evolution/ uniformitarian theory. Catastrophic events pervade world history, especially the segments of history recounted in the Bible.

The Long Day of Joshua was more catastrophic than the Jordan crossover or the Jericho decimation and was the occasion of the next comet event. There are several reasons we can identify the long day as a comet event, starting with the fact that it involved extraordinary happenings, both celestial and terrestrial.

It began with hailstones falling upon and killing more of the men in the fleeing armies of five Amorite kings who had attacked Gibeon than the Israelite troops killed with their weapons (Josh. 10:11). Like the hail of stones that fell during the ten plagues of Egypt, this was no ordinary hail, because a simple icy hail is incapable of slaughtering armored soldiers. It was a hail of explosive bolides or, less likely, a barrage of large meteorites or asteroids.

The Hebrew words here translated "hailstones" are *eben* (stone) and *barad* (hail). Considered as part of a single event, the heavenly stoning and the stoppage of Earth's rotation probably were related to the pass of a large comet close to the Earth, for a comet event involves several phases or aspects.

Astronomers debate this point. Some contend that the comas of comets do not have enough mass to affect tides on Earth, to say nothing of the planet's rotation. However, in the writings of Immanuel Velikovsky and Donald W. Patten we find frequent references to comets with considerable mass. These men proposed that the planets Mercury, Venus and even possibly Mars originally may have been comets, and it is now known that the formerly recognized planet Pluto is actually a comet. A comet of planet-size obviously has sufficient mass to create all kinds of havoc should it approach the Earth.

Mars shows no physical evidence of ever having been a comet, but it's intriguing to consider that if, indeed, Mercury and Venus originally were comets, the solar system at that time consisted of seven planets, and Earth was the one closest to the sun. The system then would have consisted of Earth, Mars, Jupiter, Saturn, Uranus, Neptune and a planet between Mars and Jupiter that subsequently disintegrated into asteroids after a clash, more than likely, with a comet.

It is significant that, on the same day as the hail of stones, in response to a prayer by Joshua, the sun and moon stopped moving in the sky with respect to their positions as seen from Earth. This gave the Israelites a chance to pursue their enemies and complete the victory with the aid of the heavenly stoning. No asteroid, nothing that is known to approach Earth other than a massive comet, is large enough, with a strong enough gravitational field, to alter the rotation of this planet.

Not only is a large comet, in close proximity, capable of creating so great a strain on the Earth, but over the course of thousands of years of clashes between the Earth and approaching cosmic objects, it should be expected to happen. And, indeed, it did happen on at least one other occasion, as we shall see in Chapter Eight.

A rotation stoppage of the Earth is no more stunning than the comet event that generated enormous new mountains worldwide during the Great Flood (Chapter One) or the comet event that resulted in the break-up of the world's land mass and the creation of new continents in conjunction with the destruction of the Tower of Babel (Chapter Twelve). It was a greater miracle that God guided the falling stones so that they killed thousands of Amorites and not a single Israelite than it was that Earth's rotation was interrupted.

After both the Jordan River crossover and the defeat of the five Amorite kings, the Israelites erected commemorative stone piles. The Bible states that the stones used in the pile built in memory of the Jordan River event were taken from the riverbed. It does not identify the origin of the ones that were piled in front of the cave where the kings were entombed, but it would make sense for them to have been chosen from among the stones that had fallen from the sky during the event.

Joshua, Jasher and Josephus

Here is Joshua's account of the long day: "Then Joshua spoke to the Lord in the day when the Lord delivered up the Amorites before the children of Israel, and he said in the sight of Israel: 'Sun, stand still over Gibeon; and Moon, in the Valley of Aijalon.' So the sun stood still, and the moon stopped, till the people had revenge upon their enemies. Is this not written in the Book of Jasher?" (Josh. 10:13).

By quoting the supportive reference in the Book of Jasher, Joshua showed that he understood that his account of the long day would be questioned, as it has been by many Bible critics. The account of Josephus supports that of Joshua:

"The place is called Beth-horon; where [Joshua] also understood that God assisted him, which He declared by thunder and thunderbolts (bolides), as also by the falling of hail larger than usual. Moreover, it happened that the day was lengthened, that the night might not come on too soon, and be an obstruction to the zeal of the Hebrews in pursuing their enemies…Now, that the day was lengthened at this time, and was longer than ordinary, is expressed in the books laid up in the temple."[1]

Josephus mentioned a second kind of hail ("larger than usual") besides the devastating bolides. This could have been a hail of meteorites or it could have been the kind of icy hail we usually associate with a winter storm. Comets are capable of precipitating both kinds of "hail," though neither is as deadly as bolides.

It is noteworthy that Josephus, apparently of the same mindset as Joshua, also sought support from secondary sources, for he mentioned books in the temple's library. Josephus translator William Whiston seems to have favored the literality of the narration because he wrote in a footnote: "The fact [of the long day] was mentioned in the book of Jasher, now lost, (Josh. x. 13) and is confirmed by Isaiah, (xxviii. 21), Habakkuk, (iii. 11,) and by the son of Sirach, (Ecclus. xlvi. 4)."[2]

The cited Isaiah reference does not stipulate to the long day but focuses on the state of mind of the Lord on that occasion in the valley, which was in the territory of Gibeon: "For the Lord will rise up as at Mount Perazim. He will be angry as in the Valley of Gibeon—that He may do His work, His awesome work, and bring to pass His act, His unusual act."

It was, indeed, an unusual act, and regardless of what intermediate causes were set into action, the Lord was the Activator. This implies that He was not finished doing unusual things and, since in context it referred to the Day of the Lord (His Second Coming), we should expect some remarkable things on that day.

Habakkuk's declaration was clear: "The sun and moon stood still in their habitation; at the light of Your arrows they went, at the shining of Your glittering spear." The arrows could refer to the appearance of the falling meteors and bolides, as they flashed through the sky. A spear was commonly used as a figurative depiction of a comet, referring to the shape of its appearance in the sky and its ability to send missiles thrusting at the Earth.

In the cited apocryphal book of Ecclesiasticus we find these vivid words: "Never before had a man (Joshua) made such a stand, for he was fighting the Lord's battles. Was it not through him that the sun stood still and made one day as long as two? He called on the Most High, the Mighty One, when the enemy was pressing him on every side, and the great Lord answered his prayer with a violent storm of hail. He overwhelmed that nation in battle and crushed his assailants as they fled down the pass, to make the nations recognize his strength in arms, and teach them that he fought under the very eyes of the Lord, for he followed the lead of the Mighty One." (Ecclesiasticus 46:3-6, NEB)

Christians tend to go to extremes regarding the Apocrypha. Some treat it like Scripture; others scoff as if it were bogus. The truth lies between: Though most of Christendom today considers it unscriptural, it is not spurious. It's a good collection of writings, perhaps second to the Holy Scriptures themselves, for it was given consideration to be included with the Scriptures—no other ancient writings were—and is quoted by at least two Bible writers and by respected historians such as Josephus. Leaders of the reformation movement, in an introduction to the Geneva Bible in A.D. 1560, declared that the apocryphal books were written by godly men. We indulge no second thoughts about quoting the works of godly men.

Adam Clarke

Another reputable source was Adam Clarke, whose famous *Commentary on the Holy Bible* was written and published about two centuries ago. Clarke did not speculate on the source of the event, but his comments gave credence to the Scriptures describing it and to the conclusion that the highlight was a stoppage of earth's rotation:

"Joshua does not say to the sun, 'Stand still,' as if he had conceived him to be running his race round the earth; but, 'Be silent,' or 'inactive'; that is, as I understand it, 'Restrain thy influence'—no longer act upon the earth, to cause it to revolve (rotate) round its axis, a mode of speech which is certainly consistent with the strictest astronomical knowledge. And the writer of the account, whether Joshua himself or the author of the book of Jasher, in relating the consequence of this command is equally accurate, using a word widely different when he speaks of the effect the retention of the solar influence had on the moon. In the first case the sun was 'silent' or 'inactive,' *dom*; in the latter, the moon 'stood still,' *amad*. The standing still of the moon, or its continuance above the horizon, would be the natural effect of the cessation of the solar influence, which obliged the earth to discontinue her diurnal rotation, which of course would arrest the moon; and thus both it and the sun were kept above the horizon, probably for the space of a whole day.

"As to the address to the moon, it is not conceived in the same terms as that to the sun, and for the most obvious philosophical reasons; all that is said is simply, '…and the moon on the vale of Ajalon,' which may be thus understood: 'Let the sun restrain his influence or be inactive, as he appears now upon Gibeon, that the moon may continue as she appears now over the vale of Ajalon.' It is worthy of remark that every word in this poetic address is apparently selected with the greatest caution and precision."[3]

Immanuel Velikovsky

Velikovsky, a brilliant man, went straight to the issue of causation: "A departure of the earth from its regular rotation is thinkable, but only in the very improbable event that our planet should meet another heavenly body of sufficient mass to disrupt the eternal path of our world."[4]

Next he discussed the question of whether a comet could have been the secondary or intermediary cause of the Long Day of Joshua: "That a comet may strike our planet is not very probable, but the idea is not absurd. The heavenly mechanism works with almost absolute precision; but unstable, their way lost, comets by the thousands, by the millions, revolve in the sky, and their interference may disturb the harmony. Periodically they return, but not at very exact intervals, owing to the perturbations caused by gravitation toward the larger planets when they fly too close to them."[5]

So, while Velikovsky is explaining his reasons for believing the cause of the long day could have been a comet, he takes time out to mention the phenomenon of perturbations. Velikovsky was a serious student of the heavens and of events involving the clash of celestial bodies. He quoted mythology related to the issue, with the intent of showing that the so-called myths had a basis in reality.

Velikovsky believed that a comet, or an object that today is a planet but at that time was a comet with a 52-year orbit, was the cause of some of the catastrophes described in the Bible. This comet, he thought, was responsible for the plagues of the Exodus and the Long Day of Joshua. Since there were only 43 years between the two events, one of the perturbations of which he speaks must have occurred when the comet came perilously close to the Earth during either the ten plagues or the Red Sea incident that followed soon after.

Velikovsky next undertook the issue of whether it is possible for stones to fall from the sky, as many of his predecessors had questioned. He concluded that they could, for they had "before the eyes of a crowd" on Nov. 7, 1492 and again on July 24, 1790.[6]

Velikovsky stated: "Since the year 1803, however, scholars have believed that stones fall from the sky. If a stone can collide with the earth, and occasionally a shower of stones, too, cannot a full-sized comet fly into the face of the earth?"[7]

He continued: "If the head of a comet should pass very close to our path, so as to effect a distortion in the career of the earth, another phenomenon besides the disturbed movement of the planet would probably occur: a rain of meteorites would strike the earth and would increase to a torrent. Stones scorched by flying through the atmosphere would be hurled on home and head."[8]

He concluded, as we have, that this is what happened on that most bizarre of all days. With regard to the question of whether it could have been a localized event in the Middle East, he cited parallel ancient references to an unusually long night in the western hemisphere.

He also quoted a prayer of Joshua, thanking God for directing all aspects of the event, including the thunderous noise made by a hail of stones (bolides and meteors), the sun and moon standing still, an earthquake and a whirlwind.

He wrote: "A torrent of large stones coming from the sky, an earthquake, a whirlwind, a disturbance in the movement of the earth—these four phenomena belong together. It appears that a large comet must have passed very near to our planet and disrupted its movement; a part of the stones dispersed in the neck and tail of the comet smote the surface of the earth a shattering blow."[9]

The whirlwind was a gigantic tornado, similar to the ones the same comet had produced, during a previous visit to Earth, first in Egypt amid the ten plagues and then a few days after the Exodus, opening the way for the Israelites to pass through the Red Sea.

Patten, Hatch and Steinhauer

A comprehensive study of Joshua's unusual day is featured in the book *The Long Day of Joshua and Six Other Catastrophes* by Donald W. Patten, Ronald R. Hatch and Loren C. Steinhauer. Their study traverses much of the same ground we have covered so far in this chapter and moves on from there to some new territory.

The three scientists estimated that a third of a million men met on the battlefield that day and that most of them were Canaanites, under the leadership of five kings. They estimated that 100,000 Canaanites were killed, most of them by celestial fallout: "Some we believe were slain by meteoric hits, some by sweeping prairie fires, but most by exploding bolides. Bolides, like the Tunguska Bolide, can explode with forces rivalling nuclear bombs."[10]

Perhaps it would have been more precise to state that some were killed by the firestorms often associated with such events. Prairie fires, though destructive, are not nearly as deadly as comet-generated firestorms.

Concerning the bolides the three men wrote: "The Scriptural account suggests the major spin axis shift started in the very early morning, whereas the bolidic and meteoric dumps arrived some two to three hours later, arriving at relative speeds of about 30,000 miles per hour. It was a long afternoon, especially for the Canaanite forces which were decimated, if not annihilated…This particular conflict was not just a battle, but was the 'Gettysburg', the 'Stalingrad', the 'Waterloo' of the entire campaign."[11]

The three scientists associated the so-called mythological story of Phaethon with the Long Day of Joshua. In the Phaethon story, Zeus "had to stop a careening chariot to save the earth from destruction, and he threw a thunderbolt at it. In a shower of sparks, the chariot flew apart and Phaethon plunged into the river Po…Hephaestus had to work the whole night through to mend the broken chariot so Helios could drive it again the next day."[12]

Helios, in Greek lore, was the sun god who drove his solar chariot across the sky each day. So the idea that the chariot was broken so that it could not be driven until the next day implies a lengthy stalling of the sun's progress across the sky.

Patten, et al, wrote: "We favor the conclusion that the Phaethon story is just the Hellenized version of the Long Day of Joshua, but our confidence is in the range of 80% as to the particular, specific catastrophe which the Phaethon story describes. With 100% confidence, however, we can affirm that modern cynics, radicals and rationalists, who ascribe this story to mere fancy, are entangled in a mistaken set of assumptions."[13]

In conclusion, they wrote: "Our analysis is that neither the traditional Biblicists (advocating an unexplained braking effect) nor the rationalists (advocating a uniformitarian rationale) have properly understood the nature of that catastrophic day."[14]

Henry M. Morris

Morris was an early leader of the contemporary creationist movement. Like Patten and Velikovsky, he believed that the so-called mythological stories of ancient peoples had a basis in reality. In his book, *The Bible Has the Answer*, he wrote: "Traditions of a long day (or of a long night, among the American Indians and the South Sea Islanders) are quite common among early nations and tribes. Immanuel Velikovsky, in his book *Worlds in Collision*, gives abundant documentation of this fact, as have many other writers."[15]

Morris did not think God's use of the sun to enable the Israelites to gain victory over the Amorites was coincidental because the Amorites were sun-worshippers: "For the chief object of their worship to be used as an agent in their defeat must have implied that the God of Israel was the true God, not only to the Amorites themselves but also to the other peoples of the region who had been intimidated by them."[16]

Morris wrote this about the possibility that the earth's rotation could have been miraculously halted for a day: "To deny the possibility of the miraculous (and, after all, how do we measure the dynamics of one miracle as against another?) is to deny the existence of God. That the earth should stop rotating on its axis for a time is no more inexplicable than that it should start rotating in the beginning. The Creator who started it could also stop it if He so desired. The question is not whether an alleged miracle *could* occur, but whether it *did* occur. The testimony of Scripture, as well as the many supporting traditions, confirms that it did."[17]

Concerning the veracity of the Bible's account of the Long Day of Joshua, Morris wrote: "It is found in the Word of God! Furthermore it is found in the context of the other events in Israel's conquest of Canaan, the general outline of which has been remarkably confirmed by archaeological discoveries in recent years. Dr. Nelson Glueck, probably the greatest living Palestinian archaeologist, president of the Hebrew Union College, has written: 'As a matter of fact, it may be stated categorically that no archaeological discovery has ever controverted a Biblical reference. Scores of archaeological findings have been made which confirm in clear outline or exact detail historical statements in the Bible.'"[18]

Summary

Christians believe that with God all things are possible, and this was one of the times when He seems to have done something that to human minds seemed impossible. But if we recognize that the orbit of a comet may be altered during a close brush with a planet, or that it might even be changed from a comet orbit to that of a planet, like Pluto and possibly also Venus and Mercury were changed, it becomes less difficult to believe. If a comet's orbit could be perturbed by a decade after one close call with the Earth, why should it be difficult to believe that Earth's axis of rotation might have been altered or even interrupted during the next visit by the same comet?

Here is a summary of the key points of this chapter:

- Providential earthquakes unrelated to a comet event enabled Joshua and the Israelites to ford the Jordan River and destroy Jericho.

- The biblical account of the Long Day of Joshua featured a barrage of bolides from the heavens and a stoppage of Earth's rotation.

- The combination of celestial bombardment and terrestrial disturbance indicated that its secondary cause was a comet.

- Also supporting the comet theory were two other aspects of the event—an earthquake and a whirlwind (tornado).

- Joshua and a Josephus translator both cited other sources backing their statements that Earth's rotation was halted.

- Adam Clarke wrote of the biblical account of the Long Day that every word was "selected with the greatest caution and precision."

- Immanuel Velikovsky asserted that Earth's rotation could be stopped only if it contacted a large celestial body such as a comet.

- Donald W. Patten and two other scientists contended that the "myth" of Phaethon was an imaginative chronicling of the Long Day.

- Henry M. Morris joined Velikovsky and Patten in finding ancient versions of the Long Day in literature of cultures worldwide.

Chapter Six

The Double Cycle

IT WAS POSSIBLE to make reasonably good estimates for the dates of Noah's flood and the bolide that destroyed Sodom and Gomorrah. The Sodom cataclysm may or may not have been the initiator of the series of events occurring usually at 54-year intervals. Probably, it was not. More likely, the comets causing the deadly Flood and Sodom events were broken apart and destroyed during those events.

Dates became much clearer after that. We know that the Exodus happened 480 years before Solomon began to build the temple (1 Kings 6:1, 2 Chron. 3:1-2). The temple was completed about 960 B.C. and took seven years to build, so it must have been begun circa 967 B.C. This implies the Exodus took place probably in 1447 B.C., though there is some scholarship favoring 1446. We can state with confidence that it was one of those two years.

The comet that had been making regular appearances at 53—or 54-year intervals for 430 years, since 1877 B.C., doing severe damage upon every fourth appearance, was perturbed while making a frightfully close pass to Earth during the Exodus plagues. Its orbital pattern was shortened, thus reducing its next period to 43 years, so that the Long Day of Joshua took place in 1404 B.C.

We are presuming the next event, because the Bible gives no details about it. Circa 1296 B.C., 108 years or a double-cycle after the Long Day of Joshua, the Book of Ruth opens with a description of a famine. There is nothing other than mention of famines in 1877 B.C. and 1662 B.C. to indicate that there were comet events at those times. But the timing was correct and famines often were caused by comets, so it is a reasonable surmise that the 1296 famine also may have been caused by the destruction of food sources during a comet event.

Two cycles later, in 1188 B.C., a major comet episode occurred involving the prophetess Deborah and the timid warrior Barak. It happened during the spring of the year, as did most of the events described in this chapter as well as many others in this book. The spring was described in the Bible as the time when kings go forth to war (2 Sam. 11:1). This was a favored time for initiating a conflict because of the weather. Napoleon once made the mistake of invading Russia at a time that would result in his troops having to spend the winter months there. However, favorable weather was not the only reason kings in ancient times chose the spring season for military operations.

Before engaging their enemies, kings sought omens of victory from the gods. Prophets, priests and magicians performed occult rituals to win favor with these gods, especially those that happened to loom largest in the heavens on ominous occasions. Foremost were the sun, moon and comets. In at least one instance, ancient artwork was mistakenly identified as depicting sun worship. It was actually drawn in reverence of a tailed object that could only have been a comet. Religious sites, or temples, were built to contain idols of the popular celestial gods. One of these was the image of the goddess Diana—probably a large meteorite—that had been recovered after falling from the sky (Acts 19:35).

In order to position themselves as close as possible to the celestial gods, the better to be seen and heard by them, the sky-watchers built "high places." Anyone who has spent time in mountainous regions knows that celestial objects appear with greater clarity and intensity in proportion to the height of the peak from which they are observed.

Comets were the most revered and feared of all celestial objects. This was because of the destruction they wrought. They often appeared in spring. A diagram showing the pattern of revolution of Earth and comets around the sun shows clearly that the most likely times for comet orbits to intersect with that of the earth were near the spring and fall equinoxes. The dangerous comet with the 54-year orbital cycle often, but not always, chose the spring.

Barak: 1188 B.C.

The name Barak meant *lightning* or *flashing sword*. Like many other Hebrew names, it was appropriate for the role played by the man in the history of Israel. He lived during an era when the Israelites were domineered by Canaanites or were led by military leaders who brought deliverance to them. Barak was one of the deliverers, and the deliverance came by means of a flashing sword in the sky.

Barak had a faith problem. Upon being told by the prophetess Deborah that he should lead Israel out of the bondage it was in at that time, Barak responded that he would do so under one condition—that Deborah would accompany him. She warned him that his reluctance to assume responsibility would result in personal loss of acclaim, and so it has been: In the lore of Judaism, Deborah is much more fondly remembered than Barak and is included among the judges of Israel.

According to the account of the battle in Judges chapter four, a Canaanite king named Jabin gained control over Israel after the Israelites did evil and "the Lord sold them" into Jabin's hands (Judges 4:2). The Canaanite army, commanded by Sisera, oppressed the Israelites for twenty years, but then Deborah sent for Barak and told him that with an army of 10,000 men he would subdue the Canaanites. Recognizing the inferiority of such a force in comparison with the Canaanites, Barak told Deborah he would do so only if she went with him.

The Bible did not attach numbers to the forces of Sisera, but the account of Josephus did: "Jabin came out of Hazor, a city that was situate over the Lake of Semechonitis, and had in pay three hundred thousand footmen, and ten thousand horsemen, with no fewer than three thousand chariots. Sisera was the commander of all the army, and was the principal person in the king's favor."[1]

Humanly speaking, Barak's reluctance was understandable. His ground forces were outnumbered by 30-to-1, and Sisera had as many cavalry as Barak had infantry, besides 3,000 iron chariots and charioteers. This battle was a no-brainer: The Canaanites were a sure thing to win. But the Bible's description of the battle at the River Kishon was carefully worded in attributing the triumph to Israel's heavenly Judge, Jehovah:

"And the Lord routed Sisera and all his chariots and all his army with the edge of the sword before Barak; and Sisera alighted from his chariot and fled away on foot. But Barak pursued the chariots and army as far as Harosheth Hagoyim, and all the army of Sisera fell by the edge of the sword; not a man was left." (Judges 4:15-16)

The Song of Deborah

The victory song sung by Deborah and Barak after the great triumph was lengthy. For our theme these were the pertinent excerpts:

"Lord, when You went out from Seir,
When You marched from the field of Edom,
The earth trembled and the heavens poured,
The clouds also poured water;
The mountains gushed before the Lord,
This Sinai, before the Lord God of Israel…
The kings came and fought,
Then the kings of Canaan fought
In Taanach, by the waters of Megiddo;
They took no spoils of silver,
They fought from the heavens;
The stars from their courses fought against Sisera."
The torrent of Kishon swept them away,
That ancient torrent, the torrent of Kishon."
—Judges 5:4-5…19-21

Much more was involved in this battle than one army against another, and the Lord used every factor in obtaining the victory for Israel. First, the Earth quaked. Though it was a universal event, we may say with assurance that it did extensive damage to the camp of the Canaanites, in contrast to the camp of the Israelites, which, by reason of the Lord's intervention, it did not touch. The quake produced groundswells and crevasses that must have terrified the horses of the Canaanites and impeded the movement of their chariots.

Next, *the heavens poured*. The King James Version translated this as *the heavens dropped* and in this case the old KJV was correct. The Hebrew word meant *to ooze, fall* or *drop*. These were not drops of water, because the next phrase, using the same word, refers to rainwater dropping from clouds. What, then, were these other droppings from the heavens above the clouds? Apparently, this was a comet event: The sword of the Lord, the most common of all images of a comet, was present in the sky, and its fiery droppings facilitated the work of Barak's undermanned militia.

Next, *the clouds also poured water*, miring the wheels of the Canaanite chariots, so that even their leader, Sisera, fled on foot. This rainfall was intensified by the presence of the comet. Its icy elements, after breaking off the coma, melted during freefall in a way similar to what happened during the first forty days of the Great Flood of Noah. The presence of a source of cold air, probably from icy parts of the comet, is mentioned by Josephus.[2]

And, *the mountains gushed before the Lord*. Sinai is mentioned here, and we know Mount Sinai was a volcano. This was a severe volcanic event that included ejaculations. The first thing that comes to mind is lava, but it could also refer to every fiery and rocky thing ejected from an erupting volcano. Since Mount Sinai was hundreds of miles away, this was not a local event but one with widespread repercussions that the Lord used locally against the Canaanites.

Moreover, *the stars in their courses fought against Sisera*. The Hebrew word *kowkab*, translated *stars*, referred to celestial bodies in the sense of *blazing* or *rolling*. Its root word meant *burning* and *blistering*. So, once more, we have a comet casting deadly fallout onto the Lord's enemies, as did the comet of the ten plagues. Flaming fallout from a comet can set on fire anything or anyone it lands upon. It can instigate deadly firestorms capable of consuming many people, especially those in a confined area such as that in which an army is deployed. Its sulfur content, turning to a sulfuric aerosol in the presence of rainfall, can raise painful, even deadly, blisters and boils on the skin of anyone contacted by it.

And, finally, *the torrent of Kishon swept them away.* Apparently, the river, swelled by the sudden downpour, overflowed its banks and drowned many of the Canaanites. Clad in heavy armor, they were easily knocked down by the force of the rushing water and were unable to regain their footing or even to stay afloat in the comparatively shallow torrents as they tried to flee from the celestial barrage.

In this battle the Israelites needed to do little other than mop up the leavings of the God who, the Bible said, arrived at the Kishon River *before Barak.* From the heavens, the Lord's *flashing sword* and His *stars in their courses* literally *fought against Sisera* and subdued his entire army. Even the Hebrew word translated *courses* had significance as "it could also be accurately translated, 'an orbit', or 'orbits', paths of the luminaries."[3]

Gideon: 1134 B.C.

The next appearance of the comet was the occasion for one of the strangest battles in world history, if it could be called a battle at all. Anyone having previous doubts about the Lord's ingenuity as a military strategist should have them no longer after reading the account of Gideon's victory, with 300 men, over 135,000 Midianite soldiers.

After the victory of the outnumbered forces of Deborah and Barak over an army of Canaanites, there was a 40-year period of rest, followed by an indefinite period of time during which the Israelites turned away from the Lord and, after that, seven years of Midianite oppression. If the falling away period corresponded to the period of oppression, as it often did in the providence of God—i.e., seven years of punishment for seven years of sinning—the interim between the Israelites' conflicts with the Canaanites and the Midianites was 54 years, the normal orbital cycle of the comet. This means the battle was joined most likely in 1134 B.C.

The decimation of the Midianites, however, was not accomplished through the medium of the comet but through the genius of the Israelites' heavenly Commander. His strategy enabled the forces of the Israelites, though outnumbered 450-to-one, to win a battle in which not one of them was killed. The enemy's death toll was 120,000. The Midianites fled that battlefield with only 15,000 survivors, one-ninth of their original force.

If there was indeed a comet in the sky at that time—and every detail of the biblical and Josephus records of the event makes it appear that there must have been—it helps to account for the presence of so many Midianite troops. We have observed that it was customary for ancient kings to lead their troops into battle during the spring season because of the good weather, besides favorable omens, which could be sought through occult means by their magicians.

But there was one other thing that could influence a decision to make war—the presence in the sky of a comet. The reason for this was that, by now, after many bombardments from comets, including one just 54 years before, everyone familiar with that event, including the Midianite kings, knew that a comet with a martial attitude could destroy their kingdoms and possibly kill everyone in an entire region (as the Sodom comet had done). Or, if they were fortunate, it could destroy their enemies. They were expecting destruction of one kind of another, and so they took to the field diffidently, as if they had no other choice.

They knew about the many deadly facets of the comet that had given victory to Deborah and Barak. Their parents had witnessed it. Perhaps, this time, they hoped, if the prophets of Baal could send skyward more influential entreaties than the priests of Israel, and if they could muster sufficient military forces, the "god" they saw in the sky would bless them and send its onslaught, for the first time in more than 500 years, upon their enemies, the Israelites, instead of themselves.

It was with this thought in mind that kings from Midianite (Arabic) cities southeast of Israel got together

135,000 troops, including many Amalekites, and encamped in the valley between the mountains of Gilead and the Jordan River. The mountain range was like a wall to their East, towering over the valley. The peaks range from 2,000 to 3,000 feet above sea level, but are much higher than that in relation to the valley, which is hundreds of feet below sea level: "Now the Midianites and Amalekites, all the people of the East, were lying in the valley as numerous as locusts; and their camels were without number, as the sand by the seashore in multitude." (Judges 7:12)

It was their intention to cross the River Hieromax to their north and attack the Israelite tribes of Gad, Reuben and Manasseh. The ragtag Israeli force recruited for the defense was led by Gideon, a reluctant warrior who had been hiding in a winepress when he was recruited by the Lord.

The Midianites and Israelites knew from reconnaissance reports that the Israeli force was much smaller than that of Midian. We cannot be sure whether or not the Midianities knew that God had decided 12,000 Israelites were too many for this battle and had reduced the number to 300. But, either way, the Midianites believed their numbers were sufficient to demolish the Israelites after dawn broke the next day. They had no idea that a nocturnal deception would prevent most of them from again seeing the sun.

In addition to the geography of the region, which placed the Midianites in a vulnerable position, there was an emotional edge favoring their enemy. Besides an awareness of what had happened 54 years before, they knew about the similar disaster that had befallen another force of Canaanites during the Long Day of Joshua. And, never to be forgotten by Middle Eastern peoples were the series of events during the Exodus that had wiped out the Egyptians, and then, forty years later, two Arab armies in the same area where the Midianites were encamped (see Joshua 2:8-11).

The Israelites, acting on instructions by Gideon, given to him by the Lord, "armed" themselves with trumpets, pitchers and torches. Gideon and his troops were on much higher ground than the camp of the Midianites: They were on the heights of Gilead, while the Midianites were in the valley below (Judges 7:3-8).

This was important.

After receiving instructions from Gideon, the Israelite troops arrayed themselves on the high hills due east of the camp of the Midianites. Upon their leader's signal, 100 of them blew the trumpets (ram's horns) that they held in their right hands. Then they broke the pitchers in their left hands revealing the blaze of torches inside the pitchers. In unison they shouted, "THE SWORD OF THE LORD AND OF GIDEON!"

Each of the other two groups of 100 men did the same, and then all 300 blew their trumpets together and continued trumpeting and displaying the torches as the made their way down the hillsides toward the Midianites.

Adam Clarke gave this account of the scene: "How astonishing must the effect be, in a dark night, of the sudden glare of 300 torches, darting their splendor, in the same instant, on the half-awakened eyes of the terrified Midianites, accompanied with the clangor of 300 trumpets alternately mingled with the thundering shout of 'A sword for the Lord and for Gideon.'"[4]

The Great Simulation

Clarke's description, while accurate, is not adequate to disclose the extremes of terror felt by the Midianites. The following is narrative explains what they saw and heard, from their perspective, and why it was so terrifying that even those aggressively trained military men yielded to panic:

In the middle of the night, when all of the Midianites except watchmen who had just come on duty, were asleep, the camp seemed at peace. The sleepy-eyed men who had just been awakened to serve guard duty noticed that the revered celestial object had made its nightly appearance above the hills east of their encampment. It appeared to be larger than it had been the previous night. Its coma was bigger than the moon and its tail stretched a head-turning distance across the sky. They cast frequent anxious upward glances, but as yet there had been no rumblings indicative of a deadly outburst.

Then, all of a sudden, they heard a noise that sounded ominously familiar to those among them who had heard their parents describe with awe the Deborah-Barak event. It was an odd trumpeting sound such as is produced by the interaction of a dangerous comet with the gravitational field of the Earth, and it seemed to be coming from the direction of the comet. They felt trapped in that valley and began to consider the possibility of making a run for it.

Next, from the same easterly direction, came explosive noises, and anxiety turned to panic: To them, nothing they could imagine was more terrifying than the thought that the rising comet had begun to unleash bolides in the hills on the east side of the valley where they were encamped. Perhaps it was too late for them to get out of there alive.

And, immediately after the explosive noises came the appearance of many torches. A trumpet and a torch were common emblems of a comet, and it wasn't only because comets had the appearance of torches or trumpets in the sky. They also were fiery, like torches, and made sounds like trumpets in full resonation. The appearance of the torches was high above the heads of the Midianites, to whose panicky eyes they appeared to be falling from the comet in the eastern sky instead of resting in the hands of Gideon's descending troops on the range of mountains.

Three times the scene repeated itself, with blaring trumpets, explosive noises and descending torches that looked like fiery emanations from the comet. During a comet event, many of the fiery precipitants look like miniature comets, as did the torches, and the Midianites were aware of that.

The clincher was the sound of the enemy shouts: "The sword of the Lord and of Gideon!"

This, to the Midianites, was a formal announcement of an impending onslaught. Comets were perceived by ancient peoples in many forms, but the most common was a sword. They were called sword-stars or sword-gods because of their shape and the way they appeared to make deadly slashes at the Earth from their exalted positions.

The Midianites' panic was total. Even while the trumpets continued to blare and now three-hundred fiery miniature comet-like objects were visible in what appeared to be the lower areas of the eastern sky above their heads than where they were first seen, the Midianites and Amalekites fled in the only direction they could, southward through the valley toward the Dead Sea.

Josephus made a curious, almost comical, statement about the flight and pursuit that makes sense only with a clear understanding of the comet scenario. He wrote: "[The Hebrews] set upon their enemies with their lamps."[5]

The Midianites and Amalekites spoke diverse languages, so upon bumping into each other during their frantic flight in the pitch-darkness of the valley they could not tell friend from enemy. They slaughtered each other even as they fled. The Israelites, still blowing trumpets and waving torches, pursued until the surviving 15,000 had disappeared into the night, leaving 120,000 dead on the floor of the valley.

As far as we know, during its 1134 B.C. appearance, the comet did nothing but hover menacingly in the sky. It was a pseudo-event, but there were 120,000 actual victims. Only the Lord could devise such an astounding battle plan. He has said that the battle is His, and on this occasion it most decisively was.

Samuel: 1080 B.C.

The comet, though threatening, was placid during the Gideon event, so its new pattern was to wreak destruction during every other orbital cycle. This was more severe than the original four-cycle pattern that was interrupted by the extreme event involving the Exodus plagues and the Red Sea pass-through. The comet was perturbed by the plagues and returned ahead of schedule for the Long Day of Joshua in 1404 B.C. Then, unless it was indeed responsible for the famine mentioned in the book of Ruth, it went back to its one-in-four format and did not do major damage until Deborah and Barak opposed the Canaanites in 1188 B.C.

Starting with the Deborah-Barak victory, however, the comet did serious physical damage to earth and its inhabitants every other 54-year cycle, or every 108 years, for the next 432 years. The next relevant incident for us to consider was Samuel's victory over the Philistines in 1080 B.C.

The Israelites were worshiping foreign gods. Samuel told them the Lord would deliver them from the hands of the oppressive Philistines if they would cease their idolatrous practices, and they obeyed: "[They] put away the Baals and the Ashtoreths, and served the Lord only." (1 Samuel 7:4)

Samuel then gathered the Israelites at Mizpah and, after a day of fasting and repentance, he offered a burnt offering to the Lord and prayed. While he was doing this, the Philistines drew near to attack the Israelites, who were unarmed and totally unprepared to defend themselves. The Bible states simply that the Lord "thundered with a loud thunder upon the Philistines that day, and so confused them that they were overcome before Israel." (1 Samuel 7:10).

Two different Hebrew words were translated *thundered* and *thunder*. The first, *raam*, meant to tumble or be violently agitated, or it could also mean to crash or roar, as the sound of thunder. The second word, *qowl*, meant to call aloud like thunder. Based on the simplest definitions of these words, the source of thunderous noise could have been anything ranging from ordinary thunder during a rainstorm to exploding bolides. The Philistines would not have fled from ordinary thunder, but this doesn't mean that the only thunderous sound that could have frightened them so badly would have been made by an exploding bolide.

The account of Josephus, who gathered his information from biblical and non-biblical sources, clarified the issue: "God disturbed [the Philistines] with an earthquake, and moved the ground under them to such a degree, that he caused it to tremble, and made them to shake, insomuch that by its trembling, he made some unable to keep their feet and made them fall down, and, by opening its chasms, he caused that others should be hurried down into them;

after which he caused such a noise of thunder to come among them, and made fiery lightning shine so terribly round about them, that it was ready to burn their faces; and he so suddenly shook their weapons out of their hands."[6]

Once again, we have a multi-faceted event. First, there was an earthquake, affecting only the Philistines. It was such a severe quake that many of the Philistines were killed, some of them dying a horrible death by being swallowed up by fissures in the ground. Next, there was the noise of thunder among them, which, in this context, seems to have been some kind of explosive substance, perhaps sulfurous rocks. And, finally, there was a "fiery lightning" that threatened to and probably did burn exposed parts of their bodies, most notably their faces. This, of course, was not ordinary lightning, but the words that should be emphasized are *fiery* and *burning*. Sodium, sulfur or methane mixing with rainfall could have created this effect.

Support for this thesis was provided by Samuel in the aftermath of the event. After the unarmed Israelites had routed the fleeing Philistines, "Samuel took a stone and set it up between Mizpah and Shen, and called its name Ebenezer, saying, 'Thus far the Lord has helped us.'" (1 Sam. 7:12)

Josephus wrote that Samuel referred to it as the *Stone of Power* "as a signal of that power God had given them against their enemies."[7] The memorial stone may have been one of the large rocks that had fallen from the sky during the assault.

The co-authors of *The Long Day of Joshua* were more definite in their identification: "The 'stone of power' was a large, impressive meteorite, and it was selected, appropriately enough, for an historical monument."[8]

The same authors also emphasized the importance of the timing of the battle: "Philistine armies like later Assyrian armies, were given over to the idea of confronting their enemy (Israel) on the date of expected cosmic intervention: 'Let the deities be involved in the decision of battle.'"[9]

Once more, with such a diversity of familiar and frightening cometic aspects, timed to coordinate the expected arrival of the cosmic intruder with another military conflict, the odds mount almost to the degree of certainty that God used His favorite celestial weapon, a comet, to rout the Philistines in 1080 B.C.

Summation

Between 1188 B.C. and 1080 B.C. there were two terrible comet events and one pseudo-event that turned out to be as lethal for the enemies of God as the other two. All three occurred on battlefields, giving victory to Israeli forces led by Deborah/Barak, Gideon, and Samuel over armies from Canaan, Midian and Philistia. These were the highlights:

- In ancient times kings often went to war in the spring of the year beneath the looming presence of dangerous comets.

- The name Barak meant *flashing sword*, which, probably not coincidentally, was a common epithet for a comet.

- In 1188 B.C., Barak mobilized 10,000 Israelites and watched the Lord unleash a heavenly bombardment upon 300,000 Canaanites.

- Besides the celestial outpourings, Barak's forces were assisted by comet-induced earthquake, volcanism and flood.

- In 1134 B.C., a battle tally was: Midianite troops total 135,000, killed 120,000; Gideon's Israelite troops total 300, killed zero.

- The Lord decided this battle with strategy simulating a fusillade from a comet that turned the panicky Midianites against one another.

- In 1080 B.C., a large force of Philistines surrounded an unarmed group of Israelites who were fasting and praying.

- The Lord's comet slaughtered the Philistines by earthquake and fiery fallout before they could launch an attack.

Chapter Seven

David & Elijah

DAVID WAS BORN in 1040 B.C. and died in 970 B.C. He witnessed two approaches of the deadly comet, which by that time had become feared and revered. Astronomers of our time keep close watch on comets, such as Halley's, even though they do no harm. In ancient times the science of astronomy was taken more seriously than it is today, because of the potential for cataclysmic happenings from the heavens. Even great leaders such as Abraham and David did a lot of sky-watching, especially during the anxious years before a dangerous comet's return.

David got his first look at the comet with the 54-year orbit during an "off" cycle, in 1026 B.C., when he was 14 years old. Even though that was not a catastrophic occasion, the comet must have impressed him because several of the psalms he wrote before its next appearance in 972 B.C. contained cosmic imagery. He also wrote at least one psalm late in life describing his second look at the comet two years before his death.

The 150 biblical psalms were organized according to themes. This was an ancient version of a hymnal, and hymnals are arranged categorically, not chronologically. Whether a hymn is old or new, it is equally likely to be in the rear of the hymnal as in the front. There is no point in even attempting to order all of the psalms chronologically. But let's take a look at a few of David's.

In a condensed section of one psalm, David mentioned two common images of a comet—a bow with arrows and a sword: "If [God] does not turn back, He will sharpen His sword; He bends His bow and makes it ready. He also prepares for Himself instruments of death; He makes His arrows into fiery shafts." (Psalm 7:12-13).

Of course, not all of the Bible's references to a sword and a bow with arrows refer to a comet. But the image of an arrow with a fiery shaft is distinctly like the discharge from a comet. During ancient warfare arrows were ignited to make them more deadly, but it was not the shafts but the tips that were set ablaze. Even though the comet of 1026 B.C. did not do severe damage, its fiery fallout was dangerous.

David was cognizant of history. He wrote this about the activity of Mount Sinai upon the approach of the Israelites: "O God, when Thou didst go forth before Thy people, when Thou didst move through the wilderness, the earth trembled; even the heavens dropped before God; Sinai (quaked) before God, the God of Israel." (Psalm 68:7-8, MLV) The Modern Language Version is quoted here because it omits the word *rain,* which is not in the original Hebrew text.

Even more vivid was a single verse of another Davidic psalm: "Upon the wicked [God] will rain coals; fire and brimstone and a burning wind shall be the portion of their cup." (Psalm 11:6) David recognizes the presence of God during an event that, from a human standpoint, appeared to be catastrophic. Psalm 11 was either written after the comet event of 972 B.C. or was based on written descriptions of earlier appearances of the comet. Since it is in the future tense, it may also contain prophetic reference to the Day of the Lord.

972 B.C.: What and Why?

There is little question about the timing of Psalm 18. It was written after the terrible comet event of 972 B.C. and so also found placement within the context of the Bible's narration of that event, in 2 Samuel 22:8-19, more than a half-century after the comet's other appearance during David's life. 2 Samuel 22 and 23 are interconnected and we know they happened after chapter 24 because 23:1 contains a reference to David's last words. Chapter 24 refers to a decision David made three or four years before he died, and the outcome of that decision.

David committed a sin in the sight of God by ordering Joab to oversee a census of the armed forces in Israel and

Judah. Joab objected, but David insisted. Joab's census disclosed that there were 800,000 men in Israel capable of participating in warfare and another 500,000 in Judah. Afterward, the Holy Spirit convicted David of his sin and he confessed it to God. The next day, the prophet Gad informed David of a message he had received from the Lord. David could choose among three options:

- Seven years of famine throughout Israel and Judah.
- Three months of defeats at the hands of enemy forces.
- Three days of plague.

David chose the third option. "So the Lord sent a plague upon Israel from the morning till the appointed time. From Dan to Beersheba seventy thousand men of the people died. And when the angel stretched out His hand over Jerusalem to destroy it, the Lord relented from the destruction, and said to the angel who was destroying the people, 'It is enough; now restrain your hand.'" (2 Sam. 24:15-16)

David himself may have been physically affected by this plague because he wrote an appeal to God: "There is no soundness in my flesh because of Your anger, nor any health in my bones because of my sin…My wounds are foul and festering because of my foolishness." (Psalm 38:3, 5)

This sounds like the plight of Job, when his skin was blistered by comet fallout. The biblical text does not describe the cosmic carnage. It simply gives the outcome:

70,000 fighting men dead, which probably equated to 300,000 people in total, including women, children and the elderly. It was a major disaster.

The biblical account leaves many questions unanswered, including the most basic ones: Why did David order the census in the first place? And, why was David's census order such a serious sin in the sight of God?

First and foremost, for David to order this census was a sin of blatant unbelief for a man of God who had been faithful his entire life, but was perhaps weakening in old age.

David studied the history of his nation. There are many historical allusions in his psalms. He knew about the comet. He could hardly *not* know, having seen it once as a teen-ager at a time when it did little damage. He also knew about it from history, not only the Exodus, but the much more recent incident, recorded in the book of the Judges, in which Gideon defeated 135,000 Midianites with a force of 300 men. Since it had been returning with a regular orbital pattern, David may also have known when it was due to return.

David probably knew all of these things, but even if he knew none of them, the comet would have reminded him when it was spotted in the sky months before making its approach to Earth. David ordered the military census because, disregarding the comparatively recent Gideon victory, he wanted to know his nation's numerical military might because he thought he might be attacked during that spring's comet event. We know that it was customary for kings to engage in warfare beneath the looming shadows of comets. Authors of *The Long Day of Joshua* wrote this explanation of such conflicts:

"Rather often in ancient history, two battling nations would tacitly arrange to have their military encounter on a day of expected cosmic visitation, concluding that the side which would be decimated was the one which the cosmic gods disfavored."[1]

On this occasion, David committed the sin of doubting God. Knowing that the comet was approaching, he ordered the census, instead of kneeling, reminding the Lord of what He had done for Gideon, and expressing trust that He could do the same again. This is a sin common to man. It's called seeing-is-believing, in direct opposition to trusting an invisible God.

The Three Options

This is opinion, but it seems worth mentioning because of its relevance to what happened in 972 B.C.: When the Lord gave the three options to David, He already had decided to use the comet in punitive judgment, regardless which of the three David chose. This had become His custom since the Great Flood.

David chose the third option, so God's "plague" was a direct aerial assault from the comet. The Hebrew word translated *plague* often, though not always, referred to comet events. It rarely referred to diseases. In this case, involving catastrophically sudden deaths, it is certain that no disease was involved, although the fallout may have caused painful lesions on the skin of victims, David included.

But even during this event, as David continued to pray, God in His mercy decided to terminate it after 12 hours, instead of permitting it to continue for three days, according to the account of Josephus.[2] Otherwise, Jerusalem would have been destroyed and so, too, would have been most of Israel and Judah. The damage done during those twelve hours was considerably more than any disease could have done in so short a time.

If, instead of choosing three days of plague, David had picked three months of defeat at the hands of enemies, it is almost certain that many more than 70,000 Israelite soldiers would have fallen on the battlefield. An entire spring of losing battles would have represented an astronomical death toll for Israeli men. As we have seen, the relation of the comet to the battlefield is that kings were inclined to go to war beneath the shadow of comets, and it would have been a simple matter for a sovereign God to persuade some of them to attack David's kingdom.

If, as his option, David had decided on seven years of famine, that, too, might have been worse than the actual death toll from the comet assault. Famine, too, could have been a comet option. Among all the other things it did, the Passover comet killed the crops and food-producing animals in the fields of the Egyptians.

The same comet in earlier appearances produced famines in Israel causing Abraham to travel to Egypt 430 years before the Exodus and Jacob to go there four comet-cycles or 215 years later (Gen. 12:10, 41:54). The latter of these, like the option offered to David, was a seven-year famine. And between the two, there was a famine in the time of Isaac. The Bible mentions the Isaac famine in the same sentence with the Abraham famine. It may or may not have occurred 108 years (two comet cycles) after the Abraham famine (Gen. 26:1).

A comet created a famine after the Sodom assault, which afflicted Job (Job 5:20-22, 30:3). We have seen, too, that it is possible that the 54-year-cycle comet caused the famine mentioned in the first verse of the book of Ruth, circa 1296 B.C. Had David chosen the famine option, God could have utilized the comet so that it destroyed the land's food supply.

What Actually Happened

Like the song of Moses and Miriam, and the one of Deborah and Barak, David wrote a song after the major comet event he witnessed. It appears twice in the Bible, as Psalm 18 and as chapter 22 in the second book of Samuel. It mentions deliverance from Saul, which occurred much earlier in David's life, but it must have been written toward the end of his life because it cites deliverance from all his enemies. Here are some relevant excerpts:

"Then the earth shook and trembled;
The foundations of heaven quaked and were shaken,
Because He was angry,
Smoke went up from His nostrils,
And devouring fire from His mouth;
Coals were kindled by it.
He bowed the heavens and came down
With darkness under his feet.
He rode upon a cherub, and flew;
And He was seen upon the wings of the wind.
He made darkness canopies around Him,
Dark waters and thick clouds of the skies.
From the brightness before Him
Coals of fire were kindled.
The Lord thundered from heaven,
And the Most High uttered His voice.
He sent out arrows and scattered them;
Lightning bolts, and He vanquished them.
Then the channels of the sea were seen,
The foundations of the world were uncovered,
At the rebuke of the Lord,
At the blast of His nostrils."

—2 Sam. 22:8-16

This is so similar to comet events discussed in earlier chapters of this book that we don't need to analyze it detail by detail. It describes a multi-faceted event of the most destructive order: The entire Earth must have been shaking beneath the feet of its inhabitants because, from their perspective, the heavens also appeared to shake. God "came down" and brought with him "coals of fire" and "arrows": Flaming meteorites. Out of an oppressive darkness came thunderbolts: Explosive bolides. There were volcanic eruptions from the "foundations of the world" and tidal waves exposing "the channels of the sea." The "blast of His nostrils" referred to powerful winds, probably tornadoes. There is also a reference to a cherub. Cherubim are to be discussed in Chapter Twelve.

This was a serious comet. Providentially, it did not persist for months as did those that were present during the Great Flood and the Exodus. God ended the event sixty hours before He had promised, just in time to spare Jerusalem, while an angelic hand was extended above that great city. We have discussed the arm and hand of the Lord, as the comet of the Exodus plagues made such an appearance in the sky. The reference to an angel could also refer to the comet, because the Hebrew word translated *angel* meant an agent or messenger from God. The comet was indeed God's agent: Aging King David recognized it as such.

Other Sources

The account of Josephus is less vivid than that of David. But Josephus did mention some details supporting the idea that this was a comet event. He wrote that the angel that "stretched out his hand over Jerusalem" held a sword in that hand, a sword being the most common symbol of a comet. This sword also is mentioned in the account of this event in 1 Chronicles 21:16.

The book, *The Long Day of Joshua and Six Other Catastrophes*, says this about the sword: "*Sword* is from the Hebrew word *chereb* meaning a cutting instrument or a plunging instrument. The word usually describes an axe, dagger, knife, mattock or rapier. However, this is a celestial plunger, a sword of the Lord, being quite different than the sword of Ahab or Tiglath-Pileser, for example. It is probably a description of visible phenomena, such as plunging meteorites associated with the catastrophe."[3]

Josephus described the way people perished: "One died upon the neck of another and the terrible malady seized them before they were aware, and brought them to their end suddenly, some giving up the ghost immediately with very great pains and bitter grief; and some were worn away by their distempers, and had nothing remaining to be buried, but as soon as ever they fell were entirely macerated; some were choked, and greatly lamented their case, as being also stricken with a sudden darkness; some there were who, as they were burying a relation, fell down dead without finishing the rites of the funeral."[4]

The suddenness of death, such as would be caused by exploding bolides, is noteworthy. So also is the entire "maceration" of some dead bodies so that there was nothing left to be buried, as would be the case with those who were incinerated by fiercely hot firestorms. Only ashes remain after incineration. Moreover, the references to choking and darkness are similar to details of other comet events, especially the ninth plague of Exodus.

Immanuel Velikovsky, in *Worlds in Collision*, made some insightful comments. Velikovsky wrote a chapter about Sword-gods, also known in antiquity as Flame-gods, which roamed through space. Referencing 1 Chronicles 21:16, he wrote: "Thus, in the days of David a comet appeared in the form of a human being 'between the earth and the heaven, having a drawn sword in his hand stretched out over Jerusalem.'"[5]

The actual shape of a comet probably depicts only the hand (coma) of the one seen to be holding the sword (tail), but ancient stargazers extended the imagery until it fulfilled the demands of their imaginations. One need only observe the constellations and the mystifying objects they are said to represent in order to appreciate the capacity of the human imagination.

During the final two years of David's life he gathered essentials for the temple that his son, Solomon, would build. Concerning the cornerstone of the temple, Velikovsky wrote: "The stone on which the temple of Solomon was built—Eben Shetiya, or *fire stone*—is a bolide that fell in the beginning of the tenth century, in the time of David, when a comet, which bore the appearance of a man with a sword, was seen in the sky."[6]

David's preparation for the reign of his son, and for that son Solomon to build a temple for worshipping God, helps to explain the mystifying content of Psalm 18. It is mystifying because, in context with an event that resulted in the deaths of 70,000 military men, not to mention many thousands of other people, David rejoiced.

Four times in that psalm, David praised God for deliverance from his enemies. It was not that David was unconcerned about the thousands who perished because of his sin. But his mindset was focused upon sustaining his kingdom and passing it along intact to his son. Associated with this was his desire to see a temple constructed for worshipping God. He anticipated that Solomon would build it, but it could not have been built if the kingdom, especially Jerusalem, were demolished.

It had been David's fear in the first place that such destruction could come upon his land during the dreaded year of the comet. This is what influenced him to sin by ordering a military census and to rejoice when his land, especially the capital city of Jerusalem, was spared from decimation. All of this was tied together in the mind of the aging king.

Fire from Heaven

At the outset of Elijah's prophetic ministry God thrust him into a situation that would have been scary for even the most impetuous young man. The Lord sent the young prophet to confront wicked King Ahab and diabolical Queen Jezebel with the message that there would be a drought in Israel. Three years later, the Lord sent Elijah back to Ahab to tell him the drought was about to end.

After hearing Ahab refer to him as the "troubler of Israel," Elijah said boldly to the king, "I have not troubled Israel, but you and your father's house have, in that you have forsaken the commandments of the Lord and have followed the Baals. Now, therefore, send and gather all Israel to me on Mount Carmel, the four hundred and fifty prophets of Baal, and the four hundred prophets of Asherah, who eat at Jezebel's table." (1 Kings 18:17-18)

Mount Carmel was in western Israel, overlooking the Mediterranean Sea. The view from the peak of the mountain is especially beautiful for, not only can the sea be seen from there, but also a wide vista of open sky. Because of the unobstructed view it offered of the celestial deities overhead, it was the site of a high place—a religious shrine at which those deities were worshipped. The 850 prophets who gathered there believed the visible present deity could be impressed by their wild dance, accompanied by the slashing of their bodies, so that their blood spilled into the ground.

But to what deity were they making their crude appeal?

Neither Baal nor Asherah was a sun god, and the sun was the only celestial object ordinarily visible during daylight hours. Baal was also known as Baal-Marduk, and Marduk may have been another name for the planet Mars. But Mars was not visible in the daytime sky. And even if Marduk did refer to Mars, the connection could be explained by the fact that astrologers of that day often associated celestial objects with the area of the sky in which they were first sighted. If the object being worshiped that day had first appeared in the area of the sky near Mars, it would have been afterward associated with the planet.

Nearly all of the pagan worship of that era was in reverence of gods that were feared. The celestial deity most feared at that time was the comet that had earned reverence by killing hundreds of thousands of people during its cyclical visits to earth. It is here suggested that on this particular day, in 864 B.C., this comet was close enough to Earth to be visible in the daytime sky. It could be plainly seen by the frenzied Baal and Asherah worshippers who were trying their best to catch the notice of the god they most feared— the sword-god comet. Since comets were known for their fiery discharges, the prophets apparently were expecting, or at least hoping that the celestial sword-god would send fire to burn up the bull they had placed on their altar.

Elijah waited patiently for the 850 prophets to wear themselves out without receiving any response from their god. Then he repaired an altar of the Lord that had been broken down either by misuse or disuse. He picked up twelve stones, representing the tribes of Israel, and used them to fortify the Lord's altar. He placed upon the altar some wood and a bull that he had cut to pieces and dug a trench around it.

Then, to make his task more difficult, he ordered the filling of four large water pots with water and the pouring of the water onto the bull, the wood and the altar stones. This was done three times, until the water ran so copiously that it filled the trench around the altar. No water had been poured on the bull or the altar presented by the prophets of Baal, so this was Elijah's way of emphasizing the superiority of the true God over the false ones.

It was about 3 p.m., the time of the Hebrew offering of the evening sacrifice, when Elijah said a brief prayer. As soon as the prayer was finished, "the fire of the Lord fell and consumed the burnt sacrifice, and the wood and the stones and the dust, and it licked up the water that was in the trench." (I Kings 18:38)

There were many people present, in addition to Elijah and the prophets, and when they saw this happen, they became excited and shouted: "The Lord, He is God! The Lord, He is God!" (1 Kings 18:39)

The prophets of Baal and Asherah were known to be murderers, most notably infant-killers, so Elijah wasn't just being mean-spirited when he ordered their execution. After they were dead, just as Elijah had prophesied, there was a downpour of rain that ended the drought, even as, symbolically, the spiritual drought of the nation was ended with the deaths of 850 bloodthirsty idolaters.

What Happened

So, how have we come to the conclusion that this was another comet event? Are we stepping over the bounds of credulity?

Actually, the evidence of a comet's presence was plentiful. It was seen first in the choice of the place for the sacrifices to be offered, a high place from which the celestial deities could be seen from below and were thought to be able to look down upon the top of the mountain. Close-range comets are visible from Earth during daylight hours.

The fire that descended from heaven was not a bolide. If it had been a bolide, it would have exploded and killed everyone atop Mount Carmel. It wasn't a sodium fire, for, although sodium does react with water, the result of that union is more explosive than consumptive. The description of fire falling from heaven indicates it already was aflame during its descent, so likely it was blazing methane or sulfur. The Chicago and other Midwestern fires, involving the presence of methane from a comet, in 1871, burned exceedingly hot. It would take a methane fire, or something comparable, to consume not only the wood and sacrificial bull, but also the stone altar and the water in the trench.

Bible commentator Finis Jennings Dake wrote this about the fire: "It was no ordinary fire, but one which nothing could resist; and it burned from the top down instead of the bottom up."[7] Comets are unique in their ability to drop flaming methane onto the Earth, and methane flames are all-consuming.

We have seen repeatedly that comet events are multi-faceted. Fire from heaven, it may be supposed, could come from a simple meteor, though it is doubtful if a fire produced by an ordinary meteor would ignite such intense flames.

But the event didn't end with the stone altar's consumption.

After killing the murderous prophets, Elijah climbed to the top of the mountain again to watch the sky for rain clouds. A cloud appeared, grew larger and it rained. This seems like a description of ordinary rainfall, so it is unlikely that the rain came from the comet; but the comet idea should not be summarily ruled out. Comets contain large masses of ice that, if dislodged from the coma, can cause deluges of rain, as did the one associated with the Great Flood.

Next, Elijah inexplicably panicked when Jezebel threatened to kill him and made a 40-day trek to Mount Sinai. At this point, the prophet seemed to be deceiving himself into thinking that his flight was nobly motivated. But the Lord knew better, and upon Elijah's arrival at a cave on the side of the holy mountain, He confronted the prophet.

Elijah, with his knowledge of Moses' experiences, could not have been surprised to discover that the volcanic mountain was active: "Then a great and powerful wind tore the mountains apart and shattered the rocks before the Lord, but the Lord was not in the wind. After the wind there was an earthquake, but the Lord was not in the earthquake. After the earthquake came a fire, but the Lord was not in the fire. And after the fire came a gentle whisper...Then a voice said to him, 'What are you doing here, Elijah?'" (1 Kings 19:11-13)

The strong wind blowing the mountain apart was a rock-shattering eruption. This was followed by the usual accompaniments of an eruption—an earthquake and fiery ejaculations, including lava. This happened hundreds of miles from Carmel but may have been associated with seismic disturbances caused by the same comet. If not, its timing was stunningly coincidental.

The biblical description of this Sinai eruption is more catastrophic than the one that occurred in the presence of Moses. Perhaps it was on the later occasion that Mount Sinai was reduced in size so that Mount Katherine's became the tallest peak on the peninsula. A gravitational clash between Earth and a comet could have explained the sequence of events from the fire-fall atop Mount Carmel, to the deluge of rain that ended the drought, and finally the eruption of Mount Sinai.

The fact that Elijah sought refuge in a cave showed that the mountain's eruption did not shock him. But it must have come as a surprise to the prophet when, instead of the booming voice Moses had heard coming from the fire atop the mountain, there was only a whisper identifying the Lord, asking Elijah what he was doing there and then telling him to retrace his steps and return to the frightening scene from which he had just fled. God had more for him to do.

Summary

The events of 972 B.C. and 864 B.C. continued the trend of the 54-year comet to do damage upon every other approach to the Earth. Both were significant events, but the earlier of the two, which killed an estimated 300,000 Israelites, was the more severe.

Important themes of Chapter Seven:

- The importance of a comet event late in David's life was emphasized by its narration twice in the Bible.

- Also appearing twice in Scriptures was Psalm 18, in which David described the event in vivid detail.

- All three punitive options offered by the Lord to David in punishment for his sin of unbelief could have been executed by the comet.

- About 300,000 Israelites died in the event involving an earthquake, fiery meteorites, bolides, volcanism, tidal waves and tornadoes.

- Some of the victims were "macerated," leaving no solid remains; this could happen during intensely hot cometic firestorms.

- The Lord, in His mercy, reduced the punitive comet assault from 72 to twelve hours, thus sparing the city of Jerusalem.

- The fire that fell from heaven and consumed the offering of Elijah during his contest with 850 pagan prophets came from a comet.

- This fierce fire was similar to the methane fires from a comet that killed thousands of Americans in 1871.

- After the heavenly fire-fall there was a drought-ending downpour and Mount Sinai exploded in an eruption with fiery ejaculations.

Chapter Eight

The Earth-Shaker

A PROBLEM IN researching and writing a book such as this one is the tendency to begin perceiving relevant subject matter where there is none. As we finished studying the story of Elijah it seemed that this was taking place, because the happenings toward the end of the prophet's life seemed to indicate the close presence of *another* comet. Since this was less than twenty years after the fire-fall upon Mount Carmel, it would have necessitated the appearance of a comet other than the one with the 54-year orbit. Not only did it seem unlikely; it seemed far-fetched.

But the quest here from the beginning has been to ascertain the truth regarding the role of comets in biblical events, so let's look into this matter. The Bible's account of Elijah's last days on earth starts with two incidents in which the prophet called down fire from heaven that consumed 102 soldiers sent by injured King Ahaziah to summon him to the king's aid (2 Kings 1:9-12).

Elisha, a young man who desired to succeed Elijah in his prophetic role, accompanied Elijah on a journey that they and other prophets believed would end with Elijah's departure to heaven. When the two men arrived at the Jordan River, Elijah rolled up his cloak and struck the water with it, and it parted so that both men could walk through the riverbed (2 Kings 2:8).

They walked along together and Elijah agreed to a request by Elisha that he be given a double portion of Elijah's prophetic spirit. "Then it happened, as they continued on and talked, that suddenly a chariot of fire appeared with horses of fire, and separated the two of them; and Elijah went up by a whirlwind into heaven." Elisha picked up Elijah's cloak and, as Elijah had done, struck the Jordan with it, and the river parted so that he could walk through and continue his return journey. (2 Kings 2:9-14)

There are characteristics of comets that appear in incident after incident. They have a fiery appearance in the sky and are said to discharge fire upon the earth. They are also often identified with figurative language. The most prominent figures we have so far found to identify them, both by shape and purpose, are a sword, the arm of the Lord, and the hand of the Lord wielding a sword.

From the perspective of this world, comets are seen as sources of fallout causing bolidic explosions, firestorms and dust-discolored surface waters. Their interaction with Earth's atmosphere and gravitational field may also result in earthquakes, volcanism, tornadoes and dividing waters.

If at least two of these things occur during an incidental period, the possibility of the presence of a comet should be considered. If three or more, the likelihood of comet activity increases proportionately.

During the last days of Elijah's life there are four such identifiers: The fire-fall from heaven, parting of the Jordan River, appearance of a fiery chariot pulled by fiery horses in the sky and a whirlwind (tornado). Actually the number is six, because the fire-fall and the river separation both happened twice.

The appearance of a fiery horse-drawn chariot in the sky may be explained like this: The comet's coma resembled the carriage of the chariot; the comet's tail looked to be occupied by horses pulling the carriage across the sky. When a comet is in a near approach to Earth, undulation is seen in the gaseous tail which may be likened to the gait of bounding horses or leaping locusts. A fiery horse-drawn chariot was a frequent ancient image of a comet.

The Myth of Helios

Many books could be written based on the theme of associating the imagery in so-called mythological tales with the activity of comets. Immanuel Velikovsky did this effectively in his writings more than a half century ago. For the more restricted purposes of this book, we shall limit this aspect of discussion; but it is relevant to call awareness to the story of Helios.

In mythology the Greek god Helios was a charioteer with a head and mane of golden hair framed by the sun, as if his head were partially or totally eclipsing the central object of our solar system. The chariot was viewed from the side, with a single visible wheel. It was pulled by horses.

It was thought in ancient times that Helios' chariot dragged the sun along with it in its daily trip across the sky. This, we believe, was not mythology but an imaginative picture of periods of time when the sun and a comet appeared in conjunction, as they were before and after the Long Day of Joshua. The comet's coma could be seen as the head of Helios, the wheel of the chariot or the entire chariot carriage. The comet's tail comprised the horses.

The story became more intensely cometary when Helios allowed his son Phaethon to drive his chariot. Phaethon lost control and the chariot fell out of the sky and set a large area of the Earth afire. The plains of Africa were scorched, turning them to desert. The angry Helios then struck Phaethon with a thunderbolt and the young man, his body aflame, fell into a river. This is vivid imagery of comet activity. It might even give a clue to the origin of the Sahara Desert.

Depending on relative orbital positions, from an earthen perspective a comet could appear near the sun for weeks. During portions of that time it might totally or partially eclipse the sun. Each day, during such a period of time, the sun would rise in the east at about the same time as the head of the comet and move across the sky, preceded by the tail, until the entire heavenly figure disappeared over the western horizon. The "horses" appeared to precede Helios' "chariot," in a westerly direction, because the tail of a comet always extends in the direction away from the sun.

In antiquity comets were known as "hairy stars." *The American Heritage Dictionary of the English Language* states this about the word *comet*: "Our name for it is based on a figurative resemblance between it and human beings. This figurative name is recorded first in the works of Aristotle, in which he used *kome*, the Greek word for 'hair of the head,' to mean 'luminous tail of a comet.' Aristotle then uses the derived word *kometes*, 'wearing long hair,' as a noun meaning comet."[1]

The most famous story of the ancient star-wars era was the Roman poet Homer's epic work, *The Iliad*. It was written in the ninth century B.C., the same century in which Elijah lived. In *The Iliad*, Homer described a terrible war fought primarily from chariots in the heavens:

Zeus hurled his thunderbolts. Apollo shot his arrows. Achilles, with eyes flashing fire, wielded his lethal sword. The effects were felt on Earth. There were tsunamis and floods, shouts of pain, thunderclouds, and hot winds.

The giant Chimaera entered the fray. He had the head and mane of a lion, body of a goat, and tail of a snake. Hector fought hand-to-hand against Ajax, both wielding spears. Hector also hurled heavy stones. Zeus thundered from heaven and cast lightning bolts onto the Earth.

At the height of battle, while stones fell to Earth as thick as snowflakes, "There appeared a strange marvel in the skies, for an eagle was bearing in his claws a great snake, which it had taken as a prey. But the snake fought fiercely for its life, and writhed itself about, even till it bit the eagle on the breast. Whereupon the eagle dropped it in the midst of the host, and fled with a loud cry."[2]

Zeus sent a great blast of wind that blew the dust of the plain onto the warring ships. This was followed by another terrible hail of stones. There was a thunderous noise. Then Ajax slew Epicles with a "mighty stone" and Hector threw a "great stone" at the gates of a besieged city. There was much spearing and arrow shooting and stone throwing and battle-axe swinging and sword fighting.

Caletor died with a torch in his hand. Earth flowed with "blood" like a river. Flames shot up to the sky. Achilles poured out a cup of libations to Zeus. The slain Sarpedon was covered with blood and dust. The horsehair-plumed helmet of Achilles fell to Earth and was covered with dust.

A lion with shaggy brows joined the battle. Horses' heads drooped to the ground and their manes were buried in dust. Achilles tore his hair and poured dust on his head. Athena placed a flaming golden halo about Achilles's head. Achilles shouted like the sound of a trumpet. He threw his mighty spear and it impaled the Earth. Hector's remains were burnt on a funeral pyre.

The picture of the eagle dropping a serpent indicates that this may have been an especially dangerous event. The eagle (a comet's coma with projections extending downward like taloned legs) is seen to be dropping a writhing snake (the comet's writhing tail). There is so much comet imagery in this story that it does not seem feasible that it could have been based on anything other than observation of one or more catastrophic comet events.

In antiquity there were many of those.

Amos

The plausible dating range for events prophesied in Amos 1:1-5:17 was between 747 and 758 B.C. Authors of *The Long Day of Joshua* studied the question of dating and concluded that it occurred in either 754, 756 or 758 B.C. They settled on the central year as being the most probable.

If this dating is correct, in 758 B.C., Amos delivered a prophecy from the Lord "two years before the earthquake" in which he predicted fiery devastation upon eight Middle Eastern nations, (Amos 1:1) The phrasing is significant: Usually in the Bible, when seismic activity is described, the terminology used for it is *an* earthquake, not *the* earthquake. There have been many, many earthquakes in world history; in fact, at least one occurs almost every year. But this is the only place in the Bible where, on first reference, a quake is described as *the* earthquake.

The definite article appears in association with other quakes, but only on second reference, after it has been established that the earth was quaking. Thus, with a clear point of reference, usage of *the* is called for. But the use by Amos of the definite article upon first reference requires a different explanation. It implies that this was the quake of all quakes, as far as biblical prophecy was concerned.

The prophet Zechariah also made reference to this quake in language that appeared to set it apart (Zech. 14:4-5). The Zechariah text is primarily about the Day of the Lord, that is, the day of Jesus' return, so Zechariah is going so far as to compare the quake during the reign of Uzziah with the Earth crust-buster on the climactic day of world history.

Continuing to speak through Amos, the Lord proceeded from there to prophesy against one sinful Middle Eastern land after another. The most frequently used phrase He used was: "I will send fire upon…" The nations that could expect fiery decimation were Syria, Philistia, Phoenicia, Edom, Ammon, Moab, Judah and Israel. The latter part of the prophecy of Amos, like that of Zechariah, is a mixture of imagery concerning both this earthquake-and-fire event and the Day of the Lord.

It was going to be a whopper.

Besides the earthquake and the rain of fire, according to the Lord's words quoted by Amos, there would be "a tempest in the day of the whirlwind" (one or more mighty tornadoes, 1:14), nakedness such as could be caused by severe flooding or fires (2:16), and darkness during the hours of normal daylight (5:8). All of this begs for consideration as a comet event.

And there is more. Comet-event phraseology such as *pass through* (5:17) is used: This is what the Israelites did at the Red Sea and again at the Jordan River. And also there is the phrase *sweep through* (5:6), which presents the visual image of a huge broom sweeping clean a sin-defiled land. A broom is included among the images of a comet in Chapter Fourteen.

Other comet images present in the Amos prophecy, which are also among those listed in Chapter Fourteen, are locusts (7:1), a plumb line (7:8) and that old standard, a sword (7:9). We should expect then that the great earthquake would be a part of a major comet event. And we should also anticipate extraordinary behavior by leaders aware of this prophecy, including King Uzziah of Judah, who is mentioned in Amos 1:1.

What Happened

Apart from the prophecy of Amos, predicting what would happen in 756 B.C.—precisely 108 years after the most recent significant event of the 54-year comet—there is little description in the Bible of what actually did occur. The only specific thing mentioned about the great earthquake was the comment of Zechariah two centuries later that people fled in terror, just as they will flee when the Mount of Olives is split in half on the Day of the Lord (Zech. 14:5).

The literal rendering of Zechariah 14:5 contains the Hebrew preposition meaning *before* or *aforetime*. This is an odd word to use in association with an earthquake, because at that time there were no instruments that could predict earthquakes. They happened suddenly and unexpectedly. But if the people somehow knew ahead of time that the quake prophesied by Amos was about to occur, how did they know? We suggest that they knew because the comet known to cause catastrophic events was visible in the sky and daily looming larger until that terrible day.

The account of Josephus says it was "a remarkable day, and a general festival was to be celebrated."[3] It was not a formal holy day, or Josephus would have specified which one, but an unusual day in terms of expectations, because of the presence of the ominous comet. Josephus wrote:

"A great earthquake shook the ground, and a rent was made in the temple, and the bright rays of the sun shone through it, and fell upon [King Uzziah's] face, insomuch that the leprosy seized upon him immediately; and before the city [Jerusalem], at a place called Eroge, half the mountain broke off from the rest on the west, and rolled itself four furlongs, and stood still at the east mountain, till the roads, as well as the king's gardens, were spoiled at the destruction."[4]

We shall discuss Uzziah's role in the event in the next section of this chapter. With regard to the magnitude of the event, as expressed by Josephus, the fact that the sturdily constructed temple was damaged is a good starting point. The earthquake, according to Josephus, involved a rolling or undulating motion of the earth, which resulted in the breaking in half of a mountain near Jerusalem and the movement of the western half a distance of one-half mile.

The Long Day of Joshua adds this interesting perspective: "The 'earthquake' was not a localized earth tremor as we think of today, but a planetary catastrophe, a 'day of commotion,' better translated as an 'earth-shaking.'"[5]

Immanuel Velikovsky concurred: "The word *shaog*, used by Amos and Joel [in his prophecy about the Day of the Lord], is explained by the Talmud as an earthshock, the field of action of which is the entire world, whereas a regular earthquake is of local character. Such a shaking of the earth, disturbed in its rotation, is visualized also by a 'shaking of the sky,' an expression found in the Prophets, in Babylonian texts, and in other literary sources."[6]

Velikovsky made this analysis: "If the commotion of the days of Uzziah was of global character and was brought about by an extraterrestrial agent, it must have caused some disturbance in the motion of the earth on its axis and along its orbit. Such a disturbance would have made the old calendar obsolete and would have required the introduction of a new calendar."[7]

And so it happened: "A new calendar was introduced in the Middle East, and that year is known as 'the beginning of the era of Nabonassar.' It is asserted that some astronomical event gave birth to this new calendar, but the nature of the event is not known... 'It is from that moment that the records of eclipses begin which Ptolemy used.'"[8]

Velikovsky concluded: "According to retrospective calculations, there was no eclipse of the sun in the region of Assyro-Babylonia between the years—762 and—701 (762-701 B.C.), if the earth has revolved and rotated uniformly since then, which is taken for granted."[9]

He expanded this by citing a quotation that the full duration of time without a total eclipse visible in Palestine was from 763 B.C. to 586 B.C.[10]

Even if an eclipse of the sun by the moon had occurred during that interval of time, it would not have been long remembered. Such eclipses are momentary and are not worldwide. However, as we saw in Chapter Three in connection with the darkness of the ninth plague of the Exodus, and shall see again concerning another incident involving earthquake damage to the temple in Chapter Eleven, significant eclipses of the sun, lasting for hours, can occur during a close approach to Earth of a comet.

A Good King's Bad End

Other than stating that he reigned for 52 years and "did what was right in the eyes of the Lord," the Bible has little to say about the reign of King Uzziah of Judah (2 Chron. 26:3-4). The more detailed account of Josephus indicates that Uzziah's reign was similar to that of Solomon. He began well, in obedience to the Lord, and the Lord blessed him with an abundance of good things, including the ability to expand and repair his kingdom.

By the time when the great comet was expected to appear, Uzziah's kingdom included Philistia, a segment of the Sinai Peninsula extending all the way westward to Egypt and the Red Sea, parts of Arabia to the southeast and Ammon on the east side of Jordan. In other words, it included virtually all of the lands named by Amos in his prophecy of fiery disaster.

However, by this time late in life, like Solomon, Uzziah had become attached to his blessings instead of to the One who had blessed him. "He was corrupted in his mind by pride, and became insolent, and this on account of that abundance which he had of things that will soon perish, and despised that power which is of eternal duration."[11]

Having lost his trust in the Lord, Uzziah was susceptible to anxiety over the lands and riches that, according to the prophecy of Amos, would be destroyed during the imminent event. Driven by fear and pride, he usurped the place of the high priest Azariah. He donned priestly garments and, ignoring the pleas of the priests, walked into the temple to make an offering of incense that only the high priest was supposed to offer. God showed His displeasure instantly:

"A great earthquake shook the ground, and a rent was made in the temple, and the bright rays of the sun shone through it, and fell upon the king's face, insomuch that the leprosy seized upon him immediately."[12]

This was not ordinary sunlight. Though the rays of the sun may cause severe burns to human skin after long exposure, this was instantaneous. It was not the rays of the sun that shone through the new hole that was carved in the temple roof by the terrible earthquake, but something that looked like a ray of the sun that struck the king's forehead (2 Chron. 26:19-20). Since this was a comet event, we suggest that it was a portion of the same fallout from the comet that was in process of burning up Uzziah's kingdom in all of its extremities.

It was perhaps a rain of explosive meteors and bolides, as often were present during major comet events. But the scriptural emphasis was on fire, rather than explosive blasts. The Hebrew noun *esh*, translated *fire* in Amos 1:4, 7, 10, 12, 14 and 2:2 meant *fire* or, in adjectival form, meant *burning, fiery, flaming* or *hot*. So, more likely than bolides or meteors, it was a fierce methanol flame created by the combination of gaseous methane and water from melting ice in the presence of atmospheric oxygen.

The only thing that spared Uzziah's life was that apparently only a drop or two of the flaming fluid fell upon him. It was enough to inflict an instantaneous third-degree burn which left a permanent scar that was identified as leprosy. The biblical word for *leprosy* sometimes indicated the notorious skin disease, but also included other severe skin afflictions.

As a legally-pronounced leper, Uzziah spent the rest of his life in isolation from human companionship. For a proud king this could be as severe punishment as death.

It was a just punishment for him because, in a rage, two years earlier, he had killed Amos with a red-hot iron after hearing the prophet predict that his kingdom would be consumed by flames.[13]

Summary & Preview

The fulfilled prophecy of Amos was significant. Although it is now considered less prominent than the Great Flood, the Exodus or any of the four incidents discussed in this book involving Jesus, it was, literally, an earth-shaking event. The planet's axis and orbit both may have been affected during the clash with this comet, which dealt fiery devastation to eight Middle Eastern nations—Syria, Philistia, Phoenicia, Edom, Ammon, Moab, Judah and Israel.

"According to ancient sources, Isaiah began to prophesy immediately after the 'commotion' of the days of Uzziah, even on the same day. The destruction of the land was very great."[14]

Isaiah's Day of the Lord prophecies, looking forward to the comet event of 701 B.C. and also to the Second Coming of Jesus, began in chapter two of his biblical book and will be analyzed in chapters nine and thirteen of this book. In Isaiah 1:1, the prophet reflected on the frightening event he had witnessed during the reign of Uzziah. Addressed to his fellow countrymen, here are a few comments by Isaiah quoted from the first chapter of his book, reviewing the consequences of the comet of 756 B.C.:

Why should you be stricken again?
You will revolt more and more.
The whole head is sick,
And the whole heart faints.
From the sole of the foot even to the head,
There is no soundness in it,
But wounds and bruises and putrefying sores;
They have not been closed or bound up,
Or soothed with ointment.
Your country is desolate,
Your cities are burned with fire;
Strangers devour your land in your presence;
And it is desolate, as overthrown by strangers.
—Isaiah 1:5-7

The following is a summation of key elements of this chapter—the Amos event and the one preceding it involving the latter part of Elijah's life:

- The biblical account of Elijah's last days of life implies the presence in the sky of a comet other than the one with the 54-year orbit.

- This comet caused two fire-falls, two partings of the Jordan River, the appearance of a fiery 'chariot' in the sky and a tornado.

- The 'myth' of the Greek god Helios using his chariot to pull the sun across the sky provided a preview of the next comet event.

- An earthquake prophesied by Amos as part of this event was so catastrophic it was referred to by the prophet as *the* earthquake.

- The prophet Zechariah compared this world-shaking event with the one on the Day of the Lord when Jesus will make His return.

- Besides the great quake, according to Amos, there would be a terrible rain of fire, a mighty tornado and darkness during daytime.

- During the quake, the temple was damaged and fallout from the comet landed on the forehead of Uzziah so that he became a "leper."

- The earthquake split in half a mountain near Jerusalem and moved the western portion of it a distance of one-half mile.

- The quake was not local, but affected the entire globe as an earthshock accompanied by a "shaking of the sky."

- Earth's orbit and/or its axis experienced a shift resulting in a calendar change.

- As prophesied by Amos, the sun was eclipsed, probably by the comet because there were no ordinary solar eclipses during that era.

Chapter Nine

The Single Cycle

ACCORDING TO SOME translations of the Bible, it was an "angel of the Lord" that killed 185,000 Assyrian soldiers on a fateful night in 701 B.C. (Is. 37:36) This happened during the Passover season—a regular time for comet appearances—54 years and five months after the calendar-changing event in October of 756 B.C. that fulfilled a similar prophecy of Amos.

Taking full advantage of the spring martial season, the Assyrians under the leadership of King Sennacherib were in the process of invading Egypt and Israel at the same time. Like King Uzziah of Judah in the Amos event, Sennacherib received severe burns during the incident that had been previsioned by Isaiah. The king, along with stragglers from an armed force that had appeared invincible, returned to Assyria where he was murdered by two of his sons.

We have mentioned this before, but it bears repeating that the Hebrew word usually translated *angel* meant *agent* or *messenger*. Bible commentator Adam Clarke correctly refers to this entity as *a messenger*, not *an angel*.[1] The Lord had many means of sending messages, including by means of His "hand" and/or "arm" in the sky. In this instance, as in others we have discussed, the *agent* or *messenger* seems to have been a comet with a 54-year orbital cycle.

Not only was the cyclical timing correct for a return of the same comet, but then there were those burns on the body of the king and other aspects of the event that lined up exactly with the facts about comet involvement. The agent of death, similar to the one that destroyed Sodom and the Tower of Babel, was tersely described as "the Jerusalem bolide."[2]

Isaiah, in his account of the incident in chapters 36-39 of his prophetic book, did not repeat any details of his prophecies appearing in the first 35 chapters. Perhaps he thought readers would assume that all of those prophecies would be fulfilled because they came from the Spirit of God. For our part, we do so assume. But for this work, it has value to repeat some of the most vivid and pertinent of Isaiah's prophecies. Let the reader decide if they are cometary.

The biblical book of Isaiah is divided into two parts, corresponding in some ways to the structure of the entire Bible. Chapters 40-66 look forward to the Messianic era of Jesus Christ, which is described more fully in the New Testament's 27 books. The first 39 chapters, comparable to the 39 Old Testament books, are prophetic of the event of 701 B.C. But, these also, in duality, are Day of the Lord prophecies, looking ahead to the Second Coming of Jesus (2 Peter 3:10).

The way to pinpoint the prophecies that deal with 701 B.C. is to eliminate those that are exclusively about the Day of the Lord. The Day of the Lord will be a climactic day involving a world-changing event, in some ways world-ending. Now, it is also true that the event of 701 B.C. affected the entire world. But, unlike the Day of the Lord, it did not bring about termination of life in the world as we know it. The Earth may have wobbled, but then it resumed rotating and revolving.

Using this criterion for our discussion of the celestial incident that took place in 701 B.C. eliminates the prophecies in chapters four, 11-12, 24 and 32-34 of Isaiah's book. These refer exclusively to the Day of the Lord. Even so, very much material remains of the dual prophecies referring to both events. Let's consider some of these.

The Grand Finale

In chapter two of his prophetic book, Isaiah hit some hardballs dealing with both the Day of the Lord and 701 B.C. The first thing he described was terror: Men hiding in caves and crags to evade the fiery fallout (Isaiah 2:10, 19, 21). Thus were the arrogant to be humiliated (Is. 2:17).

In chapter three, there is some background description including an array of details that smack of tribulation, persecution, poverty, warfare and forced labor. These include an offensive stench—likely a mixture of sulfur and decaying flesh—baldness of women, sackcloth and branding (3:18-25).

And then, the Lord intervenes. He strikes with upraised hand, one of the most common images of a comet (5:25). This is followed by another frequent occurrence during comet events, a deep distressful darkness (5:30). There is darkness at noon (16:3). This darkness may involve thick smoke in the atmosphere from comet-set fires because the sun, moon and constellations of stars cannot be seen from the Earth's surface (13:10).

Within the same context as the worldwide darkness is a description of terror, pain, anguish, and annihilation. The heavens tremble, and Earth is displaced from its normal axis of rotation because of the Lord's burning wrath (13:6-13). The new instability of the Earth makes the "fist" of the Lord in the sky appear to "shake." (Is. 10:32)

He executes punishment with His great and powerful sword (27:1). "Behold, the Lord has a mighty and strong one, like a tempest of hail and a destroying storm, like a flood of mighty waters overflowing, who will bring them down to earth with His hand." (28:2)

And then, "You will be punished by the Lord of hosts with thunder and earthquake and great noise, with storm and tempest and the flame of devouring fire." (29:6)

Chapter 30 provides a summation, with references to burning anger and consuming fire (30:27). And then, climactically: "The Lord will cause His glorious voice to be heard, and show the descent of His arm, with the indignation of His anger and the flame of a devouring fire, with scattering, tempest, and hailstones. For through the voice of the Lord Assyria will be beaten down, as He strikes with the rod." (30:30-31)

Finally, there is another specific reference to Assyria: " 'Then Assyria shall fall by a sword not of man, and a sword not of mankind shall devour him. But he shall flee from the sword, and his young men shall become forced labor. He shall cross over to his stronghold for fear, and his princes shall be afraid of the banner,' says the Lord, whose fire is in Zion and whose furnace is in Jerusalem." (31:8-9)

The Assyrians did indeed fall by a sword not brandished by man but by the Lord of heaven (Is. 37:21-36). All of their survivors, including the king, fled back to Assyria, for fear of the banner. The banner, like the sword, was used in ancient comet imagery because a dangerous comet looked like a fluttering banner and had a distinctly militant aspect. Other comet images cited in this section, and included on the list in Chapter Fourteen, are the Lord's upraised hand, His arm and His rod.

As for the catastrophic details, it seems as if the 54-year comet, in its final appearance, like the grand finale of a fireworks display, omitted nothing. The disintegrating celestial visitor dropped everything it had upon the trembling Earth beneath—violent storm, flood of mighty waters, thunderous noise (exploding bolides), earthquake, flame of devouring fire, tempest (tornadoes) and a hail of stones. Most of these are mentioned more than once for emphasis.

The Mysterious Mouse

The historian Herodotus lived in the fifth century B.C. He was as familiar with his subject matter, while writing about what happened in 701 B.C., as would be an American historian writing a history of George Washington. Like all good historians, Herodotus did personal research. During a visit to Egypt he saw in a temple of Vulcan a stone statue of the god Sethos with an object resembling a mouse in his hand. He was told that it commemorated a miraculous overnight event, one version of which he recounted in his history book:

"As the two armies [Assyrians and Egyptians] lay here opposite one another, there came in the night a multitude of field-mice, which devoured all the quivers and bowstrings of the enemy, and ate the thongs by which they managed their shields. Next morning they commenced their flight, and great multitudes fell, as they had no arms with which to defend themselves."[3]

This unlikely interpretation became even stranger upon being retold 500 years later by Josephus and 1900 years after that by Velikovsky. In addition to mentioning the Herodotus reference to mice, Josephus quoted Chaldean chronicler Berosus: "Now when Sennacherib was returning from his Egyptian war to Jerusalem, he found his army under Rabshakeh his general in danger [by a plague,] for God had sent a pestilential distemper upon his army; and on the very first night of the siege, a hundred fourscore and five thousand, with their captains and general, were destroyed."[4]

Zeroing in on the mouse image and the word *plague*, which only parenthetically was used by Josephus translator William Whiston, Velikovsky added the word *bubonic* as an adjective for the word *plague*, thus erroneously attributing to Josephus the ridiculous idea that overnight a bubonic plague incited by diseased mice ran its full course and decimated the Assyrian army.

The phrase *pestilential distemper* used by Berosus did not necessarily refer to a disease plague, and in this instance it did not. The image of a mouse cited by both Herodotus and Berosus is one that may depict a dangerous comet in very close proximity to Earth. As the comet draws near, gases in the coma are drawn off in the direction of Earth, as the weightier body's gravitational field becomes dominant. Unless the coma is directly overhead, viewers from Earth will see it becoming distended. It will assume an elongated shape similar to the body of a mouse, and the comet's tail will complete the rodent-like picture.

A bubonic plague does not run full course overnight. It is not directly transmitted to human beings by mice, but through the medium of fleas. Moreover, the iconic mouse would not explain the terrible burns inflicted upon Sennacherib; a comet would. There is also, as we have noted, a vast amount of comet imagery associated with the event in Isaiah's prophecy of it. And, in conclusion we have the words of the prophet affirming his own prophecy: The Lord sent a *blast* upon the army of Sennacherib. (cp 2 Kings 19:7 and Isaiah 37:7, KJV)

This Hebrew word in some Bible translations is rendered *spirit* instead of *blast*. But this is not the same word used to mean *spirit* or *breath*. Although it is similar, its usual meaning is *wind* or *blast* in the sense of an angry exhalation. This word is perfect for it implies both the violence of the bolidic blast and the wrath of the One who unleashed it. It describes the Jerusalem bolide.

Minus Ten Degrees

Side by side with the story of the big blast, in the writings of Isaiah and Josephus, is the account of King Hezekiah's ailment and its cure. We do not know the nature of Hezekiah's *distemper*, a word used often but not definitively by Josephus in stories involving comets. And so, unlike the leprosy of Uzziah, we can't be sure whether or not it was caused by fallout from the mouse-shaped comet. All we know for certain is that Isaiah told the king he was going to die and the king pleaded with God to be granted an extension of life long enough to beget a son who would succeed him on the throne.

The request was granted, and even in the telling of this story there are subtle clues as to why God had intended for Hezekiah to die childless. The son he sired, Manasseh, became one of the most evil kings in the history of Judah. And, to make matters worse, the aging king unwisely showed all of his treasures to Babylonian envoys, and when they felt the time was right they invaded Jerusalem and carried off the plunder. If Hezekiah had died according to Isaiah's initial prophecy, there would have been no Manasseh, and perhaps no Babylonian captivity. It is doubtful if Hezekiah's successor would have been so foolish as to expose his treasures to the militant Chaldeans.

In response to a grief-stricken prayer by the king, the Lord told Isaiah to inform him that he would live for another fifteen years. As a sign sealing the promise, the Lord said, "Behold, I will bring the shadow on the sundial, which has gone down with the sun on the sundial of Ahaz, ten degrees backward." (Isaiah 38:8) And it happened as He said.

We saw in Chapter Five, concerning the long day of Joshua, that a comet's gravitational interaction with Earth could disrupt the normal axial movement of the planet. On that occasion, the Earth's rotation was interrupted for hours so that there was a long day in the eastern hemisphere and a long night in the western hemisphere. In the instance involving King Hezekiah the Earth received a backward jolt, perhaps resulting from a change in the angle of its axis, but its regular rotation continued. Both types of events can be caused by close contact between Earth and a comet, but not an asteroid. Asteroids are not bulky enough to change Earth's axial angle or disrupt its rotation.

The concurrent incident of the backward movement of the sun's rays on the sundial supports the idea that it was a rodent-shaped comet, not a mob of mice, which accounted for the deliverance of Jerusalem from the invading Assyrians.

Four Times

In the next paragraph of his history, after attributing the death of 185,000 Assyrian troops to field-mice, Herodotus wrote that, "on four several occasions, [the sun] moved from his wonted course, twice rising where he now sets, and twice setting where he now rises."[5]

We have discussed four incidents in which, from the perspective of Earth, there was movement of the sun. All of them probably were caused by close calls with the same comet:

- Referring to the comet event that had just destroyed Sodom, Job said, "[God] commands the sun, and it does not rise." (Job 9:7)

- During a comet incident involving Joshua, the sun "did not hasten to go down for about a whole day." (Joshua 10:13)

- Speaking of the comet that caused *the* earthquake, Amos said, "[God] makes the day dark as night." (Amos 5:8)

- In fulfillment of a prophecy of Isaiah, "The sun returned ten degrees on the dial by which it had gone down." (Isaiah 38:8)

In our study of the Uzziah incident, it was disclosed that the disturbance of Earth's axis was so great that it required a change in the calendar that was researched by Immanuel Velikovsky. Another calendar change occurred a few years after the Hezekiah incident: It was explained by the authors of *The Long Day of Joshua* as having happened during the reign of Numa Pompilius, the second ruler of Rome:

"During Numa's reign, another important function, the calendar, required reorganization. As a result of the Isaiahic Catastrophe, earth's spin rate changed and earth's orbit expanded ever so slightly. The net result was that, after the cosmic holocaust of 701 B.C., 365 ¼ days were required for one orbit-year, whereas previously 360 completed an orbit-year...Numa did what we might consider the most logical adjustment; he added five days per year. His contemporary, King Hezekiah of Jerusalem, made a different kind of adjustment. He added one month every six years."[6]

Velikovsky concurred: "All over the world we find that there was at some time the same calendar of 360 days, and that at some later date, about the seventh century before the present era, five days were added at the end of the year, as "days over the year," or "days of nothing."[7]

It makes an interesting study to ascertain the comparative impact of the four incidents that involved alteration of the normal movement of the sun from an earthly perspective. A chart on the back cover of *The Long Day of Joshua* compares the catastrophic achievements of the most severe celestial events involving the Earth, including these four. No. 1 is the Great Flood. The next six, shown as about equal in intensity, are the Tower of Babel, Sodom, the Exodus, the Long Day of Joshua, and the events prophesied by Amos and Isaiah.

Besides the bolide that destroyed the tower and the city of Ur, the Babel incident probably was accompanied by worldwide continental drift. The ten plagues of the Exodus did just about everything except stop the sun. The other four were the sun-shifters. It takes a huge comet, in close contact, to alter the axial rotation of our planet so that the sun appears to make strange movement.

Pertinent Commentaries

Velikovsky was Jewish. He made good use of ancient Hebrew sources. Before we move on to New Testament (Greek) references in Part Two, let's check in with him one more time. Regarding the cause of the sudden deaths of 185,000 Assyrian soldiers, he wrote that the blast described in the Bible was verified and clarified by other sources:

"The simultaneous death of tens of thousands of warriors could not be due to a [disease] plague, as it is usually supposed, because a plague does not strike so suddenly; it develops through contagion, if rapidly, in a few days, and may infect a large camp, but it does not affect great multitudes without showing a curve of cases mounting from day to day.

"The Talmud and Midrash sources, which are numerous, all agree on the manner in which the Assyrian host was destroyed: A blast fell from the sky on the camp of Sennacherib. It was not a flame, but a consuming blast: 'Their souls [bodies] were burnt, though their garments remained intact.' The phenomenon was accompanied by a terrific noise."[8]

Concerning the sacred mouse, Velikovsky made this astute observation: "Both [Egyptian] cities with the cult of the sacred mouse were 'sacred cities of thunderbolts and meteorites.'" The Egyptian name for Letopolis is indicated by the same hieroglyphic as "thunderbolt," i.e., bolide.[9]

Velikovsky added: "The rabbinical sources state in a definite manner that the disturbance in the movement of the sun happened on the evening of the destruction of Sennacherib's army by a devouring blast."[10]

One of the most insightful comments regarding the Isaiah incident concerned the matter of fragmentation. The authors of *The Long Day of Joshua* concluded that since no more appearances of the comet with the 54-year cycle were recorded after 701 B.C., it must have fragmented during the Isaiah event:

"There is a principle in astronomy describing tidal interaction of two celestial bodies approaching each other. At a certain point, the cohesive force of the smaller body is overcome by the tide-raising force of the larger body, and the smaller body fragments before a direct collision occurs."[11]

Loren Steinhauer, co-author of *The Long Day of Joshua*, studied this principle and ascertained: "If an icy sphere of appropriate size approached earth, its fragmentation limit would be 2.3 earth radii. That is, the icy visitor would fragment at some distance (from the center of the earth) exceeding 2.3 earth radii."[12] That is a close call, indeed—less than 10,000 miles—and no wonder it was so frightening.

Finally, *The Long Day of Joshua* deals with a subject so obvious it is easy to overlook: After the sun moved backward ten degrees, or ten steps, how did it happen to return to its normal spin axis, or almost normal? The book's co-authors wrote: "The twisting force exerted on the bulge of the earth would cause the spin axis to begin to precess. We believe the spin axis is an easily displaced, easily relocated function, partly because it is precessing several meters under current conditions for no known, observable reason at all."[13]

Part One Summation

As we conclude Part One, let's review its first eight chapters before itemizing the key themes of Chapter Nine.

In Chapter One we discovered a number of firsts that occurred during the most catastrophic comet event to date.

There was the first rainfall, the first earthquake, the rising of the first tall mountains, the first volcanism, the first ice age, and the first and only universal watery deluge. In such a terrible event, it is near certain that the comet disintegrated for we have no clear evidence of its making another visible approach to Earth.

Next, in Chapter Two, we discussed a bolide that carved a thousand-foot-deep crater in the earth where Sodom and Gomorrah had been. The blast was witnessed by Abraham and was the likely cause of most of Job's woes. This may have been the first of two-dozen approaches to Earth made by a deadly comet with a normal orbital cycle of 54 years.

In Chapter Three, we considered the ten plagues caused by a comet that appeared at precisely the right time to be used by the Lord to assist Moses in delivering the Israelites from their bondage in Egypt. This occurred nine cycles after the Sodom event. It was such a major event that the comet's orbit was perturbed and it made its next appearance 43 years later instead of 54.

Chapter Four was about a series of incidents related to the Exodus comet during the Israelites' wanderings the next year on the Sinai Peninsula. These incidents featured a tornado that precipitated the Red Sea pass-through and comet-launched volcanic activity throughout the peninsula, especially at Mount Sinai while God was delivering the Ten Commandments to Moses.

In Chapter Five, we considered the source of the Long Day of Joshua and concluded it was the same comet as was featured in the previous three chapters. On this occasion the comet's gravitational field interacted with that of Earth and caused the planet to cease rotating for about twelve hours, resulting in an apparent stoppage of the sun in the sky that was witnessed and recorded throughout the world.

Chapter Six featured events involving the 54-year comet giving battlefield victories to undermanned forces led by Deborah and Barak over the Canaanites, by Gideon over the Midianites, and by Samuel over the Philistines. The second of the three events was most remarkable in that 120,000 of 135,000 Midianite troops were killed while not a single one of 300 Israelite soldiers lost his life.

Chapter Seven changed the focus from the battlefield to more personal matters. As punishment for a sinful act, David lost 70,000 armed men during a comet assault in 972 B.C. In the shadow of the same comet, in 864 B.C., God responded to a brief prayer by Elijah and sent "fire from heaven" to give His prophet victory over 850 prophets of Baal and Asherah, who were slain after entreaties to their false gods went unheeded.

The theme of Chapter Eight was an appearance of the 54-year comet in 756 B.C. that resulted in perhaps the most terrible earthquake in world history to date. The quake was so severe that the entire Earth was shaken. A mountain near Jerusalem split and the two pieces moved a half-mile apart. The prophet Amos referred to it as *the* earthquake as if to set it apart from all others. The prophet Zechariah compared it with the quake that will occur on the Day of the Lord.

As recounted in Chapter Nine, the following is a summary of important aspects of the 54-year comet's final appearance before disintegrating in 701 B.C.:

- The "angel of the Lord" that killed 185,000 Assyrians was an appearance of the 54-year-cycle comet in 701 B.C.

- The agent of death, similar to the one that destroyed Sodom and the Tower of Babel, was identified as "the Jerusalem bolide."

- Isaiah foresaw all aspects of the event in his prophecies, including the terror felt by Earth's inhabitants. (Isaiah 2-31).

- Some historians mistook an idolatrous image of the elongated comet for that of a mouse carrying bubonic plague.

- Velikovsky concluded that it was not bubonic plague that killed the Assyrians but "a consuming blast" that fell from the sky.

- In response to Hezekiah's prayer, the Lord used the comet to cause Earth to move so that a shadow cast by the sun backed up ten degrees.

- This was the fourth time the same comet disturbed Earth's rotation and altered the sun's regular movement across the sky.

- Earth's axial rotation was altered so much that the calendar was changed from a 360-day year to one with 365¼ days.

- In *The Long Day of Joshua* it was asserted that the celestial object with the 54-year cycle disintegrated during the Isaiah event.

PART TWO

THE LONG PERIOD

DO YOU HEAR WHAT I HEAR?

Said the night wind to the little lamb,
Do you see what I see?
Way up in the sky, little lamb?
Do you see what I see?
A star, a star, dancing in the night,
With a tail as big as a kite,
With a tail as big as a kite.

Said the little lamb to the shepherd boy,
Do you hear what I hear?
Ringing through the sky, shepherd boy?
Do you hear what I hear?
A song, a song, high above the tree,
With a voice as big as the sea,
With a voice as big as the sea.[1]

Chapter Ten

The Star of Him

IN DIALOGUE BETWEEN Christians and non-Christians a question sometimes asked by an unbeliever is this: If God really did create all things, how can you possibly believe He could have made such an enormous universe with life on only one tiny planet?

God, of course, can create as large a universe as He pleases, containing life as small as He pleases. He can do as He wills, because He is God. All He had to do was speak and the universe came into existence (Ps. 33:6–9; 148:5).

In the Bible He has passed along a few things for our enlightenment about His creation. Not only does Scripture make no mention of life in the vastness of what we call outer space, but it specifies the primary purpose of the celestial objects God has created and placed out there. Those objects are there to provide light for the Earth, to separate day from night, and to "serve as signs to mark seasons and days and years" (Gen. 1:14).

This is the first time the words *sign* or *signs* appear in the Bible. The second usage occurs when God makes a post-flood covenant with Noah by placing a rainbow in the sky (Gen 9:13). And so the pattern is established: Often when God does something extraordinary, affecting the Earth and His relationship with human beings, He sets a sign in the heavens to mark the occasion.

Equally important to first usages of biblical words are last usages. The final usage of this word appears in the last book of the Bible. John sees a "great and marvelous sign" in heaven (Rev. 15:1).

The most momentous intervention by God on Earth occurred when His Son, Jesus Christ, took on flesh and blood in order to live among human beings. A sign in the sky marked the occasion of Jesus' birth.

Astrologers, studying the sky in the "East," saw this "star" and somehow knew it portended the birth of a great Jewish king. From the Jewish perspective of the Bible, the most important city was Jerusalem, which turned out to be the destination of the astrologers.

If they were Jewish, they were probably familiar with the Old Testament prophecy: "A star will come out of Jacob; a [king's] scepter will rise out of Israel" (Num. 24:17). Or maybe God communicated directly with them, as He did to biblical prophets, for the purpose of identifying the heavenly sign. The circumstances that gave them knowledge of the celestial object are unimportant. The important thing is they recognized it when they saw it in the sky.

One reason they may have recognized it is that it took on the general appearance of a scepter. We saw in the first half of this book that the shapes of heavenly objects were considered important by ancient peoples. They identified clusters of stars as constellations and associated comets of varying shapes with familiar objects. And so the comet of the Exodus was identified as the arm of the Lord, and the comet signifying the birth of Jesus, the King of kings, may have appeared to the magi in the shape of a scepter. Comets were visualized as scepters, not only because of their shape but because of their common usage. Comets were seen slashing through space before doing severe damage to Earth, as a celestial scepter might have done.

After sighting the celestial sign, the magi packed their camels for the long journey to Judea. They expected to find a newborn king, so they went to the palace of King Herod to make inquiry about the royal child. They said to Herod: "Where is the one who has been born king of the Jews? We saw *his star* in the east and have come to worship him" (Matt. 2:2, emphasis added).

The Greek words translated *his star* in most English translations of the Bible meant literally *the star of him*. Its significance is that in the ancient world there was one kind of celestial object that, in reference to a king, would be identified as *his star*. This was a comet. The appearance of a comet was considered portentous of a great event, often the birth or death of a king. A comet associated with a king's birth would have been called *his star*.

The Greek word *aster*, translated *star*, was not limited to celestial objects we call stars. It was used for a variety of objects visible in the sky—stars, planets, moons, asteroids, meteors, or comets. The root meaning of this word seemed descriptive especially of comets. It meant an object "strewn over the sky."[1]

Strewing *over the sky* was precisely what Jesus seemed to be describing in his prophecy of the object that will signify His return. No known object other than a comet would appear "like lightning from the East, flashing as far as the West." (Mat. 24:27, neb). As a matter of fact, an expanding east-to-west vista, in the final days stretching from horizon to horizon, is precisely the appearance that would be given by an Earth-threatening comet.

The plural of *aster* occurs in a New Testament letter written by Jesus' brother, Jude. Describing unbelievers, Jude wrote: "They are wild waves of the sea, foaming up their shame; wandering stars [*asteres*], for whom blackest darkness has been reserved forever" (Jude 13). The two figures of speech Jude used here are a stormy ocean and comets roaming in the pitch darkness of deep space.

After leaving Herod's palace, the magi spotted the celestial object again. From the new perspective it guided them. It seemed to hover in place over the area where Joseph's family lived until they arrived there. The object's ability to hover was important for its identification. It remained visible in the same place in the sky long enough for the magi to arrive at the residence of Joseph and Mary.

Most celestial objects appear to move from east to west as the Earth spins on its axis. However, a comet making a near approach to Earth may appear to move in almost any direction.

It may acquire synchronization with our planet and appear to hover in place. This can happen if and when its motion through space coincides in speed and direction with Earth's rotation. The comet then would appear stationary in the sky. If Earth's gravitational field captured a synchronized comet, it might seem to be in the same place in the sky for a considerable period of time before making its escape into outer space.

A comet fits the essential criterion for the Christmas "star" as a portentous sign with the ability to hover in one place in the sky. It fits the basic meaning of *aster* as an object that appears to be strewn across the heavens, like a tailed kite. We must consider the possibility, even the probability, that the sign of Jesus' birth was a comet.

Broom Stars

Superstitious astrology played an important role in the religion of the ancient peoples of Asia. They combined it with astronomy, the legitimate scientific observation of the heavens. When something out of the ordinary happened in the sky, it was considered portentous of a significant event about to take place on Earth. The appearance of comets, which then were more frequent and menacing than they are today, disturbed the order of the cosmos more dramatically than any other celestial phenomena.

Some comets in ancient times passed close enough to Earth to cause terrible upheaval on our planet. The closer they came, the more likely they were to disintegrate, launching cascades of ice, torrents of rain, fiery precipitation, bolides and meteoric stones onto the earth. As we saw in the first part of this book, crumbling comets may have been involved in the extinction of mammoths and the start of the Ice Age, in the destruction of the tower of Babel and the city of Sodom, the plagues of Exodus, Elijah's "fire from heaven" incident, the long day of Joshua, the Joel-Amos catastrophe, and the worldwide Flood of Noah. If comets were involved in any or all of these events, it is no wonder they came to be considered omens of terrible happenings.

Because of their frequent appearances and perceived importance, sightings of comets were recorded by ancient peoples. Starting in about 1600 B.C., the Chinese kept a meticulous record of them, calling them "broom stars."[2] This metaphor came from the broom-shaped appearance of comets and the belief that they signified calamitous events such as the sweeping away of kingdoms. Chinese records of comets mention 581 of them between 1600 B.C. and A.D. 1600.[3]

However, no comets appeared within three years of the Lord's birth, according to the Gregorian calendar, which has been the accepted method of historical dating in the world since A.D. 1582.

Comparing the Chinese record with the Gregorian calendar, the closest appearances of comets to Jesus' birth occurred in 4 and 5 B.C.[4] None appeared in the year zero, when it used to be thought He was born.

The Gregorian calendar does not even include a year zero. There is a 1 B.C. and an A.D. 1, but no zero. Moreover, historical evidence shows that Jesus actually was born several years "before Christ." Herod, the king who tried to kill Him, died an agonizing death in 4 B.C. Many years after the Gregorian calendar replaced the Roman calendar, it was discovered that Dionysius Exiguus, the man commissioned to revise the calendar, had erred by at least four years in placing the birth of Christ. It is now thought the Lord's birth occurred between 4 B.C. and 6 B.C.

A comet appearing in 12 B.C. has been identified as Halley's.[5] Scientists attempting to identify the comets of 4 and 5 B.C. have been unable to do so. These two must have been long-period comets, because they have not reappeared in more than two thousand years.[6] Many comets with periods of thousands of years are known to exist.

According to Chinese records, the comet of 5 B.C. appeared between March 10 and April 7, and, with its vertical tail, was visible for several months.[7] According to ancient Korean records, the tailless comet of 4 B.C. made its appearance almost exactly one year later, probably on March 31.[8]

In 1977, British researchers Clark, Parkinson, and Stephenson concluded that these two comets were one and the same.[9] Working as a team, they based their conclusion on the fact that both appearances were reported in the same season of the year. And, remarkably, both objects seemed for a while to be fixed in one place in the sky instead of making constant east-to-west movement from the perspective of Earth.

The fact that the comet of 5 B.C. had a tail, and the one that appeared a year later did not, wasn't important. A comet, during a close approach to the sun, may lose its tail. Or a comet may appear not to have a tail while it is in alignment with the Earth and the sun. The tails of most comets point away from the sun. The tail of the 5 B.C. comet gave it an arrow-like appearance, pointing down as if from God's own hand in heaven to the residence of His Son on Earth.

Comets are unique among celestial objects in being able to appear and reappear from an earthly perspective. This may happen as they approach the sun and circle around it in a tight arc after arriving from and before departing to deep space. Intervals of several months to one year between appearances of the same comet are possible. It's a literal illustration of the goes-around-comes-around principle.

If the British researchers' study was competent, the so-called star of Bethlehem almost certainly was the comet of 5/4 B.C. Its movement was such to fulfill the strange statement of Matthew that it appeared to hover in place in the sky long enough for the magi to make a pilgrimage from Jerusalem to wherever the family of Jesus was residing (Matt. 2:9). They completed this trip probably about one year after His birth.

If Jesus' family was still living in Bethlehem at this time, the magi could have made the trip from Jerusalem in a single night. However, it seems unlikely that the family was still in Bethlehem. Joseph and Mary were not wealthy. They could not have afforded to pay for a full year to live in an inn comparable to a modern motel or hotel.

They certainly would not have stayed that long in a stable. Luke wrote that they returned to their hometown of Nazareth after circumcising the baby and dedicating Him to the Lord (Luke 2:39). This process took forty days (Lev. 12:1–6). They probably arrived home more than ten months before the *aster* made its second appearance, leading the magi to Jesus. Matthew's account specifies that they were living in a house, not a stable or an inn, when the magi arrived (Matt. 2:10). Their permanent residence was in Nazareth.

Capricorn Caravan

If the magi had to travel from Jerusalem to Nazareth to find Jesus, the trip probably would have taken four days, because Nazareth is about seventy miles north of Jerusalem. Under normal conditions they would have been able to travel only at night while the celestial objects were visible. However, comets are exceptional in that many of them sustain visibility during daylight hours, when it is likely that the magi would have preferred to do their traveling over rough terrain unfamiliar to them.

We saw in the chapter about the Flood of Noah that a comet could be captured and held for as long as eight months in Earth's gravitational field before escaping into space. However, remaining in conjunction with Earth and appearing to hover in the same place above the Earth are different matters.

According to ancient Chinese records, the comet of 5 B.C. appeared fixed in one place in the sky for seventy days in the constellation of Capricornus.[10] This is one of the most ancient constellations to have been identified by human eyes. It's a dim constellation appearing normally at about twenty degrees South latitude. It is the constellation that lent its name to the Tropic of Capricorn.[11]

Capricornus is visible from southern parts of the northern hemisphere for much of the year. However, if the birth of Jesus occurred near the end of March, as some evidence indicates, Capricornus might not have been visible from Jerusalem at that time. It could have been just out of view beneath the southern horizon.

This would explain the puzzlement of Herod upon hearing the magi's account that they saw the celestial sign of a Jewish king's birth somewhere in the East. Herod questioned them about its appearance. He obviously had not seen it, nor had anyone else in his palace.

The magi probably lived to the southeast of Jerusalem in a place where Capricornus was visible, although it was not visible at that time from Jerusalem. Based on geography, astronomy and logic, the most likely candidates for their place of residence was the southernmost extremity of China or Korea.

China, the nation in which the stars were studied most closely in ancient times, is the strongest candidate. A trip from southern China, about five thousand miles from Jerusalem, would have taken ten months at the normal rate of travel, about twenty miles a day, six days a week. Planning, organizing, and packing supplies for the caravan could have accounted for the other two months.

A comet appearing at first in Earth's southern hemisphere is not necessarily going to appear south of the equator every time it passes the Earth. After rounding the sun and making a second pass by Earth from the opposite direction a year later, there is a good chance it will cross Earth's equatorial plane and depart toward outer space while it is visible from the opposite (northern) hemisphere.

If this comet made its departure due north, it would have appeared to hover in place for as long as it was still visible from Earth. Polaris, the North Pole star, is used in navigation, because it always occupies the same place in the sky.

A due-north departure would have placed the comet low above the northern horizon, as seen from the Jerusalem area, as if it were hovering over something on Earth. By using the comet as a direction finder, the magi eventually would have come to Nazareth, which is due north of Jerusalem.

This would confirm the idea that by this time, a year after Jesus' birth, Joseph had returned with his family to his hometown. Ironically, this implies that the so-called "star of Bethlehem" did not appear over Bethlehem from the perspective of the magi. Perhaps we should call it instead the "comet of Nazareth."

Perfect Timing

The sign of Jesus' birth, upon its first appearance to the magi, made them think an important event had happened. In the ancient world, comet sightings often were connected with historical events. They were a source of anxiety for Roman emperors. Caesar Augustus associated a comet sighting with the death of Julius Caesar.[12] Believing the comet proved Julius was a god, Augustus ordered the minting of a coin with a comet emblazoned on its surface along with the words *deified Julius*.[13] Nero became so worried about the appearance of a comet that he reacted by slaughtering the Roman nobility.[14]

Traditions are sometimes based on fallacies, but sometimes they are meaningful. During Nero's reign, one generation after the resurrection and ascension of Jesus, the apostle Paul was preaching the gospel in Rome and Christian traditions were being established there. One Italian tradition that has survived to the present day is the inclusion of a comet in Christmas nativity scenes.

A living *presepio* in the Italian mountain town of Barba, in northwestern Tuscany, involves a procession through the streets behind a man and woman portraying Joseph and Mary. "Everybody winds up in the piazza just in time to see a comet star lead the Wise men to the Baby Jesus' manger."[15]

In Rome there are similar celebrations. Some of the city's largest churches have elaborate nativity displays with "tiny fireplaces ablaze, the heavenly host floating above waxing and waning stars, rosy dawns, and even a comet endlessly leading the way across the sky."[16]

Uba Kaess, who grew up in Italy during the 1950s, remembered that the nativity observance of her youth included a comet: "The star on top of the tree automatically became a comet." Mrs. Kaess told the author this after they met at Coral Ridge Presbyterian Church in Fort Lauderdale.

Whatever celestial object marked the sign of Jesus' birth, it must have been distinctive. The magi recognized it immediately when it made a second appearance on the night after they left Herod's palace. Other than the sun and moon, comets are the most easily distinguishable objects in the heavens because of their varying shapes and irregular motion.

Having made inquiry about the time of the comet's appearance and fearing the newborn would be a contender for his throne, Herod ordered the slaying of all Jewish male children two years old and younger. This was overkill, for it does not seem possible that two years could have passed between the first and second appearances of the *aster*. But it was in character for the fanatical Herod, who killed one of his own sons. If it was the comet of 5/4 BC, we know there was a one-year interval between its two appearances.

The Greek word used by Matthew to describe Jesus at this time was not the word customarily used for a nursing baby. The King James Version translators accurately rendered it as *young child*. It was the same word Jesus used later in His life to call a child to Himself (Matt. 18:2). Jesus no longer was an infant.

Jesus must have been more than six months old but less than two at the time of the arrival of the magi. A logical guess is He was one year old, as calculated by Herod from his conversation with the magi. It would fit the character of a psychopath like Herod to kill two-year-old boys superfluously in his determination to eliminate a one-year-old. It would also fit the timing of the two appearances of the comet.

Ironically, Herod's death proclamation may have proved fatal for himself. Less than a month after he ordered the mass murders, in April of 4 B.C., he died a horrible death in Jericho. If God did not ordain divine punishment for Herod in response to his murderous decree, his death was an amazing coincidence.

If the *aster* that led the magi to Herod was indeed the comet that first appeared in spring of 5 B.C. and then reappeared around the time of the Passover in 4 B.C., it rules out the traditional dating of Jesus' birth on December 25. That date is actually even more lacking in historical certainty than the year of His birth.

Matthew and Luke, the two biographers of Jesus who mentioned His birth, did not specify the year or the day. They did mention enough historic details (a census and the death of Herod) for us to be able to fix the event between 4 and 6 B.C. and make a solid surmise of 5 B.C.

Caesar Augustus ordered the census in 8 B.C. The organization and completion of ancient censuses took several years, so it is feasible that Joseph, a resident of Nazareth, could have taken his family to Bethlehem to be counted for the purposes of taxation three years later. It's likely that he correlated the census trip with a visit to nearby Jerusalem to observe the Passover.

In respect to the season of the year in which Jesus was born, a detail mentioned by Luke is interesting. Luke wrote that shepherds were taking care of flocks in fields near Bethlehem on the night of His birth. Shepherds did not usually take their flocks out to graze during cold months, so it was unlikely that Jesus was born in December.

If not December, when?

This returns us once more to the idea that the comet appearing in late March or early April of 5 B.C. could have signified the birth of Jesus. It would have been an appropriate time for His advent. The Christ who perished at the exact time when the Passover lamb was being slain could have been observing the anniversary of His own birthday at that time, perhaps on that very day.

God is orderly. It would be just like Him to choose this day for both the birth and death of His Son, as a double reinforcement of the fact that Jesus is the Lamb slain from the foundation of the world. He is the Passover, sacrificed for us, the Lamb of God who takes away the sin of the world.

Comet, Yes! Occultation, No!

At least two recent studies have resulted in findings favoring the 2 B.C. occultation of the planets Jupiter and Venus as the astral object that has come to be known as the Christmas star. Are these studies credible or is it more likely that the "star" heralding the birth of Jesus Christ was the comet that appeared in 5 B.C. and then again in 4 B.C.? The etymology of the Greek word *aster*, a generic word translated in the English Bible as *star*, allows either event to have been the one, although it seems to favor a comet because of its basic definition as an object "strewn over the sky."

Let's examine the two possibilities with a series of questions. *Yes* answers to these questions increase plausibility. *No* answers decrease plausibility and may even preclude possibility.

Was the known date of Jesus' birth timely with the event? Herod, the king who attempted to murder babies two years old and younger to kill the Christ child, died soon after issuing this decree in April of 4 B.C., two years before an occultation (total eclipse) of the planet Jupiter by the planet Venus. This was one year after the first appearance of the comet. The timing was right for the comet, but the occultation occurred too late for it to have been the Christmas star.

The year of Herod's death has been contested by those who have theorized that the occultation heralded Jesus' birth. However, it is verifiable. The ancients kept meticulous records of the birth and death of kings.

According to Chinese records, the comet appeared in spring, around the time of the Passover. The occultation occurred June 17. *Is either date plausible for the birth of Christ?* Passover, yes; June 17, no. No one knows the exact date of Jesus' birth, but there is a lot of scholarship favoring a spring birth, presaging his Passover-season death: "Christ our Passover lamb has been sacrificed for us." (1 Corinthians 5:7) Similar reasoning prevails for the Dec. 25 date for His birth, near the season of Rosh Hashanah, the Jewish festival of light. Jesus is "the light of the world." (John 9:5) There is no rationale favoring a birth date for Jesus in mid-June.

Astrologers came from "the East" to Jerusalem seeking a newborn babe of royal birth. Jerusalem was in the Middle East, so "East" of Jerusalem may have implied the Far East. *By Far Eastern peoples, were comets or occultations considered harbingers of important events?* In ancient eastern cultures comets were viewed as omens of great events, including the birth and death of kings. Planetary occultations were not.

Were comets or occultations considered worthy objects for intensive study by ancient Far Eastern peoples? Comets, yes: Koreans kept careful records of comets. Chinese kept records of hundreds of comets for more than three-thousand years, including precise details about the comet of 5/4 B.C. Occultations, no. There was no Asian record keeping of the appearance of occultations. In fact, there are no extant historical records from anywhere in the world pertaining to the three occultations of Venus and Jupiter that have occurred since 2 B.C. Occultations aren't impressive enough to the naked eye to stimulate much interest.

The "star" appeared in the sky where the astrologers could see it from their homeland. Then, probably about a year later, after they had prepared for and completed a long journey, it made a second appearance. *Did the occultation of 2 B.C. or the comet of 5 B.C. make reappearances about a year later?* Comet, yes. Chinese and Korean records mention appearances of comets in 5 and 4 B.C. British researchers Clark, Parkinson and Stephenson concluded that the two comets were one and the same. Occultation, no. The next occultation of Venus and Jupiter after 2 B.C. occurred in A.D. 1210.

One proponent of the occultation theory for the sign of Jesus' birth associates the planetary occultation of 2 B.C. with a conjunction of the star Regulus and the planet Jupiter in September of 3 B.C. *Is this theory credible?* It states that the conjunction was the sign of Jesus' birth and the occultation served as the reappearance of the sign described in the Bible.

The Bible makes clear that a single sign made two appearances. Upon its second appearance, the Asians recognized it as the "star they had seen in the East" (Matt. 2:9). An occultation of two planets is not identical in appearance to a conjunction of a star and a planet. Even if it was, the two different events required for this theory contradict the Bible's single-sign statement, and the Bible, as the original source, must take pre-eminence over all other sources. Moreover, planet-star conjunctions are no more visually impressive than planetary occultations, and the timing was two years too late for both the occultation and the conjunction.

Joseph and Mary went to Bethlehem to be registered in a census for the purpose of taxation. During the reign of Caesar Augustus he ordered three censuses, in 28 B.C., 8 B.C. and A.D. 14. Clearly, the census alluded to in the Bible was that of 8 B.C. It was five years too early for the conjunction/occultation theory to have been correct. *But wasn't it also three years too early to agree with the theory that the comet of 5 B.C. was the sign of Jesus' birth?*

Actually, it wasn't too early for the comet. In those days transportation and communication were much slower than today, and even now it takes many months to conduct a census of hundreds of millions of people. A three-year time span was probably close to the norm for conducting a census of the Roman Empire during the reign of Augustus. But it is doubtful that it took as long as five years, the duration necessary to uphold the conjunction/occultation theory.

The Bible says after the Asian men saw the *aster* while they were in Jerusalem, they followed it until they found the house where Jesus was living. It must have been visible in the sky long enough for them to make this trip, which likely took four days if Jesus' family had returned to their home in Nazareth (Matt. 2:11). *Were the comet and occultation visible that long?* Comet, yes: It was visible, according to Chinese records, for several months. Occultation, no. Including the time of partial occultation, it wasn't measured in days or hours, but minutes.

If the Asian men made the northward trip from Jerusalem to Nazareth, the guiding *aster* must have been visible in the northern sky. If Jesus' family was still living in Bethlehem, almost due south of Jerusalem, as tradition holds, the *aster* must have been visible in the southern sky. *Is it possible for a comet or an occultation to be visible in northern or southern skies?* Comet, yes. Comets may appear anywhere in the sky. Occultation, no. All of the planets rotate on a plane around the sun coinciding with the area near Earth's equator, between the Tropic of Cancer and the Tropic of Capricorn. Planets are seen always in eastern and western skies, never due North or South.

The *aster* appeared to hover in place above the house where the Asian men found Jesus (Matthew 2:9). *Can a comet or an occultation appear to hover motionless in the sky?* Comet, yes. Comets are the only celestial objects other than the North Star that can appear stationary in the sky, and Chinese records show that the comet in question did appear to hover during both of its appearances, in 5 and 4 B.C. Occultation, no. The occultation lasted only a few minutes before the occulted Jupiter and Venus appeared to elongate and began to separate from each other. Both then appeared to move in a westerly direction across the sky.

Can an apparently moving object—a comet or occultation—be followed to a fixed point? This was not a problem for the comet, as it appeared stationary, according to ancient Chinese and Korean records. But if the astrologers attempted to follow the general direction of the separating planets in an occultation, they would have traveled westward and would have wound up on the shore of the Mediterranean Sea. That is, if they didn't become confused the second night of their journey when Venus and Jupiter no longer appeared in occultation and were no more visually prominent than bright stars.

The claim that retrograde motion by the occulting bodies could have made them appear stationary is absurd. Other than a very brief optical illusion, there is no such thing as retrograde motion by a planet in the sky. They always appear to move across from east to west. They do not hover for four nights in a row, or even for the few hours that would have been necessary for the magi to journey from Jerusalem to Bethlehem, if, as unlikely as it seems, the family of Jesus had remained living in Bethlehem for a full year.

Speaking of the ordinary visibility of the *aster*: Which is more likely to attract attention to sky-watchers—a close-range comet, with a tail stretching millions of miles across the heavens, which can be seen by more than half of the inhabitants of Earth, and which appears to hover in the same place in the sky for seventy days; or an eclipse of two planets with brightness comparable to stars, lasting for minutes and visible only in a small area of the Middle East? Full occultation or eclipse isn't even measured in minutes but seconds. Blink and you might miss it. Conjunctions are so commonplace that they are easy to ignore. There were nine of them during the years 3 and 2 B.C.

In summation, the comet of 5/4 B.C. scores 100% on the Christmas Star Test, while the conjunction/occultation of 3/2 B.C. gets a zero. In terms of simple logic, it was impossible for either an occultation or a conjunction of planets to have been the source of the Christmas star. The odds were much more favorable for the comet of 5/4 B.C.

Here is a review of the major points of this chapter:

- Eastern astrologers saw an object in the sky that they recognized as the birth sign of a Jewish king.

- They prepared for and completed a long journey to Jerusalem with the intention of honoring the royal infant.

- While in Jerusalem, they saw the celestial object again and followed it to the home of the baby as it hovered in the sky.

- Of all known celestial objects, only a comet can appear stationary; all others appear to move from east to west as the Earth rotates.

- A comet that first appeared in 5 B.C. and reappeared a year later was most likely the "star" seen by the astrologers.

- By ancient peoples, comets often were associated with the birth and death of kings and other important events.

- There are ten logical reasons to believe that the Christmas "star" was a comet and not a conjunction or occultation of planets.

Chapter Eleven

Two Mighty Earthquakes

THE BIBLE SAYS enough about the death and resurrection of Jesus for us to know that natural calamities occurred on Earth and in the heavens during that three-day period. For three hours on the day of Jesus' death the sun was "darkened," and on both the day of His death and the day of His resurrection there were earthquakes (Mat. 27:51, 28:2; Luke 23:44-45).

The two earthquakes probably were related in some way to each other, as often they are when they occur a few days apart. From first reading of these Scriptures, it appears that the quake at Jesus' resurrection, which was described by a Greek adjective as a "great" or "violent" quake, was primary, and the one accompanying his death may have been a lesser foreshock. However, closer study reveals that both quakes were of major proportions. In fact, the one accompanying His death could have been described as a mega-shock.

The Bible is carefully worded. Regarding the event that occurred at Jesus' resurrection, Matthew wrote: "There was a great earthquake." (Mat. 28:2) He described the quake at the time of Jesus' death in slightly different terminology:

"The earth quaked." (Mat. 27:51) There is a monumental difference between an earthquake and a quaking Earth.

We also saw distinctive terminology used by prophets to describe the quaking Earth aspect of the comet events of 1447 and 756 B.C. On the latter occasion, a comet caused an earthquake so severe that the prophets Amos and Zechariah referred to it as *the* earthquake. On that occasion, too, the entire Earth was shaking; and, like the event coinciding with Jesus' death, the seismic activity was so great that the temple was damaged.

In fact, when Jesus died the temple was so severely damaged that the veil separating the Holy Place from the Most Holy Place in the temple was torn in two pieces (Mat. 27:51). The veil was torn from top to bottom, so the rent must have extended vertically for thirty feet, which was the height of the Most Holy Place.

This veil was not a flimsy thing like a bridal veil. Identified as a curtain by some Bible translators, it was more like a reinforced carpet. It consisted of two layers of strong materials and was thirty feet wide, covering an area of 900 square feet. It was held in place by fastenings to two walls of the Holy Place and to the tops of four pillars, each of which was more than two feet in diameter. Besides being sturdy, the pillars occupied nine feet of floor space, that is, thirty percent of the width of the Holy Place.

Moreover, the pillars were embedded in a thick marble base, which was supported by enormous concrete arches to an underground depth of more than forty feet. Full construction of the complex of buildings, on 26 acres of ground, took 84 years. It was massive and, like many Roman construction projects, was built to last for centuries. The undergirding arches still stand, but the temple was destroyed in A.D. 70 and has not been rebuilt in nearly two millennia.

The quaking Earth that accompanied the death of Christ generated so much power that a crack appeared suddenly in the seemingly indestructible base of the temple. It was a rift of such depth that the 30-foot tear appeared suddenly in the gigantic double-strength curtain as it was ripped from top to bottom like a sheet of paper being torn by the hands of an angry child. Perhaps it was torn by the hands of an angry God, for He could not have been pleased with the "unclean" idol of an eagle that the Romans had placed within His place of worship.

This was a seismic event even more dramatic than the one on the morning of Jesus' resurrection. It probably would have registered at the top of the Richter scale, if such a seismic measuring device had existed at that time.

Christian leaders have emphasized that the tearing of the curtain symbolized the spiritual truth that the substitutionary death of Jesus opened the way into the Holy of Holies—the presence of God—for all faithful believers in Him. But for the purposes of this study, its scientific application also is pertinent.

Two other scriptural details affirm the magnitude of this quake. The Bible states that rocks were split and graves in the Jerusalem area were broken open (Mat. 27:51-51). The splitting of rocks generates a lot of noise and may accompany a powerful earthquake. This fulfilled the prophecy of Jesus that if His followers held silence instead of boldly proclaiming His divine identity, the stones would "cry out" (Luke 19:40).

The statement that the graves were opened also has broad implications. There were many graves marked by stones, many cave-tombs, and many sarcophagi in the Jerusalem area. The cracking of Earth's surface must have been extensive for it to be described as breaking open these graves. This prepared the way for the dead to rise miraculously and walk about Jerusalem as Jesus did Himself upon rising from the dead three days later when the second powerful quake occurred (Mat. 27:52-53).

Solid Ground

The Jordan River flows through a rift valley in which many earthquakes have occurred, at least three of which are mentioned in the Bible. Much of the valley was below sea level, including the Dead Sea, lowest place on the surface of the earth at 1,400 feet below sea level.

Jerusalem was only thirteen miles from the northern edge of the Dead Sea, but the city's topography was different. Jerusalem stood at the crest of the Judean hills on solid ground about 2,600 feet above sea level. Rarely was Jerusalem the scene of an earthquake.

What natural event could God have used to cause the two great quakes that happened within three days when Jesus died and arose from the dead? And what could have caused the three hours of darkness on the afternoon of his death?

The Bible says the darkness settled over the whole land from noon to 3 p.m. (Mat. 27:45). The Greek word translated *land* was used primarily to identify the entire Earth or at least the entire land area of Earth in contrast to the planet's water-covered area. It did not refer solely to the area around Jerusalem, which might have been plunged into darkness by a localized event.

In rare instances this word was used to identify a single land or country, so it might have referred to the entire land of Israel. But that is only a remote possibility. A problem with it is the need to identify a darkness with dimensions broad enough to encompass a single entire land and precise enough so that no parts of any other land are darkened. Therefore, in this context, the word almost certainly referred to the entire Earth.

When in Scriptures there is an allusion to a darkening of the Earth or moon, it concerns a celestial event. An eclipse of the moon occurs when Earth moves between the moon and the sun. An eclipse of the sun occurs when the moon moves between Earth and the sun. The eclipsed sun turns dark, that is, coal black.

While it is true that God could simply stop the sun from shining or the moon from reflecting the light of the sun, this is not what is meant by this darkening. God works within the realm of His creation. He would not extinguish the sun for three hours; indeed, if He did so, it could have catastrophic consequences. Both the Hebrew and Greek words translated *darken* have connotations meaning to *obscure, cover* or *hide*. Therefore, the darkening of the sun does not refer to the stoppage of the sun from shining, but to its being covered or hidden, i.e., eclipsed.

That this was indeed a worldwide event was affirmed by the writings of Thallus circa A.D. 52, who probably was living at the time it happened. Thallus wrote: "On the whole world there pressed a most fearful darkness, and the rocks were rent by an earthquake, and many places in Judea and other districts were thrown down."[1]

The event described here could not have been an ordinary solar eclipse by the moon. Those events usually are seen only in localized regions of the world and last less than eight minutes at a single location. The event in question lasted for three hours in Jerusalem, and, if Thallus was correct, was global in effect.

The only known celestial object in our Solar System other than the moon large enough to eclipse the sun and having an orbit that can bring it into a position between the Earth and the sun is a comet. Asteroids are not large enough to eclipse the sun.

If a large comet circled the sun and approached Earth in the early phase of its departure toward outer space, it could cause the three-hour darkness described in the Bible. While approaching the Earth, it could make an inside pass and, from the perspective of viewers on Earth, eclipse or "darken" the sun. Such an eclipse could last for several hours. This is true because many comets have comas larger in diameter than the moon or the Earth. Some are as expansive as the sun itself.

If this was a large comet, it also would explain the two great earthquakes. An event in which a large comet was in proximity to Earth while obscuring the sun from view would create great stress on the crust of the Earth. Gravitational interaction between the comet and Earth, coupled with magmatic tidal stress resulting from the direct alignment of the three celestial bodies, including the sun, might be sufficient to generate earthquakes during the time period of the eclipse. There may indeed have been four celestial bodies in alignment, for Thallus also wrote, "It was at the season of the paschal full moon that Jesus died."[2]

This providential alignment of four celestial bodies could account for the quake of such strength that it severely damaged what at that time was probably the strongest building in Israel, the Roman-built temple. It also could account for the noisily breaking rocks and the creation of large cracks in the Earth described in the Bible as the opening of graves, besides the other damage Thallus attributed to it.

After eclipsing the sun the comet would have continued on its course. Since this was an inside pass, the comet would still have been approaching Earth, and during the next few days would move past the planet. A second powerful earthquake happened less than three days later, when the comet was still in close proximity to Earth. A comet is the only credible source of simultaneous celestial (the eclipse) and terrestrial (the earthquakes) disturbances of this magnitude.

We must not overemphasize the natural over the supernatural, for it is also clear from the language of the Bible that God was responsible for the timing of these events. The darkness occurred at the exact time when Jesus "became sin" in place of sinful human beings (2 Cor. 5:21). There never has been greater spiritual darkness on Earth than those hours when the sinless Son of God became the epitome of sin and died vicariously for all believers in Him.

The Sign: What will it be?

Most comets have regular orbits around the sun. Short-period comets that stay mostly within the boundaries of the Solar System can complete an orbit in less than 100 years. Comets that plummet deep into outer space, millions of miles beyond the orbits of the most distant planets, may require hundreds or even thousands of years to complete a single orbital cycle.

It is known by astronomers that the comet of 5/4 B.C., which we have identified as the sign of Jesus' birth, has not returned to the vicinity of Earth in more than two-thousand years. There is also no extant data suggesting that the comet of A.D. 30 has made a return. Both of these then are long-period comets, and it is reasonable to conclude that one of the two could be the celestial sign of Jesus' second coming described in Mat. 24:29-30.

A logical reason to believe the comet signifying Jesus's return is the same as either the one that heralded His birth or the one that accompanied His death is that Jesus referred to it as *the* sign of His coming (Mat. 24:30). Use of the definite article indicates the intent of Jesus to include His two comings under one sign.

It is also relevant that the return of Jesus, like His crucifixion in A.D. 30, will be accompanied by a solar eclipse, that is, a darkening of the sun (Mat 24:29). The prophesied repeat performance enables us to speculate that the crucifixion comet may also be present at the Second Coming. Its first appearance was much more calamitous than that of the comet of 5/4 B.C., and in Day of the Lord prophecies throughout the second half of the Bible, Jesus' return is foreseen as the most catastrophic natural event in world history, even though it is to be a blessed event in terms of spiritual deliverance for the redeemed of mankind.

A few days before Jesus' death He told His disciples that He would come to Earth a second time. His disciples asked Him, "What will be the sign of your coming and of the end of the age?" (Matt. 24:3, NIV). The Greek word translated *age* in the NIV and the NKJV was *aion*. The end of this eon refers to the end of time or the end of the world.

It must have surprised the disciples when the Lord answered their simple question with a sermon. It wasn't a one-point sermon, which would have satisfied their request for a sign. It was a sermon in which Jesus mentioned twenty things that would be going on in the world just before His return. It was a sermon that would occupy two full chapters of Matthew's Gospel and a single chapter in each of the Gospels of Mark and Luke.

The disciples wanted a sign. Jesus gave them much more.

The singular part of the sermon was what Jesus didn't tell them. He did not reveal the exact time of His return, and said that He Himself didn't even know the precise time, which is known only by His Father (Matt. 24:36).

But the time of Jesus' Second Coming seems to be the only thing about it that He doesn't want us to know. Before telling the disciples the one thing they could not know, Jesus mentioned so many other things about the era during which He would return that it became clear He didn't want to take a chance that believers who would read these words would be caught off guard. He spoke of these things:

- Destruction of the temple (Matt. 24:2)
- False messiahs (Matt. 24:4, 24)
- Wars and rumors of war (Matt. 24:5)
- Famines (Matt. 24:7)

- Earthquakes (Matt. 24:7, 29)
- Apostasy and betrayal (Matt. 24:10)
- False prophets (Matt. 24:11)
- Increase of wickedness, decrease of love (Matt. 24:12)
- Gospel preached worldwide (Matt. 24:14)
- The mysterious abomination of desolation (Matt. 24:15)
- Persecution, flight and tribulation (Matt. 24:9-21, Luke 21:21)
- Shortening of the tribulation (Mat. 24:22)
- Earthquakes, famines, and great signs from heaven (Luke 21:11)
- Roaring and tossing of the sea (Luke 21:25)
- Light flashing across the sky from horizon to horizon (Mat. 24:27)
- Darkened sun and moon (Matt. 24:29)
- People terrified, heavenly bodies shaken (Luke 21:26)
- Falling "stars" (Greek *asteres*, Matt. 24:29)
- The sign of the Son of man, glorious and powerful (Matt. 24:30)
- Trumpet sound and heavenly gathering of the elect (Matt. 24:31)

Jesus mentioned the first eighteen things on this list without using the word *sign*. By referring to the nineteenth as "*the sign* of the Son of man," He seemed to be singling it out as the specific answer to the disciples' request. It was as if He were saying, "Look for all of these things, but especially *the* sign in the sky, because when you see that, it won't be long before you see Me."

Jesus went on to say much more. What He said next was so important that, not only did the disciples record it for their own reference, but, by inspiration of the Holy Spirit, they wrote it down in three books of the Bible for ours: He wants us to be prepared and watchful (Matt. 24:42–44; Mark 13:35; Luke 21:36).

Prepared for what? If we are in fact living in what the Bible calls the time of the end, we should expect suffering to result from events Jesus prophesied—persecutions, wars, famines, and natural disasters.

Watchful for what? Jesus told us to lift up our heads and look skyward for the most conclusive sign of His coming and our deliverance (Luke 21:28). Seven of the final eight things on the list above refer to visible happenings in the heavens.

Duration of Orbit

The orbit of the returning comet, whether it is the one that heralded Jesus' birth or the one that accompanied His death, is about 2,000 years, give or take a few years, or even decades, to account for perturbations. We know this because all of Jesus' Olivet prophecy, except the prophesied period of worldwide oppression, has been fulfilled, including the destruction of the temple in A.D. 70. According to the Bible, the final period of time, described as great distress or tribulation, will last three and a half years (Rev. 11:2, 13:5). The redeemed are believers "taken out of great tribulation," so we can expect Jesus to return soon after the end of the 42 months of distress. Therefore, it seems likely that Jesus will return in the near future, perhaps within the lifetimes of some of us.

The comets marking the birth and death of Jesus both presided over major events, so it is possible that either could have been the one that will return as "the sign of His [second] coming." But, in addition to the fact that one caused an eclipse of the sun and the other did not, the two were different in another way. The first heralded an event so placid that the word *peace* is often used to describe it. Not only did it mark the birth of the Prince of Peace, but its appearance was accompanied by no catastrophic celestial or terrestrial events.

The comet that darkened the sun and caused powerful earthquakes on the day of His death and the day of His resurrection was much more destructive. This aspect of the comet supports the idea that it was in fact the same comet biblically prophesied to herald His Second Coming.

From the book of Isaiah through the book of Revelation, in contexts associated with the Day of the Lord, referring to the return of Jesus, there are many passages describing catastrophic celestial and terrestrial events. To keep things brief at this point let's discuss just three verses, Rev. 6:12-14.

This text mentions a blood-red moon associated with a worldwide quaking of the Earth (6:12), a dramatic display of "falling stars" (6:13) and the collapse of mountains, with islands disappearing into the sea (6:14). Other Day of the Lord Bible texts describe fierce storms and a fiery deluge. This will be a cataclysmic event like no other in Earth's history, for, after the redeemed are taken up to heaven, the planet will be consumed by fire (2 Peter 3:7, 10, 12).

All of the things mentioned in Rev. 6:12-14 are associated with comet events. A single comet could produce them all. In fact, the blood-colored moon happens only during a comet event. Common eclipses of the moon resulting from a direct alignment of the sun, Earth and moon are only briefly visible in isolated areas of the world and are predominantly brown in color. Even though the term *blood moon* is in common use, it is a misnomer with regard to ordinary lunar eclipses. The eclipsed moon, brought about by Earth's movement between the sun and the moon, does not turn a brilliant blood-red (crimson) in color.

However, during a comet event, if the sun was eclipsed from the perspective of Earth's inhabitants, the moon would appear bright red because they would be looking at it through the red dust of the comet's tail. A comet's tail always extends directly away from the sun, so its dust would surround the Earth at the same time as the comet's coma eclipsed the sun.

If indeed the comet that darkened the sun and caused the Earth to quake on the day of Jesus's death is *the* sign of His coming and will mark His second advent, as seems likely from the biblical descriptions of the two comet events; and if we are correct in discerning from Matthew chapter 24 that the "great tribulation" is the only one of the preliminary events prior to His coming that has not yet occurred; then Jesus likely will return during the 21st century A.D., and perhaps in the first half of this century. That would put the comet's orbit in the anticipated range of about 2,000 years.

If the comet were to return unperturbed with an orbit of precisely 2,000 years, it would come in A.D. 2030. However, it is foolish to try to predict the year of Jesus' return. This may be repetitious, but it's important: He said no one would know the time of His return other than God the Father (Mat. 24:36). But it does appear that the comet marking His return *may* have an orbit of *about* 2,000 years.

If that is so, within the framework of the Bible, marking the beginning of the history of mankind during the 40th century B.C., we should be able to track back from the time of Jesus' death and resurrection, and find at least one and perhaps two other noteworthy occasions when this same comet appeared and caused damage to our planet, as did the one in A.D. 30. We shall do this study in the next chapter.

After that we shall discuss the Bible's many prophecies about the return of Jesus. If our interpretation is correct, Jesus' Second Coming will be previewed by the final appearance of the great comet.

In summation of this chapter are these important points:

- When Jesus died the Earth quaked so mightily that it severely damaged the sturdiest building in Jerusalem—the Jewish temple.

- The curtain within the temple was ripped in half at the same time as a three-hour solar eclipse was reaching conclusion.

- Fissures appeared in the earth resulting in the exposure of many underground graves.

- Another severe earthquake happened three days later when Jesus arose from the dead.

- Seismic events occurred worldwide at this time, lending credence to the idea that they resulted from the approach of a comet.

- A comet is the only known source of simultaneous celestial and terrestrial disturbances of this magnitude.

- Either the comet heralding Jesus' birth or the one appearing at His death could be the "sign" of His Second Coming (Mat. 24:30)

- It's likely that the comet "sign" appeared when He died because that was a more dangerous comet than the one heralding His birth.

- Moreover, the Bible says the sun was eclipsed for three hours when He died and will again be eclipsed when He returns (Mat. 24:29).

- Jesus told His followers to prepare and look skyward for the sign of their deliverance at His Second Coming (Luke 21:28).

- At that time there will be "falling stars," collapsing mountains, storms and a fiery deluge—all of which could be caused by a comet.

Chapter Twelve

Babel & Eden

HAVE YOU EVER wondered why there is so much genealogical information in Genesis, focusing on the seemingly trivial facts of who begat whom? There are reasons for all those names, and one of them is important to us: The genealogies give information helping to date and collate important historical events.

Archbishop James Ussher, in the year 1633, completed a chronological study and concluded that the history of mankind began with the creation of Adam in 4004 B.C. Later studies, based in part on biblical genealogies, differed from Ussher's: There isn't unanimity on the subject because there are periods of time about which we can only guess. The most reliable estimates date the advent of Adam between 3965 B.C. and 3975 B.C. There are specific surmises of 3968 and 3970. The truth is we can't be sure.

For the purposes of this study, the precise year does not matter so long as we can stay within close range. We are seeking ancient appearances of a comet that had an orbit of about 2,000 years. Since we know Halley's Comet has experienced perturbations of five percent, a 2,000-year orbit may have fluctuations of as much as a century. Or, it may be consistently within a few years of 2,000. As we shall see as this study progresses, the comet in question seems to have sustained a remarkably consistent orbit approximating 2,000 years.

One intriguing aspect of this subject is the traditional belief that mankind's history would last 6,000 years after which, for believers, there would be a thousand years of peace in the presence of God. This is based in part on the Bible verse that states "...to the Lord a day is as a thousand years and a thousand years as one day" (2 Peter 3:8). The God who established a week of six work days and a Sabbath of rest may have patterned it after the bigger picture of 6,000 years of human history (six Lord's "days") followed by a Millennium of rest at Jesus' Second Coming, identified in the Bible as the Day of the Lord.

Dividing 6,000 by three and you would have the potential for four appearances of a comet with an orbit of about 2,000 years, if the final one occurred in or about the 6,000th year, heralding the return of Christ. If one of the other appearances was in A.D. 30, upon the occasion of the death/resurrection of Jesus, as discussed in Chapter Eleven, we should expect an earlier appearance around 1970 B.C., give or take a decade or two, and, perhaps, an initial appearance at around the time of the events described in Genesis chapters two and three. Let's first discuss the suggested event circa 1970 B.C.

Simple addition based on the ten-generation genealogical text of Genesis chapter five shows that the period of time that was consumed between Adam's creation and Noah's flood was 1,656 years. Splitting the difference between 3965 and 3975 and using 3970 B.C. as a starting point, the passage of 1,656 years brings us to the year 2314 B.C. and is a good approximation of the year of the Flood.

Ten more generations of genealogies are outlined in Genesis chapter eleven, from the birth of Arphaxad to Noah's son Shem two years after the flood, until the birth of Abram (Abraham). The time span covered during that interval was 292 years. This means Abram likely was been born circa 2022 B.C.

The Latter Part

Based on our estimated starting date of 3970 B.C., genealogies of Genesis chapters five and eleven indicate that the patriarch Peleg, in Shem's lineage, was born in 2213 B.C. and died in 1974 B.C. It was at some time during those 239 years that the Earth was divided (Gen. 10:25).

In those days respect approaching reverence was accorded to the patriarchs as they increased in age. This may sound strange in a society such as ours that emphasizes youth over age. But in those days wisdom acquired through age was considered of more value than the physical strength and beauty of youth.

For example, God blessed the latter part of Job's life more than the beginning (Job 42:12). The most important utterances of Jacob's life were made from his deathbed (Genesis 48-49). Moses was a murderer at age 40, a deliverer at 80 and a revered leader before his death at 120. So it is not unreasonable to conclude that the dividing of Earth occurred during the latter part of Peleg's life, probably after 2000 B.C. and possibly as late as 1975 B.C., the year before his death.

But what was this dividing of the Earth? Some Bible commentators have associated it with the confusion of languages after the fall of the Tower of Babel. The peoples split into nationalities according to the new languages they spoke and scattered to the uttermost parts of the Earth.

Earth's dividing may have been related to the confusion of languages, but was not identical to it. Whenever the Hebrew word *palag,* meaning *divided*, was used in the Old Testament, it referred to a physical division or split. It was similar to the Chaldean word *pelag* which meant *a division* or *a halving*. In the Bible names often were significant, so it is not surprising that the name of the patriarch associated with this dividing process was Peleg.

The name Peleg meant *earthquake*, offering a clue of how the physical division of Earth might have taken place. We have found much evidence that comets have caused severe earthquakes. The comet under discussion eclipsed the sun and generated two major earthquakes during a later appearance. We know it was an exceptionally large comet, which upon a closer approach to Earth than it made in A.D. 30, might be capable of changing the face of our planet the way Shoemaker-Levy 9 changed the surface of Jupiter.

The event we are about to study was universal. It was associated with a split resulting from cataclysmic seismic activity. The world up to that time consisted of a single land mass surrounded by a vast sea. The word *yam* in Genesis 1:10 is singular, therefore should be translated *sea* instead of *seas*. This original sea consisted of "gathered waters," not individually identifiable oceans.

After the divisive event the Earth's land surface was split into segments. If this happened during the year after the dispersion from Babel, there would have been time for the peoples speaking common languages to reach extremities of the land mass before it was broken apart and many of them found themselves on new continents separated by large bodies of water from the original land mass.

There is good reason to believe it happened in just this way: The people who had populated the region of the Chaldeans were land-dwellers. They were not maritime peoples and would not have had the expertise to cross oceans, if the continental divide already had taken place. They would not even have had the ocean-going vessels capable of making such a crossing, even though they were descendants of Noah. God told Noah how to build the ark, but that skill faded away long before 1975 B.C. because it was not needed by inland-dwelling people who defied God by refusing to migrate toward the extremities of the land mass.

It was at about this time that Ur-Nammu's Great Ziggurat of Ur was destroyed, as recorded in ancient Middle Eastern documents. This event could have been caused by the explosion of a bolide falling from the crumbling surface of a comet in gravitational clash with the Earth. The same forces then may have launched seismic activity throughout the Earth. This activity could have continued, as did the flood of Noah, for a full year, until the ultimate result was the continental divide. This seems to have occurred between 1975 and 1980 B.C., placing it in the correct time-frame if it was indeed an early appearance of a comet with an orbit of about 2,000 years.

Ur-Nammu's ziggurat in southern Mesopotamia was apparently the Tower of Babel. The Bible says little about this enormous stepped temple tower, other than that it was built in the land of Shinar by people who had a common language. They wanted to erect a structure into the heavens to make a name for their posterity, and also to keep from being scattered throughout the Earth. The Lord confused their language and dispersed them anyway (Gen. 11:1-9).

Josephus identified the leader of these people as Nimrod, a grandson of Ham, who established kingdoms in Shinar (Babylonia) and Assyria, in the Tigris and Euphrates valleys, covering territory that today is occupied by Iraq and part of Iran (Genesis 10:10-12). According to the account of Josephus, these kingdoms developed after the Flood when the family of Noah came down from the mountains and settled on the plains.[1]

After the passage of more than three centuries, most of the people had forgotten the rainbow covenant between God and their forefather Noah. They became concerned about the possibility of being destroyed in another deluge. So, under the leadership of the rebellious and tyrannical Nimrod they began building a waterproof tower of great height and equally great width, which they believed would stand above any floodwaters God could generate. They thought the tower could withstand any assault by God.[2]

An estimated 600,000 laborers were required to build the tower. Here is a summation of the original reasons for its construction: "The purposes of the Tower were multiple. One was to make this edifice the masterpiece of world architecture. Another was to make this edifice the political and religious capitol of the world, a center of world control. A third was to worship the planets with astrology, magic and witchcraft. The religious structure at the apex of this six-storied tower was to be the observatory, planetarium and temple. Yet another purpose was to provide the elite of Chaldea a place of refuge 'if God should choose again to flood' their world, their 'world' being the flat Mesopotamian Plain within their regional context."[3]

This sturdily-constructed tower was 288 feet high and its base was 288 feet wide. No known winds of any description, not a hurricane or even a gigantic tornado, could have severely damaged this tower and positively could not have destroyed it. But God said "Come, let us go down," and destroy it He did (Gen. 11:7). The question we must consider is this: By what means did God accomplish this feat from above?

Josephus briefly quoted the Sibyl's account of the destruction of the tower. Here is a more complete account from the same Sibylline record: "The immortal one imposed a great compulsion on the winds. Then the winds cast down the great tower from on high, and stirred up strife for mortals among themselves. Therefore, humans gave the city the name of Babylon. But when the tower fell, and the tongues of men were diversified by various sounds, the whole earth of humans was filled with fragmenting kingdoms."[4]

Even though no ordinary wind could have destroyed the tower, it may have been accomplished by an explosive blast that could be described as a powerful wind. Pieces of disintegrating comets, and even some asteroids, can generate bolidic mid-air explosions capable of demolishing their surroundings. But of the two sources of bolides, only a comet could have accomplished what this blast did.

Asteroids, though they can be explosive, are not as large or as powerful as comets and are not fire-bombs. The blast that blew away the top of the Tower of Babel also left part of it in charred ruins, according to *The Book of Jasher*. The Bible twice mentions *The Book of Jasher* in contexts that show it was a legitimate source of factual information

(Joshua 10:13, 2 Samuel 1:18). This is what *The Book of Jasher* says about the destruction of the Tower of Babel and the massive burn-scar it left in the ground:

"And as to the tower which the sons of men built, the earth opened its mouth and swallowed up one-third part thereof, and a fire also descended from heaven and burned another third, and the other third is left to this day, and it is of that part which was aloft, and its circumference is three days' walk."[5]

This seems to imply that the explosive blast demolished one-third of the tower. The force of the explosion from above, like a hammer, drove the bottom third deep into a shallow new crater it carved out of the ground, while the exposed final third was charred by incendiary gases ignited by the blast. If the Book of Jasher was correct, and the area of damage was so extensive that it took someone on foot three days to walk around it, it must have covered a ground-surface area of more than 200 square miles, about the size of the city of Chicago: A walk of three days would make the burn-scar about sixty miles in circumference.

Since this was an air blast, the pattern of destruction on the ground was different from that of Sodom, which was destroyed by an impact blast. Impact blasts leave deep craters of comparatively small circumference. Cometic air blasts, like the one that demolished Ur, leave burn scars for many miles around. Nearly four millennia later a similar air blast flattened and charred hundreds of square miles of forest land in Tunguska, Siberia.

The Tunguska Bolide

On June 30, 1908, a bolide exploded over a remote area of Tunguska, Siberia. The blast, equivalent to a thousand Hiroshima bombs, flattened hundreds of square miles of forest.[6] The earth trembled and noises were heard like guns firing. A hot blast of wind damaged vegetation. The fallen trees burst into flames.

One eyewitness description of the Tunguska event mentioned a ball of fire that left a fiery-white trail behind it in the sky. Another described "a flying star" with a fiery tail. A third was particularly graphic:

"I saw the sky in the north open to the ground and fire poured out. The fire was brighter than the sun. We were terrified, but the sky closed again and immediately afterward, bangs like gunshots were heard. We thought stones were falling ... I ran with my head down and covered, because I was afraid stones may fall on it."[7]

Scientists did not investigate the Tunguska event until 1927. Meteoriticist Leonid Kulik visited the site seven times between 1927 and 1939 and concluded that the source of the big blast had been a comet. It was later hypothesized that the entire event could have been caused by fragmentation of the comet Encke. Eyewitness accounts favored the comet theory. Of the possible causes of this event, none but a comet puts on a sensational aerial show like this one did, and shows evidence of having a tail as did this one.

Western scientists ridiculed the idea of a Tunguska comet. Some were willing to accept the idea of an asteroid, but not a comet, as if there were a substantive difference. One scientist thought the entire incident was caused by the earthquake, but could not persuade others to agree with him since a tremor seemed to be a peripheral consequence of the event, not its cause.

A particularly imaginative author wrote a book in 1958 suggesting that the Tunguska forest was flattened by an exploding UFO.

One scientist excluded a comet from consideration for the reason that in his opinion the incident was not catastrophic enough. Zdenek Sekanina of the Jet Propulsion Laboratory at Caltech said:

"[A comet incident] would have been a global catastrophe, comparable to a nuclear winter. The effects on mankind would have been so overwhelming that we could not discuss the topic, because we would not be here."[8]

Sekanina's reflections are illogical with respect to the Tunguska event, because there is no fixed limit on the dimensions of comets. Like planets, they come in all sizes— small, medium, large, and extra-large: One size does not fit all. However, his comments are sobering when we think about potential consequences of a huge comet conflicting with Earth on the Day of the Lord.

Ur-Nammu's Great Ziggurat

The Book of Jasher's account of the destruction of the Tower of Babel is probably the same event alluded to by the Chaldean account of the destruction of Ur-Nammu's Great Ziggurat. The name Babel, or Babylon, was not attributed to that part of the world until after this event, when the confounding of languages, which today might be called *babble*, persuaded the people finally to be obedient to God's command to leave the tyrannical dominion of Nimrod and repopulate the entire Earth (Gen. 9:1, 7).

Accurate maps exist of the area of Babylon and Ur based on archaeological discoveries. Superimposing a map identifying the location of ancient Ur over one showing the remains of Babylon indicates that both were in almost exactly the same location. This supports the theory that the ancient city of Ur was renamed Babylon when it was rebuilt, apparently on a nearby site, after the destruction of Ur-Nammu's ziggurat, which was thereafter called the Tower of Babel.

Ur, besides being the name of the city before it was rebuilt as Babylon, also was the name of a pagan deity revered by King Nammu and attached to his name and that of the temple tower. The similarity of the Chaldean name Nammu to the Hebrew Nimrod was noteworthy. Both could have referred to the same rebellious tyrant.

An ancient clay tablet contains panels depicting Ur-Nammu's activity. One panel shows him setting out to start construction of the gigantic tower. Another tablet states that the gods were offended by the tower, destroyed it, scattered the inhabitants and strangely altered their speech.[9] This is identical in major details to the biblical and Josephus accounts.

The common dating of Ur-Nammu's reign is from about 2044 to 2007 B.C. We are talking about the end of his reign because it concluded with the dispersal following destruction of the tower. Thus, in the traditional account, the date of the tower fall would have been 2007 B.C., about 30 years before the date we have postulated.

Dating of ancient events frequently is off by that much or more because archaeological dating methods, especially radiometric dating, are imprecise.[10] These methods often indicate age greater than a known reality.[11] The difference between our estimate of 1975-80 B.C. and the more official dating of 2007 B.C. is insignificant for a comet with an estimated orbit of 2,000 years, and this is especially true considering the imprecision of the dating methods currently in use.

One More Thing

There is one more intriguing fact that seems to verify the essentials of our interpretation—the story of Abram, whom God later renamed Abraham. Terah, Abram's father, was one of the rebellious, idolatrous people who refused to leave their Mesopotamian homes and repopulate the Earth at the command of God.

We have concluded that the comet event that destroyed the Tower of Babel and then caused the land masses of Earth to drift apart and form the new continents of North and South America, Antarctica and Australia, probably occurred between 1975 and 1980 B.C. This dating fits into the time frame of the Bible's story of the migration of Abram's family.

The Bible states that Abram was 75 years old when he completed his journey to the land of Canaan after Terah had decided to stop along the way and pitch his tent at a place named Haran (Gen. 11:31, 12:4). What we do not know is how old Abram was when Terah left his home in Ur of the Chaldees, the capital city of Ur-Nammu (Nimrod) and site of the giant ziggurat later known as the Tower of Babel.

The Bible gives no details about the length of Terah's family's sojourn in Haran, so it must not have been as long as they lived in Ur of the Chaldees before the local tower was blown apart. This reasoning is valid because the ancient scriptural account gave many details about the family's life in Ur.

According to the Bible, Terah had three sons, who were born, grew up and married while living in Ur. One of them, Haran, bore a son, Lot, who later was prominent in the story of the destruction of Sodom and Gomorrah. After fathering Lot, Haran died in Ur (Gen. 11:27-29).

It seems as if the many things that happened to Terah's family while living in Ur must have consumed most of the 75 years between the birth of Abram and his arrival in Canaan. If he was 47 years old when he left Ur and journeyed to Haran, that would have been in the year 1975, at the precise time when we think the Tower of Babel was blown apart and the frightened inhabitants of Ur and its suburbs were scattered over the face of a soon-to-be-divided world.

Haran, Abram's youngest brother, had enough time to be born, grow to adulthood, marry and father Lot before his untimely death in his hometown of Ur. Abram lived to age 175, which was not exceptional for his generation. So if Haran died at about age 40, as seems likely, it would have been a very young age for people of that era. Also, it would have happened around the time of the blast that must have demolished the city of Ur, since it destroyed the city's seemingly most indestructible building. The Bible does not say what caused the death of Haran, but the timing is right for it to have been the terrible blast that destroyed the tower.

And then, with his home city in ruins and one of his family members dead, a grieving Terah was finally, reluctantly willing to obey God, leave the desolate Ur and travel at least part of the way to the family's ultimate destination of Canaan. Did he stop along the way in order to bury the body of his youngest son? Did he feel remorse, believing that if he had obeyed God in the first place and departed Ur for Canaan, Haran would not have been killed in the blast? Did his remorse influence him to remain living near the grave of his lamented son and to name that place Haran?

Abram, in an early sign that he would be more faithful to God than his father, took his nephew Lot, Haran's son, and other members of the family the rest of the way 28 years later. Terah, who was still alive, continued living in Haran. Otherwise, the Bible would state that it was he, the patriarchal head of the family, who led the trip from Haran to Canaan.

This mixture of fact and supposition is supported by actual circumstances. First of all, it links the departure of Terah from the rubble of Ur with the departure of many other peoples from the same area, at the command of God, immediately after the Tower of Babel and their homes in the shadow of the tower were destroyed.

It accounts for the remarkable coincidence that the place where Terah pitched the family tent after leaving Ur was named Haran, the same name as that of his dead son. If Haran's death occurred during the blast that destroyed Babel, his father would have been grieving throughout the trip and likely gave the place where he pitched his tent the name Haran in memory of his recently-deceased son, who would have been buried there.

It could account for the conversion in faith of Abraham and Lot from belief in the moon god Ur—the god of Terah—to the clearly superior Jehovah, Creator God of the universe, who guided the destructive bolide into position to destroy Ur's idolatrous temple tower.

Also, it explains the curious fact mentioned by Josephus that Abraham was interested in astronomy.[12] The frightening thing Abraham witnessed in the sky over Ur, especially if it did in fact take the life of his youngest brother, could have stimulated his interest in sky-watching.

The same event also could have accounted for the astrological fixations developed in ancient times by many frightened peoples. Preserved records show that this same interest in celestial activity was shared by peoples throughout the world at that time. All of them, or their recent ancestors, had been living in the Middle East before the dispersion that followed the fall from the sky of the bolide that destroyed the Tower of Babel. They either witnessed it or received first-hand accounts from relatives who had been there.

Eden

So far in this study we have seen that large comets, including one that has an orbit of about 2,000 years, can cause worldwide catastrophes. We have suggested that, in addition to demolishing the Tower of Babel, this comet eclipsed the sun for three hours on the day of Jesus' death and caused two violent earthquakes that resulted in widespread damage, perhaps worldwide. One of these events happened in A.D. 30 and the other circa 1975 B.C.

Tracking back about another two-thousand years, is it possible that the same comet put in an appearance shortly after the creation of Adam and Eve, which scriptural genealogies and other time-related sources indicate probably happened between 3965 and 3975 B.C.?

Before the worldwide flood described in Genesis chapters six through nine, which we propose also involved the approach to Earth of a great comet, there is no description in the Bible of catastrophes. The youthful Earth seems to have been a placid place, with no violent storms, not even thundershowers. There is, however, one scriptural verse that is worthy of study because it refers to an occasion when Adam and Eve, the only two people alive on Earth at that time, became terrified and fled for their lives.

In the New International Version this verse reads: "After [the Lord God] drove the man out, he placed on the east side of the Garden of Eden cherubim and a flaming sword flashing back and forth to guard the way to the tree of life." (Gen. 3:24)

The Garden of Eden was not limited in area to the acreage of a zoo or zoological garden. It was vast. We know this because it served as home breeding grounds for at least one pair of every air-breathing creature, animals and birds, created by God (Gen. 2:19). There were thousands upon thousands of these species—more than exist today because many have become extinct.

The Bible says while Adam was dwelling in Eden, before Eve was created out of a rib of his body, the Lord brought to him each animal and bird and allowed him to name them. In order for Adam to name every kind of bird and animal, he must have taken a close look at each of them. Perhaps there was a bonding process at this time between God's newly-created beings.

The Bible also says that in Eden a large river was a source of water for four other rivers that flowed out from it. Two of the four have been identified as very large ones, the Tigris and Euphrates (Gen. 10:14). A similar but probably much smaller place in the U.S.A. would be Pittsburgh, where there is a confluence of three rivers, two feeding into the third, the Ohio. From these details about the air-breathing creatures and the five rivers we may assume that the Garden of Eden covered at least as much territory as a very large city and perhaps was as big as a state or small nation.

The Hebrew word *gan* referred to a fenced or enclosed garden. We don't know what kind of enclosure secured Eden, but it must have been beautiful, as was the rest of the garden. The word *eden* meant a pleasurable or delightful place. Three Hebrew words with the same linguistic roots all have the connotation of yielding pleasure. It was a gorgeous place with lush landscaping, for in the Revelation, referring to the heavenly dwelling prepared for believers, the description is similar to that of Eden in the book of Genesis (Rev. 21:1-8, 22:1-5).

Apparently, the primary entrance/exit to the garden was on the east side. The Hebrew word translated *eastward* or *east side* also meant *front side*. After Adam and Eve sinned, God decided they could no longer dwell in Eden lest they be tempted to eat the fruit of the tree of life while in their spiritually decadent condition, and live forever in that condition. So He expelled them. (Gen. 3:22-23).

The Bible does not give details of the process of this banishment, but it may have been associated with what happened next. The Hebrew word *mahpekah*, which in Amos 4:11 described the "overthrow" of Sodom and Gomorrah, also appears in Genesis 3:24. Here it describes the event that immediately followed the hasty departure of Adam and Eve from Eden.

We concluded in our chapter about Sodom and Gomorrah that the "overthrow" of those cities and simultaneous establishment of the Dead Sea and surrounding saline desert almost certainly resulted from substances discharged from a comet, including a heap of salt that buried Lot's wife.

Use of this same word may not prove the event described in Genesis 3:24 also involved a comet, but it stimulates curiosity. This word is used as a verb to describe the movement of the "flaming sword" that appeared in a position to guard the eastern side of Eden so that the man and woman could not return, even if they had a mind to do so.

A sword traditionally has been the most common symbol of a comet. Many comets looked like swords and so these were called "sword stars." The shapes of celestial objects, especially comets and constellations, often determined the names and descriptive words used for them by ancient sky-watchers.

If this "sword" was a comet, descending toward Earth in a position that made it appear, from the perspective of the fleeing Adam and Eve, to be coming down over the eastern edge of Eden, then the rest of the description of this event in the final verse of Genesis chapter three is important.

The NKJV Bible translation says this was a "flaming sword which turned every way." The adjective *flaming* is significant, in part because it can describe the brilliant appearance of a comet. In Genesis 3:24 the Hebrew word *lahat* is translated "flaming." It meant *blazing, burning,* or *flaming*.

We have seen that comets produce incendiary effects. Their lethal contents include methane and methanol, sulfur, ammonia, formaldehyde, ethanol, carbon monoxide and hydrogen cyanide. Intelligent human beings don't want to be anywhere in the vicinity of a fiery comet discharge, such as the one that may have taken place on the east side of Eden after Adam and Eve left the area. It likely was similar to the devastating seventh plague that God called down upon Egypt shortly before the decisive Passover.

The phrase *turned every way* also is important. Its primary meaning is *turned over* or, as in Amos 4:11, *overturned*. The only place in the Bible where translators render it *turned every way* (NKJV) or *flashing back and forth* (KJV) is in Gen 3:24. As it did in the Amos text, it can describe a comet approaching Earth. Because of gravitational interaction between the two celestial bodies, the comet will discharge dangerous, fiery missiles. It will appear to turn over in the sky and stretch out horizontally before passing overhead. Or, it may appear stationary for days, weeks or even months, as did the comet signifying Jesus' birth.

Another possibility is that this Hebrew word, in the context of a comet event, could have meant *overthrew* or *overwhelmed*. These are meanings of the word that have been used by translators in other parts of the Bible. Perhaps this word was used in Genesis 3:24 to denote both the visual overturning of the comet in the sky and the terrible destruction it did to the Earth beneath. When a comet makes a change of position, from the perspective of sky-watchers below, it appears to be striking a downward blow, like a sword being swung lethally at the Earth.

The cherubim mentioned in this verse were probably not angels. They were mysterious beings or objects described by Bible commentator Adam Clarke as "utterly unknown" creatures with "formidable appearances."[13]

The biblical book of Ezekiel provides an important clue for us about the function of the cherubim. When they first appear early in the book, the cherubim are described as "living creatures, their appearance like burning coals of fire, like the appearance of torches." (Ezek. 1:13). Then, later in the same book, God instructs a man to "fill your hands with coals of fire from among the cherubim and scatter them over the city." (Ezek. 10:2)

A torch can symbolize a comet. But even if here it doesn't, this text emphasizes the fiery element of the cherubim, which is also mentioned in the context of Gen. 3:24. When you combine this with the other image of a comet—a flaming sword—the picture you have is of a comet dropping fiery coals upon at least the east side of Eden and probably a much wider area including the entire original garden.

These cherubim may have been similar in appearance to the Leonids discharged from the remnants of comet Tempel-Tuttle on Nov. 13, 1833. At that time the sky over a large area of North America was filled with bright objects resembling meteorites, but much more spectacular. An observer described the sight at Niagara Falls: "The exhibition was especially brilliant, and probably no spectacle so terribly grand and sublime was ever before beheld by man as that of the firmament descending in fiery torrents over the dark and roaring cataract."[14]

Prints of two paintings depicting the awesome event are reproduced in the same book.[15] The Leonids look like miniature comets or "torches." Each has a head with a tail flaring out behind it as it falls. Turn these objects over and you have a different look. Some comets, appearing in vertical or near vertical position in the sky, head up and tail down, look like human beings wearing long robes.

An Earth-threatening comet, during its approach, would develop appendages protruding from the area of the coma extending downward toward the planet. This happens because the larger object, Earth, has a stronger gravitational field than the comet and begins to tear it apart. The rending of Shoemaker-Levy 9 by Jupiter is an example of such an event. The twin extensions from the head or shoulder area of the comet may resemble the horns of a bull, wings of an eagle, or arms of a human being. A bull and an eagle were commonly used as depictions of a comet.

A dangerous comet, such as the one discussed in our chapters about the great Flood and the Exodus, may appear in outline very much like the statues of cherubim atop the Ark of the Covenant in the tabernacle the Israelites erected after leaving Egypt. These could have been representations of the comet they observed in the sky as they made their escape. The appendages resemble wings. Ancient peoples tended to personify, and even deify, objects in the sky that resembled the human shape.

Conversely, the cherubim atop the ark could not have represented angels because the Bible makes clear that angels do not have wings. If they did, they could not be mistaken for human beings (Heb. 13:2). The angels sent by God on a mission to decadent Sodom looked like men and were called men (Gen. 18:2, 16, 22). Their identity as angels was made clear in Genesis 19:1. And after this they were again viewed as men (Gen. 19:5, 8, 10, 12, 16).

The Leonid scene in 1833 was so frightening that many people panicked. Some unbelievers sought to make peace with God because they thought they were going to die. A 12-year-old boy, a believer in Jesus, jumped up and down for joy because he thought the thousands of raining objects were "falling stars" previewing the return of the Lord (Rev. 6:13, 12:4).

This was only a secondary event, however. The remnants of the comet posed no danger to the populace. But, had the comet still been intact, raining millions of incendiary objects onto the Earth, many people would have died in the resulting inferno. The peril of such a comet assault may have been what terrified Adam and Eve as they fled from Eden, so that they and their descendants gave no consideration thereafter to returning to their pleasurable first home.

There is a part of the human psyche that longs to return to its roots, especially those people who experienced joyful childhoods. This urge can be so strong that it is manifest even in some people who had miserable experiences in their hometowns. It is the basis for such things as high school and college reunions. Biblical examples of it are the Israelites yearning to return to Egypt even though they lived in oppression there, and Lot's wife turning to take a nostalgic last look at the corrupt city of Sodom just before it, and she along with it, were buried in cosmic rubble.

A return to Eden, even if Adam and Eve longed for its pleasures, would have been inhibited by the terror of their flight from it and might not even have been possible: If this was the comet we believe it was, the Garden of Eden may have been left in charred ruins.

His Coming

We conclude this chapter in anticipation of the event that the little boy desired—the return of Jesus Christ. Many Scriptures offer evidence that His coming on the Day of the Lord will be presaged by the final appearance of the 2,000-year comet. This conclusive event of world history is to be the topic of discussion for the final chapters of this book.

Here is a summary of Chapter Twelve:

- If the comet having a 2,000-year orbit will signify Jesus's return, it probably made two appearances during Old Testament times.

- One occurred between 1975 and 1980 B.C. when the Tower of Babel in Ur was destroyed and people scattered throughout the Earth.

- A God-directed bolide blew the top off the tower, charred the middle third and, like a hammer, drove the bottom third into the ground.

- At about the same time, perhaps shortly afterward, the Earth was divided during the time of Peleg, while the people were scattering.

- Peleg's name meant *earthquake* and it was a worldwide seismic event that divided a single land mass into continents existing today.

- Abraham, living in Ur, witnessed the decimation of the tower, and his brother Haran may have been killed at that time.

- Also possibly associated with the 2,000-year comet was the event that terrified Adam and Eve as they fled from the Garden of Eden.

- God used a "flaming sword" to bring about this event between 3965 and 3975 B.C.

- The Hebrew verb meaning *overthrow* appears in connection with the Sodom and Eden events, so both may have had similar causes.

- Cherubim were present for the Eden event. They were "like burning coals of fire, like the appearance of torches." (Ezekiel 1:13)

- Burning coals of fire are seen falling from close-range comets; swords, hammers and torches all are common comet symbols.

Chapter Thirteen

That Day

If our theory is correct, the next appearance of the fiery 2,000-year comet will herald the Second Coming of Jesus Christ on what the Bible refers to as the Day of the Lord (2 Thes. 2:1-3). With celestial and terrestrial fires burning at the same time, it will be a terrifying event for unbelievers and an occasion of the utmost joy for believers who will recognize the object in the sky and rise into the presence of the Lord before the fires are kindled (2 Peter 3:3-13).

In Chapter Nine we quoted some verses from the book of Isaiah pertaining to both the terrible comet event of 701 B.C. and terminal happenings on the Day of the Lord. It was shown that many of Isaiah's Day of the Lord prophecies did not refer predominantly, if at all, to 701 B.C. Let's look at a few of these, keeping in mind that they describe occurrences on the great day of Jesus's return.

Isaiah chapter eleven contains much comet imagery, including a rod, a banner, and the fisted hand of the Lord: "He will strike the earth with the rod of his mouth; with the breath of his lips he will slay the wicked...He will raise a banner for the nations and gather the exiles of Israel; he will assemble the scattered people of Judah from the four quarters of the earth…The Lord will dry up the gulf of the Egyptian sea; with a scorching wind he will sweep his hand over the Euphrates River. He will break it up into seven streams so that men can cross over in sandals." (Isaiah 11:4…12…15, NIV)

The "exiles of Israel" refer to the new "Israel" consisting of all believers, Jewish and gentile (Romans 9-11). The image of the Lord striking the Earth with a rod held in His mouth could refer to a comet. The next verse, containing a banner, seems to relate to the ingathering of the elect. And the final one refers to the massing of troops hostile to the Lord and their crossing of Euphrates to engage in the conclusive battle of Armageddon (cp. Rev. 16:12-16). A shaking fist is the image of the coma of a comet in the sky above a quaking Earth. The fist is perceived attached to a forearm, i.e., the comet's tail.

The river crossing is facilitated by the "mighty wind" of the Lord, probably an enormous comet-spawned tornado like the one that separated and froze in place the Red Sea so that the Israelites could pass through (cp. Is. 11:15 and Ex. 15:8)

Isaiah chapter 24 opens with these words: "Behold, the Lord makes the earth empty and makes it waste, distorts its surface and scatters abroad its inhabitants." The heart of this chapter is in verses 19 and 20:

> "The earth is violently broken,
> The earth is split open,
> The earth is shaken exceedingly.
> The earth shall reel to and fro like a drunkard,
> And shall totter like a hut;
> Its transgressions shall be heavy upon it,
> And it will fall, and not rise again."

A "split open" Earth would spew lava from the depths beneath its mantle until the surface could be described literally as a "lake of fire." (See Rev. 19:20, 20:10-15 and 21:8)

Isaiah chapters 32 and 33 describe the Lord rescuing His people from "everlasting burnings" (Is. 33:14) Then, in chapter 34, beginning with the appearance of the sword of the Lord in heaven, there is the judgmental conclusion replete with comet imagery:

> "[Earth's] streams shall be turned into pitch,
> And its dust into brimstone;
> Its land shall become burning pitch.
> It shall not be quenched night or day;
> Its smoke shall ascend forever.
> From generation to generation it shall lie waste;
> No one shall pass through it forever and ever."
>
> —Is. 34:9-10

This provides a startling contrast to the description of the peaceful new heavens and new earth, joyful habitation of the redeemed (Is. 65:17-25).

Ezekiel

Most of the Old Testament prophets spoke of the Day of the Lord and, on subsequent references, *that day*. The book of Ezekiel contains one passage that has as much comet imagery as any of Isaiah's. Speaking of the battle of Armageddon on that day, here is what the Lord says, according to Ezekiel 38:19-23:

"In the fire of my wrath I have spoken: 'Surely in that day there shall be a great earthquake in the land of Israel, so that the fish of the sea, the birds of the heavens, the beasts of the field, all creeping things that creep on the earth, and all men who are on the face of the earth shall shake at My presence. The mountains shall be thrown down, the steep places shall fall, and every wall shall fall to the ground.' I will call for a sword against Gog throughout all My mountains," says the Lord God.

"Every man's sword will be against his brother. And I will bring him to judgment with pestilence and bloodshed; I will rain down on him, on his troops, and on the many peoples who are with him, flooding rain, great hailstones, fire, and brimstone. Thus I will magnify Myself and sanctify Myself, and I will be known in the eyes of many nations. Then they shall know that I am the Lord."

We have seen it so often that by now the comet imagery is clear. This, a prophecy of the second world judgment, reflects the first in one way—the flooding rain. In another, it is the opposite, causing mountains to collapse into the deluge instead of rising out of it. The deluge ultimately is fiery, not watery. The fire (lava) seeping from the heart of the Earth will boil away the water on the surface.

As elsewhere in catastrophic Bible prophecy where the translation is *hailstones*, the Hebrew word *eben* appears. It means literal stones, not icy hail. The phrase *great hailstones* would be better translated *hail of great stones.*

And, as we have also seen, *brimstone* is unstable sulfurous rock that may explode with greater force than nuclear bombs.

Joel

Joel's Day of the Lord prophecy contains vivid references to that day and mysterious references to locusts. Here are relevant excerpts:

"Let all who live in the land tremble, for the day of the Lord is coming. It is close at hand—a day of darkness and gloom, a day of clouds and blackness. Like dawn spreading across the mountains a large and mighty army comes, such as never was of old nor ever will be in ages to come. Before them fire devours, behind them a flame blazes. Before them the land is like the Garden of Eden, behind them, a desert waste—nothing escapes them. They have the appearance of horses; they gallop along like cavalry. With a noise like that of chariots they leap over the mountaintops, like a crackling fire consuming stubble, like a mighty army drawn up for battle." (Joel 2:1-5, NIV)

The reference is to an army of locusts, referring back to Joel 1:4 and forward to Joel 2:25. However, these are not ordinary locusts. They do not consume greenery in the usual way, but set destructive fires. They look like horses and make noise like chariots as they leap over mountaintops.

This is a reminder of what we have suggested was comet imagery in relation to the chariot that was visible in the sky when Elijah was taken into heaven. It recalls the story of Helios, pulling the sun across the sky daily with his horse-drawn chariot. A comet resembles a chariot. When it approaches dangerously near Earth, the gases in the tail begin to undulate so that the tail may be visualized as galloping horses or leaping locusts. The imagery that follows seems to confirm this interpretation, as it relates to Joel's vision:

"Before [the locusts] the earth shakes, the sky trembles, , the sun and moon are darkened, and the stars no longer shine. The Lord thunders at the head of his army; his forces are beyond number, and mighty are those who obey his command. The day of the Lord is great; it is dreadful. Who can endure it?" (Joel 2:10-11, NIV)

The comet imagery was clear in the preceding text, as it is in the following: "I will show wonders in the heavens and on the earth, blood and fire and billows of smoke. The sun will be turned to darkness and the moon to blood before the coming of the great and dreadful day of the Lord." (Joel 2:30-31, NIV)

Because of a popular teaching linking the return of Jesus with a lunar eclipse, it is worthy of our attention that the above-quoted verses, in addition to mentioning a blood-red moon, also refer to a darkened sun. Eclipses of the moon and sun are rarely seen from all parts of the world at once and *never*, in the natural order of things, concurrently. Moreover, lunar eclipses are too common to be associated with "great" or "dreadful" events and are predominantly brown in color.

Finally, there is this wonderful conclusion as unbelievers are given one last chance to commit themselves to Christ and receive forgiveness of their sins along with the promise of eternal life: "Multitudes, multitudes in the valley of decision! For the day of the Lord is near in the valley of decision. The sun and moon will be darkened, and the stars no longer shine. The Lord will roar from Zion and thunder from Jerusalem; the earth and the sky will tremble. But the Lord will be a refuge for his people, a stronghold for the people of Israel." (Joel 3:14-16, NIV)

Jesus

The first significant description of *that day* in the New Testament occurred during the week of Jesus' crucifixion when the disciples asked Him, "What will be the sign of Your coming, and of the end of the age?" (Mat. 24:3)

Jesus began His response by identifying twenty things that would preface the great event: These were itemized in Chapter Eleven. The first thing we need to consider is the duality of Jesus' sermon. In this sense it was like the prophecies of Isaiah that pertained to both the defeat of the Assyrians in 701 B.C. and the Day of the Lord.

Many but not all of Jesus' prophetic comments were fulfilled initially during the 42-month Roman siege of Jerusalem from A.D. 66 to 70 (Mat. 24:21). When the city finally fell, the destruction was so complete that it appeared as if not a single stone of the temple was left upon another stone (Mat. 24:2).

As we stay with our Day of the Lord theme—the second and primary focus of these dual prophecies of Jesus— we shall emphasize the final eight phases of the event mentioned by the Lord. All of these will either originate in the sky or be associated in some way with what will be going on up there before Jesus returns:

- Earthquakes, famines, and great signs from heaven (Luke 21:11)

- Roaring and tossing of the sea (Luke 21:25)

- Light flashing from horizon to horizon (Mat. 24:27)

- Darkened sun and moon (Matt. 24:29)

- People terrified, heavenly bodies shaken (Luke 21:26)

- Falling stars (Matt. 24:29)

- The sign of the Son of man, glorious and powerful (Matt. 24:30)

- Trumpet sound and heavenly gathering of the elect (Matt. 24:31)

The cometary aspects of these things are plain. Indeed, no known celestial object other than a comet could account for them all. Many of the comet events described in this book have involved severe earthquakes. Famines, floods, tidal waves, simultaneous eclipses of sun and moon, appearance of shaking objects in the sky brought about by a quaking Earth, fiery precipitation resembling falling stars: This covers nearly the full range of serious potential comet consequences, and all of it will take place on the Day of the Lord.

The "sign of the Son of man" in the sky will be the close-range approach of the great 2,000-year comet. Light flashing from horizon to horizon precisely describes how this comet will appear, with its tail extending across the sky for millions of miles (Mat. 24:27). The "trumpet" strains of gravitational and magnetic interaction between Earth and the comet will announce it (Mat. 24:31).

As reinforcement for the identity of this sign, it is noteworthy that in A.D. 66, at the outset of the Roman siege of Jerusalem, a comet appeared in the sky. This is mentioned twice in the description of the event by Josephus, who witnessed it: "Thus there was a star resembling a sword, which stood over the city…[It was]…a comet that continued a whole year."[1]

The sword-star was the comet. But to make sure it was not misidentified, Josephus mentioned the comet a second time. It was not, however, the 2,000-year comet. Historians have identified it as an appearance of Halley's Comet.

Jesus wants us to keep watch for the age-ending comet, and so He also made a comet a focal object of the first fulfillment of this prophecy in A.D. 66. Not only are we to watch, but we are to be prayerfully and pragmatically prepared. Recognizing it and preparing our responses in advance are two distinct things. (Mat. 24:42-44, 25:13)

The Scroll Unrolled

The plagues of Exodus were almost certainly caused by a comet. The three sets of plagues that comprise half of the Book of Revelation also seem cometic in origin, because the patterns of all four sets are similar. There is one major difference: The plagues of Revelation, referring to happenings at the time of the end up to and including the Day of the Lord, are much more severe than those of Exodus. There is no "Goshen" on Earth that will escape the effects of cataclysmic events described in the Revelation's plague texts.

In the final hours of world history, dangerous things will drop out of the heavens. The apostle John described it in the sixth chapter of the Book of Revelation: "I watched as [Jesus] opened the sixth seal. There was a great earthquake. The sun turned black like sackcloth made of goat hair, the whole moon turned blood red, and the stars in the sky fell to earth, as late figs drop from a fig tree when shaken by a strong wind. The sky receded like a scroll, rolling up, and every mountain and island was removed from its place." (Rev. 6:12-14, NIV)

The quoted text appears within a context of a heavenly scroll being unsealed (Rev. 5:1-8:5). It describes fallout from a disintegrating comet ("stars" falling from the sky). A rolled up scroll, with a knobbed end, provides a good picture of the tail and coma of a comet. To imaginative eyes a scroll being unrolled looks like a shattering comet. Gravitational forces would cause the broken pieces to fall to Earth in thick precipitation like sheets of rain from a gigantic thundercloud.

A comet's tail may be longer than one hundred million miles—more than the distance between the Earth and the sun. It is likely that Earth would pass through the tail before encountering the coma of an approaching comet. The tail consists of gas and particles ranging from dust to pieces of rock, so a tail pass-through would result in a dense dust-fall and a rocky hail that could be perceived from Earth as the unrolling of a scroll with sheets descending.

The heavenly scroll of Revelation must have been important, for God the Father sealed it with seven seals and would not let anyone unseal it other than His Son.

Jesus broke the seals, disclosing these contents as written in Rev. 5:1-8:5:

- Seal One: A rider on a white horse goes forth to make conquests.

- Seal Two: A rider on a red horse causes men to kill each other.

- Seal Three: A rider on a black horse brings famine to the Earth.

- Seal Four: A rider on a pale horse represents a huge death toll.

- Seal Five: Christian martyrs appeal to God to avenge their blood.

- Seal Six: God responds with an earthquake and a "star-fall."

- Seal Seven: A censer filled with fire is hurled onto the Earth.

The sixth and seventh seals contain details relevant to comet events. The most important difference is that, instead of fire on Earth, the seventh seal discloses a censer containing the prayers of the saints. A censer may be a depiction of the coma of a vertical comet with rising incense appearing as its tail.

This, then, is the end: On the Day of the Lord, when a cascade of incendiary meteorites falls to the Earth followed by huge pieces of the coma of a great comet, the sky will roll up like a scroll in a symbolic gesture of completion as if God were wrapping things up (Rev. 6:14).

This present Earth no longer will be habitable.

Some of the imagery of the world-ending scroll also shows up elsewhere in the Bible. In the midst of Day-of-the-Lord prophecies, Isaiah admitted the things he was prophesying were difficult to understand. He compared them with the words in a sealed scroll:

"If you give the scroll to someone who can read, and say to him, 'Read this, please,' he will answer, 'I can't; it is sealed.' Or if you give the scroll to someone who cannot read, and say, 'Read this, please,' he will answer, 'I don't know how to read'" (Isa. 29:11-12, NIV).

Isaiah promised that the unsealed scroll would be understood by everyone on the Day of the Lord: "In that day the deaf will hear the words of the scroll, and out of gloom and darkness the eyes of the blind will see" (Isa. 29:18, NIV).

Isaiah prophesied the final event of this world eight hundred years before John received his equally-difficult-to-understand revelatory visions on the island of Patmos. Isaiah declared: "All the stars of the heavens will be dissolved and the sky rolled up like a scroll; all the starry host will fall like withered leaves from the vine, like shriveled figs from the fig tree" (Isa. 34:4, NIV; also see Rev. 6:13–14).

A sealed scroll also appears in the final chapter of Daniel's prophecy. Referring to the time of the end, the angel Gabriel said to Daniel: "Multitudes who sleep in the dust of the earth will awake: some to everlasting life, others to shame and everlasting contempt. Those who are wise will shine like the brightness of the heavens, and those who lead many to righteousness, like the stars for ever and ever. But you, Daniel, close up and seal the words of the scroll until the time of the end." (Daniel 12:2-4, NIV)

The most mysterious reference to a scroll in the Bible is that of the prophet Zechariah. In a context in which he identifies the four horsemen of the Apocalypse as the "four spirits of heaven," Zechariah mentions a scroll. He calls it "a flying scroll" and describes it as "the curse that is going out over the whole land" (Zech. 5:2-3; 6:5, NIV).

Why call it a flying scroll unless it appears in the sky?

Why not call it a flying scroll if it is a picture of a comet?

Trumpet Plagues

After the seven scroll-unsealing plagues are seven trumpet-sounding plagues (Rev. 8:7-11:19, cp. Mat. 24:31). The trumpet plagues begin with hail and fire mixed with blood falling onto Earth. This fiery precipitation is tinted a blood-red hue by the elements of the same color in the comet's tail. So, right away, we have a description of meteoric activity (Rev. 8:7).

Next, a blazing mountain plunges into the sea. Sea creatures die and, though it is here left unsaid, a piece of a comet falling into an ocean would generate a series of enormous tsunamis, fulfilling one part of the Olivet prophecy of Jesus (Rev. 8:8; Luke 21:25).

Third, a great star, blazing like a torch, casts pollutants into surface waters worldwide. Because of its contamination of the fresh water supply, the torch-star is called Wormwood (bitterness). It incites bitter enmity in the hearts of people who aren't prepared to meet God (Rev. 8:10-11).

In the fourth plague the sun, moon, and stars are darkened. This involves a massive eclipse of the sun and moon. It is perhaps associated with severe air pollution caused by smoke and dusty fallout from the eclipsing comet's tail as it even obscures the visibility of stars throughout the sky (Rev. 8:12).

During plague five, a star descends to Earth carrying a key to unlock the abyss. It's a mountain-sized meteoric bolide, released by the crumbling coma of the comet. It penetrates Earth's crust to the magma core (Rev. 9:1).

The sixth plague involves mobilization of two hundred million demon-driven troops at the Euphrates River. They initiate the world-ending battle of Armageddon in which all of them will fight for the losing side (Rev. 9:13-16).

And finally, the appearance of a mighty angel coming down from heaven, robed in a cloud with a rainbow above His head, is the Second Coming of Jesus Christ (Rev. 10:1).

The only one of the seven that needs more explanation is the first, which is almost identical to the seventh plague of the Exodus. Approaching the sun, the tail of a comet is created by vaporization of ice from the coma. As the icy surface vaporizes, large quantities of carbon and hydrogen and other gases are expelled, forming an enormous atmosphere around the coma and the long tail. The tail contains large amounts of water vapor, carbon, hydrogen, other gases, dust, and smaller quantities of sand and rock.

Passage of Earth through a comet's tail generates "falling stars," i.e., meteorites. Such a pass-through results in "fire mixed with blood" falling to Earth. Upon contact with Earth's atmosphere, water vapor in the comet's tail condenses. As it falls, it picks up red dust and takes on the appearance of bloody rainfall.

A fall of rain resembling blood has occurred several times in recorded history. Such precipitation containing comet dust probably accounted for turning the surface waters of Egypt a blood-red color at the command of Moses. Another bloody rainfall happened at the time of the establishment of Rome. On the day of Rome's founding, in the eighth century B.C., the sun was eclipsed and the world was darkened.[2]

A comet approaching the Earth could eclipse (darken) the sun long enough to be a history-altering event. This darkening may also have been part of the eighth-century-B.C. comet event prophesied in the book of Amos and discussed in the eighth chapter of this book in connection with King Uzziah (Amos 5:8).

The gases in the tail of a comet are combustible. When they come in contact with an atmosphere containing oxygen, they are set ablaze. As they burn, they bind the available oxygen. The unconsumed gases turn to liquid and fall to earth as the fiery element mixed with the blood-colored rain.

Meanwhile, a large portion of the precious ozone layer of the atmosphere, which has been an object of careful preservation by environmentalists, is consumed by the conflagration in the sky. It's a reminder of Who is really in charge. Without the protection of its Creator God, this world would be doomed. He will sustain it until, according to His sovereign decision, it is time for it to be replaced with the new heaven and earth (Rev. 21:1).

Many biblical texts containing trumpets can be associated with the age-ending comet. Isaiah prophesied that on the Day of the Lord there will be a trumpet blast (Isa. 27:13). He linked a trumpet with a raised ensign. It was customary in ancient times for one soldier to lift an ensign and another to blow a trumpet at the start of a battle. However, it has never happened that a literal battle ensign was seen in the sky *above* the mountains, as described by Isaiah. It will happen as part of the comet's imagery when the last trumpet sounds (Isa. 18:3).

In a great Second-Coming reference, the prophet Zechariah wrote: "Then the Lord will appear *over them*; his arrow will flash like lightning. The Sovereign Lord will sound the trumpet; he will march in the storms of the south" (Zech. 9:14, NIV, italics added). This is yet another reminder that these Day-of-the-Lord events will be initiated from the heavens.

There are still two more things to be mentioned about trumpets.

First, the whining noise heard just before projectile impact, such as a bolide rushing toward Earth, is similar to the sound of a trumpet. The clashing of gravitational and magnetic force fields of Earth and the comet would produce weird noises that could resemble the blaring of trumpets: "All you people of the world, you who live on the earth, when a banner is raised on the mountains, you will see it, and when a trumpet sounds, you will hear it" (Isa. 18:3, NIV).

Second, the shape of a trumpet is prototypical for a comet. It has a narrow tube like the tail of a comet and an open rounded end like the coma.

Bowls Poured Out

The bowl plagues are described in Revelation 15-18, including a long description of Babylon the harlot, which seems to emanate from the fifth bowl. Revelation chapter 16 is another version of the same end-time events we have just seen described under the imagery of a cosmic scroll and a trumpet. Jesus considered these events important enough to repeat them for us. This time they are presented as the effects of seven celestial bowls pouring out their contents onto the Earth.

First, painful sores break out on the bodies of unredeemed people. By this time, the redeemed have been whisked off to heaven. Seen in context with the two pollution plagues that follow, these sores likely will result from contact with caustic comet dust (Rev. 16:2).

During the second bowl plague the sea turns to blood and sea creatures die. The dust-fall affects surface waters (Rev. 16:3).

In bowl plague No. 3, rivers and springs turn to blood, implying more water pollution (Rev. 16:4).

The sun scorches people with fire during the fourth plague. Atmospheric fires damage the ozone layer, and the sun blazes through the gaps (Rev. 16:8).

There is agonizing darkness that results from extreme air pollution in plague No. 5. The sulfurous pollutants of a comet may produce sulfuric acid. Deadly acid also could be produced when sulfurous pollutants from a comet or volcanism initiated by the comet are inhaled into moist human lung tissue (Rev. 16:10).

The sixth-plague Battle of Armageddon begins with the attack of demon-driven kings. Jesus intervenes, however, for we hear him declare: "Behold, I come like a thief" (Rev. 16:15).

The cosmic conclusion involves flashes of lightning, peals of thunder, and the worst earthquake (quaking Earth) in world history. And, "From the sky huge hailstones of about a hundred pounds each fell upon men. And they cursed God on account of the plague" (Rev. 16:21).

A common interpretation of the hundred-pound hailstones is they are nuclear bombs, perhaps hundred-megaton or hundred-gigaton bombs. However, the God who created the universe and knows its destiny is not going to relinquish final control to human beings and their miniscule weapons of warfare. A better interpretation is that the number one-hundred is symbolic of explosive objects with sufficient power to achieve the Lord's purpose. Most of the numbers in the Book of Revelation are symbolic.

One hundred is ten times ten, or ten squared. Ten, along with seven and twelve, is a scriptural number of completeness or fullness. Use of the number one-hundred in this text then is an indication of the complete fulfillment of the Lord's judgmental purposes by means of the bowl plagues.

"Hailstones from heaven" is more severe precipitation than "falling stars" or "fire mixed with blood." It is more catastrophic than the hail of stones that destroyed every living thing exposed to them during the plagues of Egypt. It is much worse than the hail of stones that decimated the Amorite troops as they fled from Joshua.

For the Earth, the huge explosive bolides will represent a history-ending event. We saw a preview of coming attractions through telescopes when 21 gigantic bolides struck the planet Jupiter in 1994. The comet that disintegrates on the Day of the Lord may be comparable to the one that left Earth-sized scars on Jupiter. One such scar would be sufficient to apply the word *terminal* to our planet. Twenty-one, if there are that many, would be massive overkill.

The New Testament equivalent of the Hebrew *barad* is the Greek *chalaza*. This word is used four times by John in the Book of Revelation, each time referring to a barrage of explosive rocks tumbling from the sky onto the Earth—first, in Rev. 8:7 in connection with seventh scroll-seal plague; second, in Rev. 11:19 during the seventh trumpet plague; and the final two times in Rev. 16:21 while the seventh bowl is pouring out its contents onto the beleaguered Earth.

You have to appreciate the Bible's emphasis of a three-times-repeated event.

Take a bowl out of a kitchen cabinet. Run water into it from a tap. Now turn it sideways and watch as the water spills out and falls into the sink. Except for the omission of explosive rocks and fiery rainfall, the view of the bowl's contents being poured down the drain is remarkably like the cosmic picture of a comet dump onto the Earth.

Year of Jubilee

The Jewish year of Jubilee may have been a type of the final year of human history culminating with the Day of the Lord when Jesus returns. The Hebrew word for *jubilee* meant *trumpet blast*. In this chapter we already have mentioned two ways a clash between Earth and a comet can produce trumpeting sounds. And a comet bears a remarkable visual likeness to a trumpet.

The Jubilee year was announced every fiftieth year in ancient Israel after seven seven-year cycles. It was a time for the proclamation of liberty to all Israelites who were in bondage. It was a time for a return of ancestral possessions, including land, to those who had been compelled to sell them. And it was a year of rest for the land.

The year of Jesus' return will feature the release from earthly bondage of all believers in Him, even the confinement of the grave. Those who are alive, even if they are being persecuted or oppressed, will receive instantaneous liberation and ascend into the presence of the Lord Himself. They will find heavenly mansions awaiting them. This event will usher in a millennium of rest.

Jonathan Cahn's book, *The Mystery of the Shemitah*, shows a remarkable pattern of dramatic events that have occurred during Shemitah years. These were observed in ancient times and, from God's perspective, still seem to be the seventh year in each cycle. In regard to the United States, Cahn has shown how the nation arose in power during Shemitah years and how, since the Shemitah year of 1944-45, it has been in decline. Since then, in each fourth Shemitah cycle, in the years 1972-73 and 2000-01, there have been major occurrences associated with this nation's deterioration. If this pattern holds, the year 2028-29 could be climactic.

Even before reading Cahn's book, I noticed that the pattern of events related to the orbit of the comet-sign of Jesus's return was pointing toward an arrival circa A.D. 2030. Jubilee years are uncertain since for more than 2,000 years they have not been observed. However, it is known that every Jubilee year immediately followed a Shemitah year, so, if the next Jubilee year does occur in the projected pattern, we shall reach Jubilee in the year 2029-30.

There is a plus-minus variable of one year in the computations involved in this process, and since the Shemitah year overlaps from one of our calendar years to the next, we must admit to the possibility that, even if the next four-cycle Shemitah year is the one immediately preceding the Jubilee year in which the Messiah returns to this Earth, it might occur as early as 2028 or as late as 2031. And, of course, it might not happen during that cycle at all. We should not try to make exact predictions of the time of the Lord's return because we can't know it (Mat. 24:36, 42).

But we should give thought to the possibility that during autumn of a year in the not-so-distant future, at around the time of the Jewish festival of Ingathering, the Lord may come to gather His saints imto their new heavenly habitations. What a glorious day that will be! The trumpets will sound in jubilation!

Armageddon

The Battle of Armageddon is a conclusive Day of the Lord event that already has been mentioned four times in this chapter even though the name *Armageddon* appears only once in the Bible (Rev. 16:16). Thayer's Greek-English Lexicon of the New Testament states this about it:

"In the Apocalypse (Revelation) it would signify the place where the kings opposing Christ were to be destroyed with a slaughter like that which the Canaanites or the Israelites had experienced of old."[3]

The references cited in the lexicon for the typical battles include Judges 5:19 and Zechariah 12:11. Judges 5:19 was part of the celebratory song of Deborah and Barak following the comet event in 1188 B.C. in which "the Lord routed Sisera and all his [900] chariots and all his army with the edge of the sword before Barak." (Judges 4:15) Sisera, a Canaanite, had oppressed Israel for twenty years.

The Deborah-Barak victory, which was analyzed in Chapter Six, occurred at Megiddo. It served as a prototype for the battle of Armageddon on the Day of the Lord as described in Rev. 16:

- Demons gather forces from eastern lands for the battle "of that great day of God Almighty," i.e., the Day of the Lord (Rev. 16:12-14).

- They gather them together "to the place called in Hebrew, Armageddon." (Rev. 16:16).

- When the seventh bowl is poured out there are "noises and thunderings and lightnings." (Rev. 16:18)

- And there is "such a mighty and great earthquake as had not occurred since men were on the earth." (Rev. 16:18)

- The great city (Jerusalem, cp. Zech. 12-14) is split into three parts, and the cities of other nations collapse. (Rev. 16:19)

- Islands disappear, submerging into the heart of the sea, and mountains disintegrate. (Rev. 16:20)

- A heavy hail of stones falls from heaven upon men, who blaspheme God because of the terrible plague of hail. (Rev. 16:21)

The final four of the seven are clearly comet-related, as each has been observed in connection with comet events analyzed throughout this work. If any doubt remains, the language of the prophet Zechariah is plain:

"Then the Lord will go forth and fight against those nations, as He fights in the day of battle. And in that day His feet will stand on the Mount of Olives, which faces Jerusalem on the east. And the Mount of Olives shall be split in two, from east to west, making a very large valley;

half of the mountain shall move toward the north and half of it toward the south. Then you shall flee through My mountain valley…yes, you shall flee as you fled from the earthquake in the days of Uzziah king of Judah…It shall come to pass in that day that there will be no light; the lights will diminish…And this shall be the plague with which the Lord will strike all the people who fought against Jerusalem: Their flesh shall dissolve while they stand on their feet, their eyes shall dissolve in their sockets, and their tongues shall dissolve in their mouths." (Zech. 14:3-5, 6, 12)

The cause of dissolving flesh could be massive sulfuric bolides detonating with fiery force exceeding any nuclear blasts known to mankind, or they could be tornadic methane firestorms, or both.

The entire scenario is intriguing from the perspective of the misled kings of the East. They likely would include rulers of Middle Eastern nations that have launched repeated military campaigns against Israel for more than 3,000 years, many of these, as we have seen, in the looming shadows of dangerous comets.

The final event, like most of the others, will not turn out well for the enemies of God's people, even for those of militant Islam which dominate those nations today. They might also include atheistic Red China and other brutal communist-dominated lands, although these traditionally have shown less hostility toward Israel than countries like Assyria and Babylon, which parallel Iraq and Iran.

In 2006, at the end of a television show aired by The History Channel, *Comets: Prophets of Doom*, the narrator made this summary statement: "NASA has plans to deal with an asteroid, but there is nothing anyone can do about comets. They are too large and show up too suddenly...What would we do if an average-sized comet came at the Earth? We would die, or a lot of us would, anyway...[Comets] can come from any direction. We do not have the technology to defend against a comet. Comets are nature's unstoppable projectiles."

Comet events are devastating enough to provide fulfillment for the latter part of Peter's great prophecy about Jesus' return: "Looking for and hastening the coming of the day of God, because of which the heavens will be dissolved, being on fire, and the elements will melt with fervent heat." (2 Peter 3:12)

Summary

Day of the Lord is a biblical phrase identifying the time of Jesus' Second Coming and all of the things that will be happening during a cosmic clash between the Earth and a comet on that day. This phrase and its corollary *that day* do not appear in the first half of the Bible. But they occur in prophecies occupying about twenty percent of the scriptures in the second half. It is the Bible's most prophesied event and the only one that has not yet happened exactly as the Bible has predicted. Its importance cannot be overemphasized.

Here are highlights of the prophecies of *that day* mentioned in this chapter:

- Beginning with the prophecies of Isaiah, the Day of the Lord is a primary theme of many books in the second half of the Bible.

- Ezekiel made a stunningly detailed prophecy about the battle of Armageddon on the Day of the Lord.

- Joel's Day of the Lord prophecy contained references to "locusts" setting fires and leaping over mountaintops.

- Joel also prophesied a "valley of decision" in which the Lord would be a refuge for His people.

- Jesus told His disciples to watch and prepare for the appearance of the celestial "sign" heralding His return.

- The sign prophecy also referred to the comet that appeared during the Roman siege of Jerusalem in A.D. 66-70.

- Three seven-part series of Day of the Lord plagues occupy half of the book of Revelation.

- All three—seals of an unrolling scroll, martial trumpets, and bowls pouring out their contents—are cometic.

- The Jewish year of Jubilee (trumpet blast) may proclaim the return of the Messiah with fanfare during the year after a Shemitah year.

- The culminating battle of world history is described several times in the Bible, but only once is it called Armageddon.

- Jesus will strike down His enemies by a mighty earthquake and a heavy hail of stones along with consumptive firestorms.

Chapter Fourteen

Shaping Up

We have mentioned 36 objects, animate and inanimate, which are used in the Bible to present celestial images of comets. Most of them have characteristics that relate to activity occurring during specific comet events. For example, the first such picture, the sword mentioned in Gen. 3:24, is seen slashing down with deadly force near the Garden of Eden. A sword, with its handle (the coma) and its blade (the tail) provides the most common scriptural image of a comet.

When this project was begun twelve years ago, the author was reading the book of Isaiah. Within Day of the Lord contexts he took notice of many objects that seemed to be couched in figurative language. He began listing them and after the sum of these word-pictures had attained double figures, he realized that the shapes of every one of them resembled shapes often assumed by comets.

The first time through the Bible, he found forty of them. And by this time he knew it was a significant discovery. Further research showed that it was common for ancient peoples to view objects in the sky according to their resemblance in shape to objects often seen on earth. Besides constellations of stars, this was most notably true of comets, perhaps because they were known to make regular catastrophic assaults on the Earth. The Great Flood comet by itself probably was responsible for the deaths of hundreds of millions of people.

When the Bible's total of figurative comet-shaped objects reached forty, a book project was begun. Readings and re-readings of the Bible while this project was underway resulted in the addition of still more comet-shaped objects to the celestial picture gallery. At the time of this writing there are 54—a sum that far exceeds the possibility of mathematical coincidence.

Comets have been a great factor in the many cataclysmic events afflicting Earth in the past, with one yet to come: The Day of the Lord, when Jesus returns. We shall briefly identify and discuss all 54 comet-shaped objects in this chapter, keeping in mind that the combined evidence of the 54 depicts the sign of Jesus' Second Coming on the Day of the Lord. All scriptures are from Day of the Lord contexts in the New International Version of the Bible, unless otherwise noted.

Judgmental Objects

There are nine objects in biblical prophecy associated with judgmental aspects of comet events:

Ax: An ax wielded by God from heaven chops down proud and arrogant human beings. "[The Lord] will cut down the forest thickets with an ax; Lebanon will fall before the Mighty One." (Isaiah 10:34) The head of the ax represents the coma of the comet; the handle is the tail. This is in a Day of the Lord/that day context (Isaiah 30:27)

Saw: Self-sufficient men who scoff at God will be cut down from their lofty positions in this world on the day of the Lord's wrath. "Does the ax raise itself above him who swings it; or the saw boast against him who uses it?" (Isaiah 15:15) The handle of the saw is equivalent to the coma of the comet; the blade is the tail. This also concerns the time of Jesus' return (Isaiah 16:5).

Broom: A "broom star" sweeps away temporal worldly kingdoms and ushers in the eternal kingdom of God. " 'I will turn her into a place for owls and into swampland; I will sweep her with the broom of destruction,' declares the Lord Almighty." (Isaiah 14:23) The bristle of the broom represents the comet's coma; the handle is the tail.

Fork and Shovel: A winnowing fork and/or a shovel are used to separate the wheat from the chaff in the final judgment. The wheat is gathered into a heavenly "barn" while the chaff is burned or blown away. "[Jesus'] winnowing fork is in his hand, and he will clear his threshing floor, gathering his wheat into the barn and burning up the chaff with unquenchable fire." (Matthew 3:12) The pronged end of the fork and the scoop of the shovel outline the coma of the comet; the handle of each represents the tail. Fork and shovel are distinct items. In reference to the shovel, see Isaiah 30:24 (NKJV).

Fan: Another winnowing tool is the fan that blows away the chaff after it has been separated from the wheat. "Likewise the oxen and the young donkeys that work the ground will eat cured fodder, which has been winnowed with the shovel and fan. There will be on every high mountain and on every high hill rivers and streams of waters, in the day of the great slaughter, when the towers fall." (Isaiah 30: 24-25, NKJV). The fan is the comet's coma; the arm holding it is the tail.

Sickle: The Lord swings His sickle of judgment over the Earth to reap the harvest of human souls. "Swing the sickle, for the harvest is ripe. Come, trample the grapes, for the winepress is full and the vats overflow—so great is their wickedness!" (Joel 3:13) The curvature of the sickle provides an outline of the comet's coma. The handle is the tail.

Key/Star: A projection from the judgmental comet strikes a lethal blow to the corrupted Earth, penetrating its crust all the way to the magma layer beneath the mantle. "I saw a star that had fallen from the sky to the earth. The star was given the key to the shaft of the Abyss. When he opened the Abyss, smoke rose from it like the smoke from a gigantic furnace." (Revelation 9:1-2) The star represents the coma; the key is either the tail or a descending "horn" of the comet.

Hand/Chain: This image is similar to that of the key descending from the star, but there are two important differences. Instead of being attached to a star, the key is held by an angel, who also holds a chain. "And I saw an angel coming down out of heaven, having the key to the Abyss and holding in his hand a great chain." (Revelation 20:1) The angel's hand is the comet's coma; the chain is its tail. And, this time, the key clearly is a hornlike projection from the comet.

Punitive Implements

There are seven objects that may be visualized as punitive tools:

Whip and Scourge: The Lord strikes down from on high with the whip and scourge of punishment required for sin. (The Hebrew word can refer to either whip or scourge, but these are two distinct objects wielded in different ways.) "The Lord Almighty will lash them with a whip [scourge], as when he struck down Midian at the rock of Oreb." (Isaiah 10:26a) The handle of either depicts the coma of the comet; the lash or flail is the tail.

Rod: The Lord delivers punitive blows with a rod. "Every stroke the Lord lays on them with his punishing rod will be to the music of tambourines and harps, as he fights them in battle with the blows of his arm." (Isaiah 30:32) The hand holding the rod is the coma; the rod is the comet's tail. This is within one of the clearest Day of the Lord contexts (see Isaiah 30:27-33).

Club: Held in the same way as a rod, but more compact, a club also is wielded as a punitive tool. "Does the ax raise itself above him who swings it, or the saw boast against him who uses it? As if a rod were to wield him who lifts it up, or a club brandish him who is not wood." (Isaiah 10:15). There is much comet imagery here. The hand brandishing the club is the coma; the club is the tail.

Staff: A staff may be used punitively, but also in the Bible it represents an extension of the Lord's arm when held by a leader such as Moses. "The Lord Almighty will lash them with a whip, as when he struck down Midian at the rock of Oreb; and he will raise his staff over the waters, as he did in Egypt." (Isaiah 10:26) The next reference is to *that day*, so this is a Day of the Lord text. The curvature of the crook of the staff represents the comet's coma; the stick is the tail.

Scepter: The Lord wields His heavenly scepter to administer blows of punishment. "The voice of the Lord will shatter Assyria; with his scepter he will strike them down." (Isaiah 30:31) The rounded top of the scepter is the coma; the wand is the tail. The reference to Assyria is about the comet event of 701 B.C., but this is in a Day of the Lord context that makes it also about Jesus' Second Coming.

Ball/Chain: The combination of ball and chain is a single object of punishment. The chain binds, while the ball immobilizes. "And the angels who did not keep their positions of authority but abandoned their own home— these he has kept in darkness, bound with everlasting chains for judgment on the great Day." (Jude 6) The ball represents the coma; the chain is the tail.

Familiar Things

There are seven cometic depictions having various uses that may be included under the category of familiar things:

Hammer: The Lord strikes blows with His celestial hammer. It breaks the oppressors of His people before being broken itself. "How broken and shattered is the hammer of the whole earth!" (Jeremiah 50:23) The head of the hammer depicts the comet's coma. The handle is the tail.

Tent Peg: Overwhelmed by its burden, the cosmic tent peg breaks loose from its position in the sky and falls to Earth on the Day of the Lord. "In that day," declares the Lord Almighty, "the peg driven into the firm place will give way; it will be sheared off and will fall, and the load hanging on it will be cut down." (Isaiah 22:25). The head of the peg is the comet's coma. The stake is the tail.

Millstone: A boulder breaks off the Day-of-the-Lord comet and falls into an ocean, generating an enormous tsunami. "Then a mighty angel picked up a boulder the size of a large millstone and threw it into the sea." (Revelation 18:21) The stone represents the comet's coma. The drive shaft is the tail.

Sieve: The shaken sieve releases destructive fallout onto the Earth and its wayward inhabitants. "[The Lord] shakes the nations in the sieve of destruction; he places in the jaws of the peoples a bit that leads them astray." (Isaiah 30:28) The vessel of the sieve may be visualized as the comet's coma, the fallout as its tail.

Potter's Jar: The Lord smashes His vessel of pottery in the heavens, and its pieces strike the Earth, killing many people. Their bodies pile up in Topheth, also known as the Valley of Slaughter (see Jer. 19:6). "This is what the Lord Almighty says: 'I will smash this [sinful] nation and this city just as this potter's jar is smashed and cannot be repaired. They will bury the dead in Topheth until there is no more room.'" (Jeremiah 19:11) The vessel of the jar is the comet's coma; the neck is the tail.

Plumb Line and Measuring Line: Although mentioned in the same context of Scriptures, the plumb line and measuring line are visually different and have different uses. As the comet descends it looks in various phases like a plumb line or a measuring line sizing up God's enemies for their demise. "God will stretch out over Edom the measuring line of chaos and the plumb line of desolation." (Isaiah 34:11) The plumb line is the comet in vertical appearance. The measuring line is the comet stretched out horizontally.

Darkness and Light

Six objects representing the dense darkness and brilliant light present during various aspects of the Day of the Lord's comet events will be viewed in the sky on that day:

Sackcloth of Hair: The sun will be eclipsed by the comet, and the moon will look ruddy through a huge cloud of comet dust. Many people will die when the Earth quakes and many more when the comet releases a barrage of bolides that look like stars falling from the sky. The dead will be mourned in sackcloth. "There was a great earthquake. The sun turned black like sackcloth made of goat hair, the whole moon turned blood red, and the stars in the sky fell to earth." (Revelation 6:12-13) Sackcloth of hair is related to the traditional view of a comet as a hairy or bearded star. The star is the coma. The hair or beard is the tail.

Candle and Lamp: A Hebrew word in Zephaniah's Day of the Lord prophecy had the optional meanings of *candle* or *lamp*. As that day approaches, He will shine the light (candle, lamp) of His truth into the dark corners of the hearts of people who have become lukewarm or complacent. "At that time [the Lord] will search Jerusalem with lamps and punish those who are complacent." (Zephaniah 1:12) The KJV uses the word *candles* instead of *lamps*. The flame of both lamp and candle may be viewed as the coma of the comet. The wax shaft of the candle and oil feeder of the lamp are seen as the tail.

Torch: "A great star, blazing like a torch, fell from the sky on a third of the rivers and on the springs of water—the name of the star is Wormwood." (Revelation 8:10) Wormwood means *bitter*. The pollution caused by dust and other debris from a descending "star" that looks like a torch will turn the waters of Earth undrinkable. The flaming end of the torch is the comet's coma, the handle its tail.

Firepot: On the Day of the Lord He will give His people a role in executing judgment on the oppressive peoples who are responsible for the terrible tribulations and persecutions at the time of the end. "On that day I will make the leaders of Judah like a firepot in a woodpile, like a flaming torch among sheaves. They will consume right and left all the surrounding peoples." (Zechariah 12:6) The hot belly of the firepot is the coma of the comet; flaming exhaust is the tail.

Flashing Rays: The power and glory of the returning Lord will be displayed by the radiance of the comet: It will resemble His hand with rays flashing from it. "[God's] splendor was like the sunrise; rays flashed from his hand, where his power was hidden." (Habakkuk 3:4) God's hand is the coma. The rays are the tail. On many occasions the tails of comets have been seen streaked with two or more "rays." So shall it be on the "day of trouble." (Hab. 3:16) Although not quoted in full, the third chapter of Habakkuk is replete with world-ending comet imagery.

The Lord

Eight comet images relate specifically to the Lord on His Day:

Sprouting Branch: "A shoot will come up from the stump of Jesse; from his roots a Branch will bear fruit." (Isaiah 11:1) Jesus is the branch emanating from the "stump" of David's father, Jesse. He bears fruit in righteousness, justice and judgment. The stump is the comet's coma; the branch is its tail.

Breath of His Lips: On the Day of the Lord's return, He will set hell ablaze with His fiery breath—a sulfurous blast from the disintegrating comet. "Topheth has long been prepared; it has been made ready for the king...the breath of the Lord, like a stream of burning sulfur, sets it ablaze." (Isaiah 30:33) The Lord's lips are depicted by the coma, His breath by the tail.

Cup of His Wrath: Before Jesus died He drank from the cup of suffering for the sake of His people. When He comes back He will pour out from on high the cup of His wrath upon His enemies. "The great city split into three parts, and the cities of the nations collapsed. God remembered Babylon the Great and gave her the cup filled with the wine of the fury of his wrath." (Revelation 16:19) Viewed from beneath, the receptacle of the cup is the coma; the handle is the tail.

Rod of His Mouth: This is slightly different from the conventional picture of a hand-held rod listed among punitive objects. The Lord is identified as the Word of God, most notably in John 1:1. The image of a punitive rod projecting from His mouth may be even more frightening to an unbeliever than one held by hand. "He will strike the earth with the rod of his mouth; with the breath of his lips he will slay the wicked." (Isaiah 11:4) The mouth is the coma; the rod is the tail.

Golden Censer: Jesus' judgmental acts on the Day of the Lord will come in response to prayers of the saints rising like incense from the golden censer in the sky. "Another angel, who had a golden censer, came and stood at the altar...The smoke of the incense, together with the prayers of the saints, went up before God from the angel's hand." (Revelation 8:3-4) A censer is the coma of a vertical comet; incense rising from it is the tail.

Golden Altar: "Then the angel took the censer, filled it with fire from the altar, and hurled it on the earth; and there came peals of thunder, rumblings, flashes of lightning and an earthquake." (Revelation 8:5) Just as it can be visualized as a censer, a comet may appear like the altar from which fire is taken to fill the censer. The comet context is identified by the thunderous rumblings, lightning flashes and earthquake of the quoted verse. The golden altar is the comet's coma; smoke rising from the sacrificial animal being burned upon it is the tail (Rev. 9:13).

His Upraised Hand: The hand of the Lord is raised in judgment. "Therefore the Lord's anger burns against his people; his hand is raised and he strikes them down. The mountains shake, and the dead bodies are like refuse in the streets. Yet for all this, his anger is not turned away, his hand is still upraised." (Isaiah 5:25) In another depiction of a vertical comet, the Lord's upraised hand is the coma; His forearm is the tail beneath it.

His Arm Stretched Out: The arm of the Lord is stretched out to receive His people into His eternal kingdom. "The Lord will lay bare his holy arm in the sight of all nations, and all the ends of the earth will see the salvation of our God." (Isaiah 52:10) Now in the final horizontal position, stretched out across the sky, the Lord's arm is the comet's tail; His hand is the coma.

Militant Objects

There are seven objects that have been associated with military operations, especially in antiquity when comets most often appeared. They may be seen as implements of the Lord for His employment at the battle of Armageddon:

Sword: The Lord assaults the Earth and slays its inhabitants by means of a double-edged sword (the Word of God) issuing from His mouth. "My sword has drunk its fill in the heavens; see, it descends in judgment on Edom, the people I have totally destroyed. The sword of the Lord is bathed in blood." (Isaiah 34:5-6) The sword's scabbard is the coma, its blade the tail. It will be seen "bathed in blood" when viewed through the red dust of the comet tail.

Banner: Every eye will see, and every ear hear the approach of the celestial object that will serve as the sign of the Lord's Second Coming. "[The Lord] lifts up a banner for the distant nations…All you people of the world, you who live on the earth, when a banner is raised on the mountains, you will see it, and when a trumpet sounds, you will hear it." (Isaiah 5:26a, 18:3) The undulating tail of the close-range comet is the banner blowing in the breeze; by implication, there must be a hand or something else holding the banner, that is, the coma.

Spear: In a text that could refer to the past event of the Long Day of Joshua or in future to the Day of the Lord, the prophet Habakkuk said: "Sun and moon stood still in the heavens at the glint of your flying arrows, at the lightning of your flashing spear." (Habakkuk 3:11) The first, of course, was a comet event, as will be the second. A "flashing spear" is a brilliant image of a comet. The deadly head of the spear is the coma and the handle is the tail.

Bow/Arrows: The Lord will take aim with His celestial bow and shoot flaming arrows onto the Earth. The Habakkuk verse cited above about the spear also effectively describes the flying arrows launched by the Lord's bow. And there is also this extension of the first part of the celestial text about the banner: "Their arrows are sharp, all their bows are strung; their horses' hoofs seem like flint, their chariot wheels like a whirlwind." (Isaiah 5:28) The bow is the comet with a curved tail; the arrows are the fiery missiles launched by the bow.

Chariot: The second half of Isaiah 5:28 introduced the chariot, and there is also this marvelous biblical image of the fiery wrath that will be unleashed from on high on the Day of the Lord: "See, the Lord is coming with fire, and his chariots are like a whirlwind; he will bring down his anger with fury, and his rebuke with flames of fire. For with fire and with his sword the Lord will execute judgment upon all men, and many will be those slain by the Lord." (Isaiah 66:15-16) A chariot wheel, viewed singly from one side, is the coma of the comet; the galloping horses are the undulating tail during the final phase of the event.

Arrow: Not identical to the image of the bow and arrows above, a solitary celestial arrow provides a different picture. On the Day of the Lord, an object resembling an arrow will be prominent in the sky. "Then the Lord will appear over them; his arrow will flash like lightning." (Zechariah 9:14a) The comparison of the arrow with lightning shows that its appearance will light up the sky. The head of the arrow is the coma; the shaft is the tail.

Sling Stones: The Lord uses a cosmic sling to hurl bolides down upon the Earth. He will shield His people from the onslaught: "The sovereign Lord will sound the trumpet; he will march in the storms of the south, and the Lord Almighty will shield them. They will destroy and overcome with slingstones. The Lord their God will save them on that day." (Zechariah 9:14b-16a) A stone is the coma of the comet; the sling is its tail.

Creatures Great and Small

It takes imagination to view comets as living creatures, but ancient people often did so. These seven were mentioned in the Bible's Day of the Lord prophecies:

Dragon: Satan, that great red dragon, has been cast down from heaven to Earth and seeks to destroy it. "Then another sign appeared in heaven: an enormous red dragon with seven heads and ten horns and seven crowns on his heads. His tail swept a third of the stars out of the sky and flung them to earth." (Revelation 12:3-4) The dragon's head is the coma; his body and tail comprise the tail of the comet. The "stars" falling from the sky are meteors from the comet's tail.

Scorpion and Locusts: As the cosmic "creature" descends, it holds its sting in the vertical position. It strikes painful piercing blows downward upon the Earth. "And out of the smoke locusts came down upon the earth and were given power like that of scorpions of the earth…They had tails and stings like scorpions, and in their tails they had power to torment people for five months." (Revelation 9:3, 10)

The body of the scorpion is the comet's coma; the stinger is the tail. When the comet draws near to Earth, the undulations of its tail resemble leaping locusts and it makes noises like a locust swarm.

Serpent: A fiery flying serpent, like a fire-breathing dragon, is either weird mythology or an excellent description of the comet that will bring distress into the world on the Day of the Lord. "Into the land of trouble and anguish, from whence come the young and old lion, the viper and fiery flying serpent, they will carry their riches upon the shoulders of young asses, and their treasures upon the [humps] of camels, to a people that shall not profit them." (Isaiah 30:6, KJV)

The serpent's head is the coma; its twisting body is the comet's undulating tail.

Eagle: A great eagle soars through the heavens and descends to seize the Earth in its talons. This will take place when trumpet blasts proclaim this world's termination and the establishment of the new heavens and earth. "As I watched, I heard an eagle that was flying in midair call out in a loud voice: 'Woe! Woe! Woe to the inhabitants of the earth, because of the trumpet blasts about to be sounded by the other three angels!'" (Revelation 8:13) An eagle will be one of the forms assumed by the comet during the final cataclysm of world history. The eagle's head is the coma; its body is the tail. Its wings, in the lowered position, are the comet's appendages extending toward Earth; its "talons" are comet-spawned tornadoes.

Lion: On the Day of the Lord the great comet will descend with terrible roaring noises, like a celestial lion growling over its prey. The Earth will be darkened and its peoples distressed. "Their roar is like that of the lion, they roar like young lions; they growl as they seize their prey and carry it off with no one to rescue. In that day they will roar over it like the roaring of the sea. And if one looks at the land, he will see darkness and distress; even the light will be darkened by the clouds." (Isaiah 5:29-30) Seen from in front, the head and mane of the lion form a clear image of the comet's coma. The legs and feet are downward extensions, probably tornadoes. The lion's tail is also the tail of the comet.

Mouse: It's a big fall from lion to mouse, but we saw in Chapter Nine that a mouse may represent a comet, figuratively speaking. When a comet approaches Earth, its coma distends until it assumes the shape of the body of a mouse. Its tail, of course, is seen as the tail of the mouse. " 'Those who sanctify themselves and purify themselves to go to the gardens after an idol in the midst, eating swine's flesh and the abomination and the mouse, shall be consumed together,' says the Lord. 'For I know their works and their thoughts. It shall be that I will gather all nations and tongues; and they shall come and see My glory.' " (Isaiah 66:17-18)

Yes, even a mouse.

Plagues of Revelation

There are three sets of plagues in the book of Revelation. All three are similar to the plagues of Exodus that God brought about through the medium of a comet:

Flying Scroll Unrolled: On the Day of the Lord, Jesus will open the seven seals of a celestial scroll. The opening of each seal will unleash a plague upon the Earth as described in Revelation 5:1-8:5. "I looked again—and there before me was a flying scroll! [The Lord] asked me, 'What do you see?' I answered, 'I see a flying scroll, thirty feet long and fifteen feet wide.' " (Zechariah 5:1-2) The knob of the scroll is the comet's coma; the scroll is the tail. After the unsealing, as the scroll is unrolled, its contents fall in meteoric sheets from the disintegrating tail of the comet.

Trumpet Sounding: The sound of a cosmic trumpet signals the ingathering of the redeemed and launches the seven trumpet plagues described in Revelation 8:6-11:19. "The sign of the Son of Man will appear in the sky, and all the nations of the earth will mourn. They will see the Son of Man coming on the clouds of the sky, with power and great glory. And he will send his angels with a loud trumpet call, and they will gather his elect from the four winds, from one end of the heavens to the other." (Matthew 24:30-31) The bell horn of the trumpet is the comet's coma; the air tube is the tail.

Bowls Poured Out: First the meteoric tail, then the bolidic contents of the coma of the great comet are "poured out" onto the Earth during the final bowl plagues described in Revelation 15:1-18:24. "Then I heard a loud voice from the temple saying to the seven angels, 'Go, pour out the seven bowls of God's wrath on the earth.' " (Revelation 16:1) The bowl is the coma; the outpourings come from the comet's hornlike projections and its tail.

Summary

We have committed an entire chapter to the shapes of objects mentioned in Bible texts about the Day of the Lord when Jesus returns. Primary purpose of this is to continue building evidence to affirm the premise that a comet will be the sign of Jesus' Second Coming (Mat. 24:30).It seems clear at this point that a comet will be that sign, but we shall consider the mathematical odds and other evidentiary details in the next chapter. For now, it is enough to know that 54 comet-like objects have been found in Day of the Lord biblical texts, and that 36 of them (two-thirds) were mentioned during the discussion of comet events in the first thirteen chapters of this book. These are the 54:

- **Judgmental Objects (9)**: Ax, saw, broom, shovel, fork, fan, sickle, key/star, hand/chain.

- **Punitive Implements (7)**: Whip, scourge, rod, club, staff, scepter, ball/chain.

- **Familiar Things (7)**: Hammer, tent peg, millstone, sieve, potter's jar, plumb line, measuring line.

- **Darkness and Light (6)**: Sackcloth of hair, candle, lamp, torch, firepot, flashing rays.

- **The Lord (8)**: Sprouting branch, breath of lips, cup of wrath, rod of mouth, censer, altar, upraised hand, stretched out arm.

- **Militant Objects (7)**: Sword, banner, spear, bow/arrows, chariot, arrow, sling stones.

- **Creatures Great and Small (7)**: Dragon, scorpion, locusts, serpent, eagle, lion, mouse.

- **Plagues of Revelation (3)**: Flying scroll unrolled, trumpets sounding, bowls poured out.

Chapter Fifteen

Facts & Figures

DAY-OF-THE-LORD PROPHECY OF Jesus' Second Coming begins with and is a focal point of the Book of Isaiah. From Isaiah we learn these facts about life on Earth during the era just preceding and including that day:

- There is rampant idolatry and occultism (Isa. 2:6–8)

- Terrified people hide in caves and bunkers (Isa. 2:19)

- Injustice, greed, drunkenness, unbelief, and arrogance (Isa. 5)

- Desolation, plunder, mourning, defilement, burning (Isa. 24)

- War, tribulation, crime, treachery, and insolence (Isa. 33)

- Thunder, earthquake, windstorm, and flames (Isa. 29:6)

- Consuming fire, cloudburst, and hail of stones (Isa. 30:30)

- Sky trembles, earth shakes off its axis (Isa. 2:19, 21; 13:13; 24:1)
- Sky rolls up like a scroll, "stars" fall to earth (Isa. 34:4)
- Streams turn to pitch, dust to burning sulfur (Isa. 34:9)
- Heavens disappear amid thick smoke, people perish (Isa. 51:6)
- Mountains and high hills crumble (Isa. 54:10)
- The Lord comes to execute judgment (Isa. 66:15–16)

It is not the purpose of this book to dwell on the distresses of the prophesied tribulation before Jesus' return. It is described by Isaiah and by Jesus Himself in a sermon quoted extensively by three New Testament writers. It won't be a pleasant time, and Christians should prepare for the worst, including the possibility of persecution (Mat. 24:9-22).

The bad news is that some Christians will suffer. The good news is that those who suffer will do so *for the honor of the name of Jesus*. Early Christians welcomed persecution because they believed that by participating in the sufferings of Christ they would insure a resurrection with nearness to Him commensurate with their sufferings.

Peter, who according to ancient tradition was crucified upside down, wrote this: "Rejoice to the extent that you partake of Christ's sufferings, that when His glory is revealed, you may also be glad with exceeding joy." (1 Pet. 4:13)

Except for John, every faithful apostle was martyred for the sake of Christ. The martyrdom of Christians has pervaded history since the ascension of Jesus. It escalated during the 20th century A.D. and has continued at a high level to the present day.

Recommended reading on this subject begins with the biblical book of 1 Peter. Also, the writings of Richard Wurmbrand, Corrie ten Boom and Dietrich Bonhoeffer. A daily devotional book that beautifully portrays positive aspects of tribulation is *Streams in the Desert*. There are several versions in print of John Foxe's books about Christian martyrs, including one distributed by an organization established by Wurmbrand, Voice of the Martyrs, in Bartlesville, OK.

Reading such books contributes to the readiness recommended by Jesus for believers expectantly awaiting His return (Mat. 24:44). And we are encouraged to pray so that we may be found worthy to escape some of the prophesied distresses (Luke 21:36).

How Then Should We Live?

Many books have been written about Christian living under various circumstances. For the issue at hand, it is good to focus on the words of Jesus, especially as they pertain to the time of the end. In His response to the disciples' question of when He would return and what would be the sign of His coming, Jesus emphasized that they couldn't know when

(Mat. 24:36, 42, 44). He said to ignore false prophets who claim to know the time element (Mat. 24:23-27).

This should forestall holding one's breath in eager anticipation on every day in which there is a regularly scheduled lunar eclipse. Jesus is not going to return on a day predicted by anyone, so we should disregard this and all other such forecasts. Ignoring false prophecy is rule No. 1 for end-time living.

In His end-time sermon, Jesus also told His disciples that they should watch for the signs of His coming and prepare for it. When Jesus returns, His believers will take the longest trip of their existence, to the heavens above. Whatever preparations we make for shorter, less important trips on this Earth should be multiplied many times over in readiness for our heavenly journey. We should study the "road map" outlined in the Bible, and we should discuss our trip with the Planner of the event. We should talk to Him about everything that is going on in our lives until the time comes to meet Him in the sky.

Since tribulation involving all nations is to be a part of the preparatory phase for the journey, we should be in prayer about that (Mat. 24:21-22). Whatever nation is our homeland should be a featured subject of our prayers. As a citizen of the United States, I am disappointed by the sparseness of prayers being offered to God on behalf of this spiritually ill land. Though it once was plentiful in the ways of God, it has become a place of pervasive sin and lethargy.

Many have denied Jesus, as Peter did, or even betrayed him, as Judas did. All of us should pray for ourselves that we may be found faithful to the end (See the sixth highlighted item below).

The book of Revelation was written near the end of the first century B.C., looking ahead to the days preceding Jesus' return. The warnings issued to the seven churches (early believers) are also relevant for us:

- Remember and embrace your first love for Jesus (Rev. 2:4-5).
- Do not be afraid of suffering for Jesus's sake (Rev. 2:10).
- Identify and reject false doctrines (Rev. 2:14-16).
- Avoid idolatrous greed and sexual immorality (Rev. 2:20).
- Repent of deadly indifference (Rev. 3:3).
- Persevere in faithfulness to the end (Rev. 3:10-11).
- Repent of sickening lukewarmness (Rev. 3:16-17).

The meaning of most of these is clear, but what about "deadly indifference" and "sickening lukewarmness"? They sound like different ways of saying the same thing, but what did Jesus mean by them?

These things are evident in the church today. The church on its deathbed is the one whose members ignore

God's Word, if they bother to read it or preach it or teach/ learn it at all. They do not tithe. They do not pray. Many of them do not even worship God on a weekly basis.

The lukewarm church is the dominant one right now in the U.S.A. Described by Jesus as wealthy and arrogant ("I am rich…and have need of nothing"), this is the church that makes Him sick to His stomach. It has been gifted with much but does little with it. Its members have no idea that they are spiritually "wretched, miserable, poor, blind, and naked." (Rev. 3:16-17) Jesus says He prefers them to be cold or hot to lukewarm (Rev. 3:16). To Him, it is better that we should be unashamedly dead, like the church at Sardis, than to be putting on a pretense of living faith, like Laodicea. He abhors hypocrisy.

If we do just one thing, we'll be found worthy of honor when Jesus' returns. That one thing is sustaining a fervent faith in the God and Father of our Lord Jesus Christ—a faith that demands regular worship, pervasive prayer, participation in serious Bible study, and joyful presentation of tithes and offerings so that the Lord's work on Earth can be advanced.

But that's not all we can do. We should encourage one another in the faith and continue meeting together (Heb. 10:25). We should conduct ourselves as living examples of our faith, even when falsely accused (1 Pet. 2:12). We should demonstrate love for one another (1 John 4:16-17). We should strive to keep pure, blameless and holy until the Day of the Lord (2 Pet. 3:11, Phil. 1:10).

The Last Days Narration

Worldwide tribulation has ended. The sign of Jesus' return—a great comet—is visible in the sky. Each night it grows larger. It is expected to make a close approach to Earth in about one year. Astronomers have computed and recomputed its orbital pattern. They see planet and comet coming together on a near-collision course during the autumnal season.

One wishful-thinking scientist has acquired instant fame. He dares to question the others' near-unanimous proclamation that this comet is large enough to render the Earth uninhabitable if it approaches within a few thousand miles and disintegrates, splattering the Earth with deadly bolides; and that it will, indeed, come closer than the computed minimum.

The lone voice, of course, is the popular one. He is invited to appear on network programming of all national television and radio media. He is being paid a lot of money for his cheerful prognostications that Earth will survive and thrive. Recognizing the value of saying what people want to hear, he embellishes his comments with more and more optimism each day until he views the comet as no threat whatsoever to the prosperity of the planet.

Meanwhile, the comet grows a smidge larger in the sky every night.

The popular scientist has convinced a majority of the world's population that they have nothing to worry about. Discerning Christians, however, aren't listening to him. Recognizing in the comet potential fulfillment of the Bible's Day of the Lord prophecies, they are preparing for the great event. There is no anxiety among them for they understand that they will rise into the presence of the Lord before the comet unleashes the assault that writes an end to human history.

Inspired by the Holy Spirit, believers in all parts of the world are studying biblical imagery extending beyond the 54 comet shapes. They are impressed by the figurative use of the word valley *in four parts of the Bible. In the twenty-third psalm they find the valley of the shadow of death. They compare this with the valley of weeping (Psalm 84:6) and the valley of slaughter (Jer. 19:6). They come to understand that these three "valleys" have meaning for themselves and their planet. But the most significant of the four is that of the prophet Joel.*

They read and re-read Joel's prophecy: "Multitudes, multitudes in the valley of decision! For the day of the Lord is near in the valley of decision. The sun and moon will grow dark, and the stars will diminish their brightness. The Lord also will roar from Zion, and utter His voice from Jerusalem; the heavens and earth will shake; but the Lord will be a shelter for His people." (Joel 3:14–16a)

Word spreads among joyful Christians: They believe the comet is to be the greatest tool for revival in the history of the world, and they begin praying for this. When unbelievers finally recognize the truth and begin cowering in fear of what is coming upon the Earth, believers will have a chance to tell them about Jesus and offer them an opportunity to make the *most important decision of their lives: Believe in the Lord Jesus and accept His offer of forgiveness for sins with assurance of eternal life, or refuse the offer and doom themselves to the wages of sin. (John 3:36, Romans 6:23)*

The believers can hardly wait for the great opportunity to participate in the last-chance harvest of millions of people into the kingdom of God. During the final weeks before the Day of the Lord—a day they know is coming though they cannot pinpoint the exact one—they concentrate on praying about Jesus' arrival, living holy lives, and providing examples of faithfulness and love for multitudes who are struggling to hold their heads above the surging waters of unbelief. And so it happens, during the final days, that fearful unbelievers are impressed by the calm faith and compassion of believers. Many unbelievers open their hearts to the gospel message as it is boldly proclaimed by the Lord's faithful remnant:

"God demonstrates His own love toward us, in that while we were still sinners, Christ died for us…For He made Him who knew no sin to be sin for us, that we might become the righteousness of God in Him." (Rom. 5:8, 2 Cor. 5:21).

And multitudes are saved in the valley of decision while the great Day of the Lord draws near!

How Many?

We have mentioned the Prophet Joel's "valley of decision" three times in this book. Like the valley of the shadow of death of Psalm 23, it is not a literal place but a figurative or spiritual one. Indeed, the "valley of decision" is a place of spiritual death for all of those who refuse Jesus' final offer, through His faithful witnesses, to forgive their sins and give them eternal life. If this is the correct interpretation, the "multitudes, multitudes" refer to an uncountable number of people, including all except those who have been redeemed by the blood of the Lamb, Jesus Christ (Rev. 7:14).

This indefinite number's contrast is the number of the redeemed in heaven, "ten thousand times ten thousand and thousands of thousands." (Rev. 5:11) Ten thousand times ten thousand is a phrase indicating an uncountable number. Literally, it equals a hundred million. But with these must be included thousands of thousands, so this extravagant language seems to imply that we must add at least one more decimal place, perhaps more, for a sufficiency to include the full number of the redeemed from all eras of world history.

If at present there are one-billion redeemed persons alive in the world, it leaves at least six-billion unredeemed. All of these, if they survive the tribulation and are still alive as the Day of the Lord approaches, will be viewed from the perspective of the God in heaven as the "multitudes, multitudes" in the valley of decision. They will have one more chance to decide where to spend eternity.

The Hebrew word *hamon* translated *multitudes* appears only a few times in the Bible, most of them in the book of Ezekiel. A key verse is Ezekiel 39:11, which refers to "the valley of Hamon Gog," i.e., the multitudes of Gog. This falls within a clear passage about what is referred to in the book of Revelation as the Battle of Armageddon, which will take place on the Day of the Lord.

The multitudes of Gog are led by the demonic "princes" of Gog, along with Magog, Rosh, Meshech and Tubal. They are allied with the pagan peoples of Persia, Ethiopia, Libya, Gomer, Togarmah, Sheba, Dedan and Tarshish. This encompasses the uttermost parts of the Earth as was known to the Prophet Ezekiel and his contemporaries. For us, therefore, it means everybody who is not committed to God the Father and His Son, Jesus Christ.

Talk about an opportunity for revival!

The only other place in the Bible that mentions Gog and Magog is Rev. 20:7. Here, too, it accompanies a futuristic description of troops massing in opposition to the Lord. "And fire came down from God out of heaven and devoured them." (Rev. 20:9)

Repeatedly in this book we have seen that consumptive fires fall from the skies during a comet event. Are we correct then in our conclusion that the Day of the Lord will feature a comet, streaked across the sky, signifying the return of Jesus? (Mat. 24:27-30)

Here's what Ezekiel prophesied about this Day-of-the-Lord event: " 'Surely in that day there shall be a great earthquake in the land of Israel, so that the fish of the sea, the birds of the heavens, the beasts of the field, all creeping things that creep on the earth, and all men who are on the face of the earth shall shake at My presence. The mountains shall be thrown down, the steep places shall fall, and every wall shall fall to the ground.'

"I will call for a sword against Gog throughout all My mountains," says the Lord God. "Every man's sword will be against his brother. And I will bring him to judgment with pestilence and bloodshed; I will rain down on him, on his troops, and on the many peoples who are with him flooding rain, great hailstones, fire, and brimstone. Thus I will magnify Myself and sanctify Myself, and I will be known in the eyes of many nations. Then they shall know that I am the Lord." (Ezek. 38:19b-23)

This is descriptive of a comet event. We know from repeated biblical exposure that the reference to hailstones means, literally, a hail of large stones, and the reference to brimstone means explosive sulfurous bolides. Everything described here is characteristic of a comet event.

For the sake of contrast, let's suppose that believers are uninformed that a comet is to signify the Day of the Lord. What would be the consequences of such ignorance?

In the first place, the believers themselves might be fearful—something that would not happen if they recognized the celestial sign. Their testimony would be negligible because they would have no vision for the "valley of decision." Instead of viewing the impending event as a great opportunity, some might see it as a great catastrophe and join unbelievers in weeping and mourning. Without the joyous testimony of believers, the multitudes in the "valley" would not even be informed that there was something important for them to decide.

Considered from this negative perspective, it becomes clear why the Lord wants believers to watch for the sign of His return, to identify it, and then to fulfill His wishes to become faithful witnesses to everyone in that "valley."

Odds and Ends

Four of the twelve houses of the Zodiac contain constellations with shapes that may be identified with comets. These four incorporate twelve such objects out of a total of sixteen. The other eight houses, in total, contain zero comet-shaped objects out of a total of 32 constellations. The odds against such a scenario being random are more than 100,000-to-one. It is near certain that the reason for the concentration of twelve comet-shaped objects in four houses is that the four were seen to be the areas of the sky from which comets emerged to make dangerously close approaches to Earth.

The four are Scorpio the scorpion, Sagittarius the archer, Capricornus the goat-fish and Leo the lion. We know that Capricornus is identifiable with comets because ancient far-eastern peoples associated the comet-sign of Jesus' birth with Capricornus. We know that Leo is identifiable with comets because the remnants of a comet seen to originate in Leo's area of the sky are known as Leonids.

It is likely that Sagittarius has cometic roots because three of the four celestial signs within its dominion have shapes often attributed to comets—an archer with bow and arrow, an altar and a dragon. Likewise, Scorpio has three comet-associated images—a scorpion and two serpents.

But we want to stay on the conservative side, so we will not quibble over the understated odds, but instead will accept the idea that these are trustworthy numbers and that one quarter (12 of 48) of the constellations are randomly comet-shaped. If this were true, it would mean the odds would be three-to-one (36 to 12) against the chance of a celestial image assuming the appearance of a comet.

We have found in the Bible's Day of the Lord texts the imagery of 54 pictures with shapes and characteristics identifiable with comets. Using three-to-one odds, this means that if the Bible's cosmic imagery is random, Day of the Lord scriptures should contain at least 162 figurative pictures bearing no resemblance to comets (three times 54).

The author has read carefully through the Bible's Day of the Lord texts numerous times during the past decade. Once, he read for the specific purpose of identifying non-cometic images. How many of the mathematically anticipated 162 has he found?

The answer, so far, is zero.

Based on the conservative three-to-one odds, we actually should find hundreds of non-cometic objects in the Day of the Lord sections of the Bible because, in total, counting repeated sightings of such objects as the celestial sword, there are a great many more than 54 cometary objects. The sword alone makes dozens of appearances in these scriptures.

At this point there is but one more thing to do: Issue a challenge to skeptics to find Day of the Lord imagery depicting anything other than comets in the Bible... anything at all. If there are none to be found or even a very few, it is because Jesus wants His people to *know* that a comet will be the sign of His Second Coming.

One of the popular lottery gambling games is known as pick-six. Out of a specified total of numbers—usually 40 or more—the game player is asked to pick the exact six that will be selected at random by a machine. If there were 54 numbers in a game of pick-six, the odds would be about 17-million-to-one against a direct hit by a game player.

This means accurate selection of six out of 54. What do you suppose the odds should be against getting *all 54*, which is an approximation of what is being asked of the "players" in the celestial game suggested by the Bible's Day of the Lord imagery?

Celestial signs are instructional (Gen. 1:14). We know that the Lord wants His people to recognize the sign of His coming, and to be watchful for it, and prepared for His appearance—not just because of the overwhelming odds favoring the comet identity, but because He said so and He does not lie (Mat. 24:29-30, 42-44; Titus 1:2).

Part Two Summation

Now, as we did at the end of Part One, let's summarize the chapters in Part Two of this book.

In Chapter Ten, we learned that ancient peoples associated comets with the birth and death of kings and other important events. A comet that first appeared in 5 B.C. and reappeared a year later was most likely the "star" seen by the magi heralding the birth of Jesus, the King of kings. There are ten logical reasons to believe that the Christmas "star" was a large comet and not a conjunction or occultation of planets. Planetary conjunctions and occultations went virtually unnoticed by ancient peoples who did not have powerful telescopes.

In Chapter Eleven, we saw that when Jesus died the Earth quaked so mightily that the sturdiest building in Jerusalem—the temple—was severely damaged. The heavy curtain within the temple was ripped in half at the same time as a three-hour solar eclipse was reaching conclusion. Another severe earthquake happened three days later when Jesus arose from the dead. Similar seismic events occurred worldwide at this time, in A.D. 30. A comet is the only known source of simultaneous celestial and terrestrial disturbances of this duration and magnitude. Ordinary eclipses of the sun by the moon last no longer than a few minutes.

We showed in Chapter Twelve that if a comet having an orbit of about 2,000 years is the one that will signify Jesus's return, it probably made two appearances during Old Testament times. One occurred between 1975 and 1980 B.C. when the Tower of Babel was destroyed by discharge from a comet. An exploding sulfurous bolide blew the top off the tower, charred the middle third and, like a hammer, drove the bottom third into the ground. Also likely associated with the 2,000-year comet was the event that terrified Adam and Eve while they were fleeing from the Garden of Eden. God used a "flaming sword"—the most common image of a comet—to bring about this event between 3965 and 3975 B.C.

In Chapter Thirteen, it was emphasized that the Day of the Lord (when Jesus returns) is a prominent theme in the second half of the Bible. Three seven-part series of Day of the Lord plagues occupy half of the book of Revelation. All three—seals of an unrolling scroll, martial trumpets, and bowls pouring out their contents—are comet events. The Jewish Year of Jubilee ("trumpet blasts") may be associated with the trumpet plagues. The culminating battle of world history is described several times in the Bible, but only once is it called Armageddon: God will use a comet to strike down His enemies by a mighty earthquake and a heavy hail of explosive stones along with consumptive firestorms.

Chapter Fourteen's theme: The 54 comet images appearing in the Bible's Day of the Lord texts concerning Jesus' Second Coming include nine judgmental objects, seven punitive implements, seven familiar things, six objects contrasting darkness and light, eight objects describing aspects of the Lord's participation in the event, seven militant objects, seven creatures of varying sizes, and three series of comet plagues described in detail in the book of Revelation.

The Big Picture

The proposition that a comet will be the sign of Jesus' return does not depend solely upon 54 individual images, or even upon hundreds of such images including repeat appearances of the 54 in the Bible's Day of the Lord prophecies. The 54 are edge pieces in the jigsaw puzzle that was introduced in Chapter One.

But there is much more.

The centerpiece of the puzzle consists so far of 24 past comet events, all of which are described in the Bible and discussed in this book, with details added from other reliable sources. Because so many of the most important events described by the Bible were accompanied by the presence of comets, it stands to reason that we should expect that a comet will also be present for the grand finale on the Day of the Lord even if there were not a predominance of comet imagery supporting this idea. But, of course, there is, as we saw in Chapter Thirteen.

And there is plenty of filler between the edges and the centerpiece. A total of 131 important facts about biblically-described comet events, highlighted with bullets at the end of chapters of this book, complete the big picture puzzle looking ahead to the Day of the Lord event, which will be the 25th.

In Chapter Fourteen we listed the 54 comet images, so everything important is mentioned on at least one of our highlight lists other than the 25 biblical comet events. Here is a list of those events as discussed in the first thirteen chapters:

- The global flood of Noah (1)
- The destruction of Sodom (1)
- The plagues of Exodus (1)
- The Red Sea crossing and subsequent Sinai events (7)
- The long day of Joshua (1)
- Events involving Barak, Gideon and Samuel (3)
- Events involving David and Elijah (2)
- The second Elijah event and Amos (2)
- The Isaiah cataclysm (1)
- The birth of Jesus (1)
- The death/resurrection of Jesus (1)
- Eden and Babel/continental separation (2)
- The fall of Jerusalem in A.D. 70 and Jesus' return (2)

Counting edge pieces (54), center pieces (25) and pieces of factual filler (131), this is a jigsaw puzzle with

210 interlocking parts. Every one of them fits in place to complete the big picture, and none of them must be driven in forcibly. Each nestles comfortably into its own niche.

All evidence related to the biblical centerpiece events mentioned above points to a comet as the sign of Jesus' return. The same evidence excludes all other reasonable possibilities.

Bibliography

Forty Books Referenced in the Writing of this One:

Atlas of the Bible, edited by James B. Pritchard; London: HarperCollins Publishers, London: 1997.

Bible Readings for the Home Circle, London: Review & Herald Publishing Assoc., 1921. Quoted from *The American Encyclopedia*, article "Meteor," 1881.

Brown, Walt, *In the Beginning: Compelling Evidence for Creation and the Flood*, Phoenix: The Center for Scientific Creation, eighth edition, 2008.

Cahn, Jonathan, *The Mystery of the Shemitah*, Lake Mary, FL: FrontLine, Charisma House Book Group, 2014.

Church, Alfred J., *Stories from Homer: The Iliad of the Siege of Troy*, New York: Thomas Y. Crowell & Co., undated.

Clarke, Adam, *Adam Clarke's Commentary*, Grand Rapids, MI: Baker Book House, 1967.

Dake's Annotated Reference Bible, Lawrenceville, GA: Dake Bible Sales, Inc., eighth printing, 1974.

Dawson, Buck, *When the Earth Explodes!* Commack, NY: Kroshka Books, 1998.

Goodrick, Edward W. and Kohlenberger, III, John R, *The niv Exhaustive Concordance*. Grand Rapids, MI: Zondervan Publishing House, 1990.

Halley, Henry H., *Halley's Bible Handbook*, New Revised Edition, Grand Rapids, MI: The Zondervan Corp., Twenty-fourth edition, 1965.

Hawass, Zahi, *Tutankhamun and the Golden Age of the Pharaohs*, Washington, D.C.: National Geographic, undated.

Josephus, Flavius *Complete Works*, translated by William Whiston, Grand Rapids, MI: Kregel Publications, 1960.

Kennedy, D. James, *The Real Meaning of the Zodiac*. Fort Lauderdale, FL: CRM Publishing, 1996.

Marshall, Alfred. *The Interlinear Greek-English New Testament;* Grand Rapids, MI: Zondervan Publishing House, 1975.

McDowell, Josh, *The New Evidence that Demands a Verdict*, Nashville: Thomas Nelson Publishers, 1999.

Morris, Henry M., *Many Infallible Proofs,* San Diego: Creation-Life Publishers, 1974.

Morris, Henry M., *The Bible Has the Answer,* Nutley, N.J.: The Craig Press, 1971.

Patten, Donald W., *The Biblical Flood and the Ice Epoch,* Seattle: Pacific Meridian Publishing Co., 1966.

Patten, Donald W.; Hatch, Ronald R., and Steinhauer, Loren C., *The Long Day of Joshua and Six Other Catastrophes*, Seattle: Pacific Meridian Publishing Co., 1973.

Pfeiffer, Charles, and Harrison, Everett, *The Wycliffe Bible Commentary*, Chicago: The Moody Press, 1962.

Pritchard, James B., *Atlas of the Bible*, London: Harper Collins Publishers, 1998.

Rehwinkel, Alfred M., *The Flood*, St. Louis: Concordia Publishing House, 1951.

Strong, James, *The New Strong's Exhaustive Concordance of the Bible*, Nashville, TN: Thomas Nelson Publishers, 1990.

Tenney, Merrill C., *The Zondervan Pictorial Bible Dictionary*. Grand Rapids, MI: Zondervan Publishing House, 1972.

Thayer, Joseph Henry, *The New Thayer's Greek-English Lexicon of the New Testament*, Peabody, MA: Hendrickson Publishers, 1981.

The American Heritage Dictionary of the English Language, Boston: Houghton Mifflin Co., third edition, 1992.

The Amplified Bible, Grand Rapids, MI: Zondervan Publishing House, first printing, 1965.

The Book of Jasher, translated from the original Hebrew into English; Salt Lake City: J. H. Parry & Co., 1887.

The Books Called Apocrypha, the authorized version; London: Oxford University Press, undated.

The History of Herodotus, translated by George Rawlinson; New York: The Dial Press, 1928.

The Holy Bible, King James Version, public domain.

The Modern Language Bible, Grand Rapids, MI: The Zondervan Publishing House, Revised Edition, 1969.

The New English Bible, with Apocrypha; New York: Oxford University Press, 1971.

The niv Study Bible, New International Version, Grand Rapids, MI: Zondervan Publishing House, 1985.

The Old Testament Pseudepigrapha, Sibylline Oracles, Garden City, NY: Doubleday & Co., Inc., 1983.

The Word in Life Study Bible, New King James Version, Nashville, TN: Thomas Nelson Publishers, 1996.

Velikovsky, Immanuel, *Worlds in Collision*, New York: Dell Publishing Co., 1965.

Vermes, Geza. *The Dead Sea Scrolls in English*. London: Penguin Books, 1987.

Whitcomb Jr., John C., and Morris, Henry M., *The Genesis Flood*, Philadelphia: The Presbyterian and Reformed Publishing Co., 1961.

Whitcomb, Jr., John C., *The World that Perished*, Grand Rapids, MI: The Baker Book House, 1973.

Notes

Chapter One: The Great Flood

1   Flavius Josephus, *Complete Works, The Antiquities of the Jews*, translated by William Whiston, (Grand Rapids, MI: Kregel Publications, 1960), 28.

2   Walt Brown, *In the Beginning: Compelling Evidence for Creation and the Flood* (Phoenix: Center for Scientific Creationism, eighth edition, 2008), 105.

3   Charles Pfeiffer and Everett Harrison, *The Wycliffe Bible Commentary* (Chicago: The Moody Press, 1962), 13.

4   Henry H. Halley, *Halley's Bible Handbook*, New Revised Edition, (Grand Rapids, MI: The Zondervan Corp., Twenty-fourth edition, 1965), 75.

5   John C. Whitcomb Jr., *The World that Perished* (Grand Rapids, MI: The Baker Book House, 1973), 54.

6   Buck Dawson, *When the Earth Explodes!* (Commack, NY: Kroshka Books, 1998), 32.

7   Donald W. Patten, *The Biblical Flood and the Ice Epoch* (Seattle: Pacific Meridian Publishing Co., 1966), 159.

8 Alfred M. Rehwinkel, *The Flood* (St. Louis: Concordia Publishing House, 1951), 290-291.

9 Whitcomb, *The World that Perished*, 84.

10 Ibid., 84-85.

11 Patten, 120-121.

12 Ibid., 121.

13 Rehwinkel, 107-108.

14 Ibid., 116.

15 Ibid., 108.

16 John C. Whitcomb Jr. and Henry M. Morris, *The Genesis Flood* (Philadelphia: The Presbyterian and Reformed Publishing Co., 1961), 122.

17 Rehwinkel, 313.

18 Ibid., 247.

19 Dawson, 33.

Chapter Two: Sodom

1 *The Wycliffe Bible Commentary*, 25.

2 *Adam Clarke's Commentary* (Grand Rapids, MI: Baker Book House, 1967), 44.

3 Flavius Josephus, *Complete Works*, *The Antiquities of the Jews*, 1-11-4.

4   Jeffrey Goodman, *The Christian Post, The Comets of God Blog: Was Sodom and Gomorrah Wiped out by a Comet?*

5   James B. Pritchard, *Atlas of the Bible* (London: Harper Collins Publishers, 1998), 118.

6   Josephus, *Antiquities,* 1-8-2.

7   Donald W. Patten, Ronald R. Hatch and Loren C.Steinhauer, *The Long Day of Joshua and Six Other Catastrophes* (Seattle: Pacific Meridian Publishing Co., 1973), back cover.

Chapter Three: The Exodus

1   Josephus, *Antiquities* 2-14-3

2   *The Long Day of Joshua and Six Other Catastrophes*, 211.

3   Josephus, *Antiquities,* 2-14-4.

4   Judith Kane, *Did a Comet Cause the 1871 Great Chicago Fire?* http//www.mysteriesmagazine.com/articles/issue9. html.

5   Ibid.

6   Wikipedia, *Great Chicago Fire*. http://en.wikipedia.org/ wiki/Great_Chicago_Fire, 2.

7   Judith Kane, *Did a Comet Cause the 1871 Great Chicago Fire?* See also Cronaca: *Chicago devastated by comet impact*. www. cronaca.com/archives/002162.html, accessed Feb. 5, 2007.

8   Kane, *Did a Comet Cause the 1871 Great Chicago Fire?*, 2.

9   Ibid.

10 Immanuel Velikovsky, *Worlds in Collision* (New York: Dell Publishing Co., 1965), 180.

11 Ibid.

12 Ibid., 181.

13 Josephus, *Antiquities*, 2-14-5.

14 *The Long Day of Joshua*, 213.

15 Josephus, *Antiquities*, 2-14-6.

16 Zahi Hawass, *Tutankhamun and the Golden Age of the Pharaohs* (Washington, D.C.: National Geographic, undated), 86, 88, 108.

Chapter Four: Sinai

1   Josephus, *Antiquities*, 2-16-1.

2   Ibid., 2-16-3.

3   Ibid.

4   Ibid.

5   The Universe in the Classroom; No. 6—Fall 1986; *What Have We Learned About Halley's Comet?* www.astrosociety.org/uitc.

6   Josephus, *Antiquities*, 3-2-7.

7 Ibid., 3-5-1.

8 Ibid., 3-5-2.

9 Ibid., 4-3-3.

10 Ibid., 4-3-4.

Chapter Five: The Longest Day

1 Ibid., 5-1-17.

2 Josephus, *Complete Works* (Grand Rapids, MI: Kregel Publications, 1960), 107.

3 Adam Clarke, *Commentary on the Holy Bible* (Grand Rapids, MI: Baker Book House, 1967), 249.

4 Velikovsky, *Worlds in Collision*, 40.

5 Ibid.

6 Ibid., 41.

7 Ibid.

8 Ibid., 41-42.

9 Ibid., 43.

10 *The Long Day of Joshua*, 179.

11 Ibid., 185...191.

12 Ibid., 181.

13 Ibid.

14 Ibid., 197.

15 Henry M. Morris, *The Bible Has the Answer* (Nutley, N.J.: The Craig Press, 1971), 72.

16 Ibid.

17 Ibid., 73.

18 Ibid., 71-72.

Chapter Six: The Double Cycle

1 Josephus, *Antiquities*, 5-5-1.

2 Ibid., 5-5-4.

3 *The Long Day of Joshua*, 169.

4 Clarke, *Commentary on the Holy Bible*, 273.

5 Josephus, *Antiquities*, 5-6-5.

6 Ibid., 6-2-2.

7 Ibid.

8 *The Long Day of Joshua*, 167.

9 Ibid.

Chapter Seven: David & Elijah

1 Ibid., 155.

2 Josephus, *Antiquities*, 7-8-3.

3 *The Long Day of Joshua*, 159.

4 Josephus, *Antiquities*, 7-13-3.

5 Velikovsky, *Worlds in Collision*, 261-262.

6 Ibid., 290.

7 *Dake's Annotated Reference Bible* (Lawrenceville, GA: Dake Bible Sales, Inc., eighth printing, 1974), commentator's notes, 383.

Chapter Eight: The Earth-Shaker

1 *The American Heritage Dictionary of the English Language* (Boston: Houghton Mifflin Co., third edition, 1992), 378.

2 Alfred J. Church, *Stories from Homer: The Iliad of the Siege of Troy* (New York: Thomas Y. Crowell & Co., undated), 70–71.

3 Josephus, *Antiquities*, 9-10-4.

4 Ibid.

5 *The Long Day of Joshua*, 133.

6 Velikovsky, *Worlds in Collision*, 215.

7 Ibid., 210.

8 Ibid., quoted text from F. Cumont, *Astrology and Religion Among the Greeks and Romans*, 1912, 8-9

9 Ibid.

10 Ibid., 215.

11 Josephus, *Antiquities*, 9-10-4.

12 Ibid.

[13] *The Long Day of Joshua*, 135.

[14] Velikovsky, *Worlds in Collision*, 212.

Chapter Nine: The Single Cycle

[1] Clarke, *Commentary on the Holy Bible*, 592.

[2] *The Long Day of Joshua*, 128.

[3] *The History of Herodotus*, translated by George Rawlinson (New York: The Dial Press, 1928), 131.

[4] Josephus, *Antiquities*, 10-1-5.

[5] *The History of Herodotus*, 131.

[6] *The Long Day of Joshua*, 22-23.

[7] Velikovsky, *Worlds in Collision*, 341.

[8] Ibid., 231, parentheses added.

[9] Ibid., 232.

[10] Ibid., 233.

[11] *The Long Day of Joshua*, 89.

[12] Ibid.

[13] Ibid., 119.

Do You Hear What I Hear

[1] Noel Regney and Gloria Shane, "Do You Hear What I Hear?" Public Domain.

Chapter Ten: The Star of Him

1 Joseph Henry Thayer, *The New Thayer's Greek-English Lexicon of the New Testament* (Peabody, MA: Hendrickson Publishers, 1981), 81.

2 Colin Humphreys, "The Star of Bethlehem," http://www.asa3.org/ASA/topics/Astronomy-Cosmology/S&CB%2010-93Humphreys.html.

3 *Formation of the Chinese Civilization: Astronomy and Mathematics*, china.org.cn/e-gudai/6. htm (accessed December 2006).

4 Kelly Whitt, "The Science of the Christmas Star," http://astronomyspace.suite101.com/ article.cfm/the_science_of_the_christmas_star.

5 Ray Bohlin, "The Star of Bethlehem." Probe Ministries: www.probe.org/docs/starbeth.html (accessed February 5, 2007).

6 Bill Hess, "Star or comet was visible in local area on night of Christ's birth."*Sierra Vista Herald*. www.svherald.com/articles/2004/12/24/local_news/news3.txt7).

7 "Chinese and Babylonian Observations," http://www.iac.es/galeria/mrk/Chinese.html (accessed February 5, 2007).

8 Ibid.

9 Ibid.

10 Ibid.

11 Information taken from various Web sites: "Capricornus, not Capricorn," www.eastbayastro .org/articles/lore/capricor.htm; "Curious About Astronomy: What Is the Significance of the Tropic of Cancer, Tropic of Capricorn, Arctic Circle, and Antarctic?" question.php?number=551; "Capricornus: a Constellation for September," www.faster.co.nz/~rasnz/Stars/Capricornus.htm; "Constellations," www .enchantedlearning .com/subjects/astronomy/stars/constellations.shtml; "Objects and Observing Tips: Constellations," http://depts.clackamas.edu/haggart/WhatsUp/ConstellationVisibility.htm; "Constellations," http:// library.thinkquest.org/J0112388/constellations.htm; "Measuring the Sky: A Quick Guide to the Celestial Sphere," www.astro.uiuc.edu/~kaler/celsph.html.

12 Ron Conte, "Biblical Chronology: Evidence From Astronomy." www.biblicalchronology .com/evidence.htm (accessed February 5, 2007).

13 William R. Newcott, "The Age of Comets." *National Geographic*, December 1997, Washington, D.C.: National Geographic Society, 96.

14 Conte, *Biblical Chronology*.

15 "Markets and Events in Christmas." www.initaly.com/regions/xmas/markets.htm (accessed February 5, 2007).

16 "Presepi e Pifferai: How to Say 'Christmas' in Rome." www.initaly.com/regions/xmas/michael.htm (accessed February 5, 2007).

Chapter Eleven: Two Mighty Earthquakes

1 Josh McDowell, *The New Evidence that Demands a Verdict* (Nashville: Thomas Nelson Publishers, 1999), 58, quoting Julius Africanus, *Chronography*, 18.1, Roberts, ANF.

2 Ibid.

Chapter Twelve: Babel & Eden

1 Josephus, *Antiquities*, 1-4-1.

2 Ibid., 1-4-2.

3 *The Long Day of Joshua*, 286.

4 *The Old Testament Pseudepigrapha, Sibylline Oracles* (Garden City, NY: Doubleday & Co., Inc., 1983) 364.

5 *The Book of Jasher* (Salt Lake City: J. H. Parry & Co., 1887) 9:38, www.sacred-texts.com/chr/apo/jasher/9.htm, accessed May 7, 2015.

6 Richard Stone, *The Last Great Impact on Earth.* Discover Magazine Online, Sept. 1996, 1.

7 William K. Hartmann, *1908 Siberia Explosion: Reconstructing an Asteroid Impact from Eyewitness Accounts.* www.Psi.edu/projects/siberia/siberia.html,2, accessed Feb. 5, 2007.

8 Richard Stone, 8.

9 *The New Evidence that Demands a Verdict,*105.

10 Henry M. Morris, *The Bible Has the Answer* , 97

11 Henry M. Morris, *Many Infallible Proofs* (San Diego: Creation-Life Publishers, 1974) 290-295.

12 Josephus, *Antiquities*, 1-7-1.

13 Clarke, *Commentary on the Holy Bible*, 24.

14 *Bible Readings for the Home Circle* (London: Review & Herald Publishing Assoc., 1921) 321. Quoted from *The American Encyclopedia*, article "Meteor," 1881.

15 Ibid., 319 and 323.

Chapter Thirteen: That Day

1 Josephus, *Wars of the Jews*, 6-5-3.

2 Velikovsky, *Worlds in Collision*, 239.

3 *The New Thayer's Greek-English Lexicon,* 74.

Printed in Great Britain
by Amazon